SEASONS

OF THE

SACRED EARTH

Photo © Cliff Seruntine

About the Author

Cliff Seruntine is a psychotherapist in private practice and an ardent practitioner of deep ecology—actively engaging with the natural world in ways that promote spiritual growth and a greener Earth. Inspired by the lifeways of ancient peoples who lived close to the land and by the insights of anthropology and experimental archeology, Cliff and his wife, Daphne, have immersed themselves in traditional living in order to understand "from the inside" the sacredness of Nature and the power of its enchantment.

Cliff, Daphne, and their two daughters reside on an old Scots farmstead deep in a misty wooded hollow of the Nova Scotia highlands, ancestral Canadian home of the Gaels. There they maintain organic gardens, raise dairy goats, and keep alive old skills such as horse driving, woodscraft, and cheesemaking. They also teach classes on how to live green while living well. In his free time, Cliff may often be found wandering with his horse, Aval, among the deep green places of the wildwood.

Other books by Cliff

The Lore of the Bard (Llewellyn, 2003)

An Ogham Wood (Avalonia Esoterica Press, 2011)

"The Maid of Ice & Meadows." *The Faerie Queens Anthology*
(Avalonia Esoterica Press, 2012)

CLIFF SERUNTINE

SEASONS
OF THE
SACRED EARTH

FOLLOWING THE OLD WAYS ON AN ENCHANTED HOMESTEAD

Llewellyn Publications
Woodbury, Minnesota

FIRST EDITION
Third Printing, 2023

Book design by Bob Gaul
Cover design by Kevin R. Brown
Cover illustration by Meraylah Allwood
Cover graphic elements of birds © iStockphoto.com/Cyro Pintos,
    leaves © iStockphoto.com, cartouche © Llewellyn art department
Interior photos and maps by Arielle, Cliff, Daphne, and Natalia Seruntine
Interior graphic elements of birds © iStockphoto.com/Cyro Pintos,
    leaves © iStockphoto.com, cartouche © Llewellyn art department
Editing by Ed Day

Llewellyn Publications is a registered trademark of Llewellyn Worldwide Ltd.

Library of Congress Cataloging-in-Publication Data
Seruntine, Cliff, 1968–
  Seasons of the sacred earth: following the old ways on an enchanted homestead/
Cliff Seruntine.—First Edition.
      pages cm
  ISBN 978-0-7387-3553-5
  1. Nova Scotia—Description and travel. 2. Seruntine, Cliff, 1968—Homes and haunts.
  3. Nature—Psychological aspects. 4. Spiritual life. 5. Magic. I. Title.
  F1037.S47 2013
  917.1604–dc23
                    2013010018

Llewellyn Worldwide Ltd. does not participate in, endorse, or have any authority or responsibility concerning private business transactions between our authors and the public.
    All mail addressed to the author is forwarded, but the publisher cannot, unless specifically instructed by the author, give out an address or phone number.
    Any Internet references contained in this work are current at publication time, but the publisher cannot guarantee that a specific location will continue to be maintained. Please refer to the publisher's website for links to authors' websites and other sources.

Llewellyn Publications
A Division of Llewellyn Worldwide Ltd.
2143 Wooddale Drive
Woodbury, MN 55125-2989
www.llewellyn.com

Printed in the United States of America

To Daphne: you make living the vision like living a dream.
I couldn't do it without you, my damsel.
And to my incredible daughters,
Arielle the Ever Reliable and Natalia the Little Warrior:
you enrich every day by simply being who you are.
My beloved girls, thank you for sharing the journey
into the green world with me. All of you together
prove that the sum is greater than the parts.

And to my friends, thank you for your support of our
work at the Hollow, for joining us for our events, and for
offering to help share the load. Working together, we can
cultivate deeper spirits and create a greener, kinder Earth.

"All truth can be found in Nature. When it happens for you, you then know, and no one else can tell you otherwise."
—Eli Gatoga, Cherokee Medicine Chief (1914–1983)

Contents

Maps of Twa Corbies Hollow

This map depicts the wild mountaintop valley in which the homestead of Twa Corbies Hollow is nestled. The map was created by the author's daughter, Arielle.

Maps of Twa Corbies Hollow

This map shows a zoomed-in layout of the farming area of Twa Corbies Hollow, and was created by the author's daughter, Arielle.

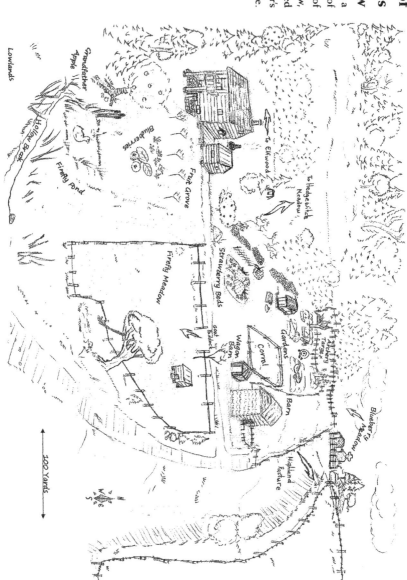

Lowlands

Grandfather Apple

Hollow Brook

Blueberries

Firefly Pond

Fruit Grove

To Eldwood

To Hedgewitch Meadow

Strawberry Beds

Firefly Meadow

Goat Paddock

Gardens

Archery Targets

Wagon Barn

Corral

Barn

Blueberry Meadow

Highland Pasture

100 Yards

Introduction

I grew up in an enchanted forest. Of course, at that time I didn't know it was an enchanted forest or that there was anything special about it at all. I just knew it as home. That particular forest was in the heart of Louisiana, in country that was part bayou woodland and part farmland, dotted with scattered villages throughout. Summer days were a delight of exploration as I rambled along copses of ancient oak and hickory and nibbled wild persimmons absconded from forgotten groves. Sometimes my wanderings took me miles from home, back into the depths of an unbroken woodland that went on for miles and miles along the banks of the Red River. My friends and I fished the river for giant catfish and roasted them at twilight on green spits made of twigs over campfires while we laughed over the day's adventures. And when it drew very late, we scared each other silly with ghost stories.

Sometimes our backcountry ramblings brought us upon ancient homes, abandoned and crumbling, and in the reckless way of boys, we were compelled to explore them. Every shadow held a phantom. Every room was steeped in mystery. Dust-covered decaying furnishings spoke of lives long since lived and gone, and disintegrating barns yielded mouldering covered wagons that yearned to tell of old ways forgotten. And surrounding it all was the forest, alive and green, promising ever deeper secrets if only we trekked on.

In autumn, we checked and rechecked our camping gear, and when the hunting season at last opened, we stowed our gear in packs and hiked out to the pinewoods in pursuit of deer. We never got one, but it didn't matter. The camp, the camaraderie, the days and nights passed among the tall trees was the real reward. I'll never forget the frosty morning my two friends and I awoke before dawn—a rare day when hoarfrost touched the subtropical foliage—and got an early start on the hunt. We encountered a stream and talked David, a gangly youth with more good nature than sense, into swimming across the icy water with a rope so that we could tie it between two trees and slide our gear across nice and dry, whereupon we would swim across ourselves. David stripped and swam the twenty feet, moaning loudly about the frigid water all the way. He reached the other bank and, goose-fleshed and shivering, tied the rope to a tree. Scott and I tied the rope off on our side and then tested the water with our toes. "Too cold!" Scott barked, and we put our boots back on and decided to hunt on our side of the brook instead while David, naked as innocence, jumped about and ranted some nonsense about us having to swim the brook also to make it fair.

And there was magic! It was everywhere, thick like the southern fogs. Tales of bayou ghosts and fey folk abounded. Gypsy fortune-tellers passed through the Acadian villages in carnivals à la Ray Bradbury. Once, down a lost dirt road on a hot summer's day, we found clay sculptures in the form of genitalia, leavings of some Acadian sorcerer's fertility rite. One evening we came across magic circles in an abandoned structure among ancient pines. These were hallmarks of vodou and Old World witchcraft, and in the Deep South, with sorcerous New Orleans only a few hours away, we were instinctively wary of occult things, with their spooky mysteries and bizarre rites. My friends were leerier than I, though. In fact, I came to feel drawn to learn about the hidden world and started reading everything I could find in the local library about witchcraft, alternative beliefs, and magic, and at my urging, we held séances and laid out our own magic circles back deep in the sequestering forest.

And then I grew up and left that world of woods and farms behind in search of education.

I traveled first to the nearby cities of Baton Rouge and Pineville to attend colleges and became aware of a whole different world. In the cities, I learned about the marvels and wealth of urban life, the richness of many cultures coming together, and the wonders of technology of which I had only been sleepily aware before. A little later, my studies launched me into traveling, first to the desert country of the American West, then to Mexico, later to French Canada, and ultimately to Europe and the subarctic. Along the way, I saw more and more cities and people, and learned that the world I knew as a youth—that vast, rambling, lazy realm of forests and farms—was, in fact, small and far from the experience of most. In the hearts of great cities such as Montreal, I met persons whose entire lives consisted only of daily treks between apartment and work. If they ever tasted magic, it had little to do with the living green enchantment I had known as a youth.

As my education progressed and I determined to undertake a career in psychotherapy, my interests in enchantment and spirituality evolved as well. I began to study the writings of Buckland, Flowers, Harner, John and Caitlin Matthews, Markale, Lady Wilde, and Evans-Wentz. I devoured books on Wicca, Asatru, shamanism, druidry, and witchcraft. As I studied, it became clear to me that most, if not all, magical and spiritual paths shared common roots in Nature. In fact, I began to perceive them as virtually inseparable. The Celtic path, with its druids and faeries under green, hollow hills, and profound seasonal cycles tied deeply to the tides of summer and winter, is an ideal example. The

Norse path, with its gods, light elves, and giants of enchanted caves and wild northern mountains, is strongly bound to primal Nature, as well. Likewise, the witch of legend and fact draws healing from wild herbs and keeps camaraderie with little Earth spirits, and so must be linked profoundly to Earth, too. And the shaman of aboriginal folk is perhaps the quintessential symbol of the link between human and Nature, for his magic and wisdom are drawn from power animals, sacred plant spirits, and vision quests in far wild places. Even the Bible has its origin in Eden, a garden of ecological harmony and splendour.

But the more I studied the various paths, the more I realized their essential foundation in Nature was slipping from the experience of modern folk. Most modern witches I had met had never picked a wild herb in the woods. Followers of Norse lore were more concerned with casting runes than wandering the wild mountains in search of wisdom, as their god Odhinn had done. The British druids, who come from a path firmly rooted in the green world, had become an almost entirely urbanized and academic lot. I recall a discussion I once read on an on-line druid mailing list. A new person asked what he should study to become a contemporary druid. Every person on the network referred him to enormous reading lists on Celtic history and culture. Not one thought to advise him to immerse himself in the green world for a spell. How very odd for a path that is considered a Nature religion to entirely neglect the essential need of Nature

In an increasingly urbanized world, is the spirit and mystery of Nature still even relevant? Or is the land little more than a resource: a source of energy and the minerals we need to contrive our cities and technologize our lives?

It was about twenty-five years ago that I first began wrestling with such questions. I was spending some time in the Adirondack forest of upstate New York. There I met a man who seemed a relic out of the past. Tall, muscular, rustic, sporting a bushy black beard, and wearing jeans, boots, and a homemade skin jacket, he looked like a mountain man of yesteryear. He owned a homestead deep in the mountains. His land was twenty acres of maple woods, and from local materials he had constructed a snug log cabin. He had no electricity, no plumbing, no refrigeration … and he wanted for nothing. Responsible forestry provided him firewood. He grew his own gardens and hunted abundant deer for meat. From the forest he gathered maple syrup, wild nuts, and berries. I spent a brief but wondrous season at his homestead and learned the true value of keeping close to the land—a life lived close to Earth keeps us tuned in to what is real and important. In the natural world, we very quickly come to understand that the next diploma, promotion, or raise, and the bigger house and the shinier car—these count for very little in the grand scheme of things. Happiness comes of life and balance. It is rooted in good friends, good family, sustainable lives, and spiritual fulfillment. Yet it is all too easy to lose track of these things if one is alienated from the living world and its sacred magic that energizes and enlightens our spirits.

In my early twenties I married Daphne, a demure but spirited Canadian redhead, and she and I moved to the Alaskan wilderness where we began our own lives close to the land. We bought a very remote cabin and harvested berries and mushrooms from the boreal forest, hunted caribou among the taiga, and fished for trout and salmon in the lake. Along the way, we had two great daughters, and as a family we spent each day immersed in the green world in as primal a way as possible in the modern era. And living far deep in that bush, I found again the truth I knew as a child—the natural world is enchanted, powerful, healing, and ultimately vital to our well-being. It does far more than just give us food and resources. It is full of mystery and powerful spirituality. I encountered great grizzlies in the primeval forest and became, in those intense moments, supremely aware of how small a man is. When I stood on the deck of the cabin and regarded an autumn night sky ablaze with the aurora, which the aboriginals call the Path of Souls, I felt the power of indescribable beauty illuminating my soul. When I walked outdoors on winter evenings beneath a huge silver moon and regarded the glowing mountains across the vast inland lake that fronted our cabin, I could feel the closeness of the wild gods and marvel at the sacred mystery of a universe beyond my ken.

Nature, experienced close and firsthand, makes magic come alive and gives life to endless, numinous, and enchanted possibilities. A friend once said, "In the city, it's all concrete and logic. But here, in the wild country, it's something deeper." Nature is a wellspring of enchantment and spirit, half-forgotten in an era of growing urban tangle. But Nature is the source of health in mind and spirit, and we would do well to keep it close.

After nearly a decade and a half in Alaska, we developed a yearning to keep a farm where we could cultivate more varied gardens and have horses and goats and chickens. It would be a lot more work than bush living, but my profession as a psychotherapist allowed me the freedom of self-employment, and I could choose my hours and work from home. (Many persons who undertake the rural lifestyle find their own ways to break out of the workaday life. With a measure of gumption and grit, it's not so hard.) That freedom would be essential to operating a farmstead, but we also had another couple assets. Daphne and I had acquired by that time a lot of experience in self-sufficient rural living. We knew all kinds of ways to work smarter instead of harder. But the most important thing was our years of living in the deep Alaskan wilderness had forged us into a very "together" family. We could function smoothly as a team, and that allowed us to accomplish a lot more than four people working as individuals.

So, being an international couple, we had the option of living in either the USA or Canada, or emigrating to another British Commonwealth country such as Australia. After careful consideration, we decided to relocate to Nova Scotia, Canada. So we went a bit south and a long way east and acquired a hidden homestead deep in the forested Maritime highlands, a small paradise we call Twa Corbies Hollow (old Scots English for "Two Ravens Hollow"). It is a place of decadent summers and bitter winters, springs that smell of earth and maple wood smoke, and autumns afire with red and gold leaves. Working in harmony with the land, we started vast organic gardens far more varied than the harsh weather of Alaska allowed, and we were soon up to our necks in goats and chickens, barn cats and horses. But if you are attentive, living in the wilds never lets you forget that the world is full of enchantment, and we were careful from the very beginning to honor the local spirits. In return, they seemed to bless our endeavors. Though we live far back in the woods where there are many predators, our livestock are always safe even though we never close the barn by night, and year after year our gardens have yielded virtually miraculous harvests despite our location atop a mountain where the weather is often fierce. And there is a fey enchantment in this woodland, too. This is a profoundly Gaelic and Acadian place, and the forest that surrounds us is rumoured to be haunted by ghosts and faeries and aboriginal sprites. Some of the local folk have warned us to be wary of them, but we have never felt a need. Why live in fear if one embraces a path of harmony and peace with those very beings? And so we have always been respectful of those entities and in return have been privileged to catch glimpses of a more magical reality, from twigs that toss themselves among the trees to the thrill of living with a barn bruanighe (pronounced BRU*nee, this is the brownie of Scots legend). The forest comes right up to the edge of our cottage, and it is so full of magic we've taken to calling it the Elfwood. But you'll read more about all those things later on ...

And living this deeply earthy lifestyle at Twa Corbies Hollow has also given us another gift ... a profound, firsthand comprehension of the power and meaning of each turn of the Wheel of the Year. When the goats birth their kids in February, we relive the heartwarming touch of Imbolg, when the gods promise there will be an end to ice and snow. When we gather the first greens during the decadent days of high summer, we experience the deep satisfaction of a well-earned Lughnasadh. When the autumn wind whispers through the bones of leafless maples, Samhain frissons turn the heart toward the otherworldly adventure of the Sacred Hunt. As the great Cherokee Eli Gatoga (1914–1983) said, all truth can be found in Nature, and then you *know*. You know the unfathomable depths of mystery concealed so elegantly in these otherwise simple natural events in a way that goes beyond words yet will profoundly reshape your life.

This book is all about getting to that *knowing*. But it is not a how-to kind of book. You will find no lessons on meditations, drumming, or magical work—there is already so much of that available. But this is a book of magic. Indeed, wild magic and wild spirituality. Only, it is a "why-to." It is a collection of true stories experienced by myself, my wife, and our two daughters relating the enchantment we have been privileged to encounter in living so close to Nature. Some stories will warm your heart. Some will be hard to hear. All are true, though I have changed a few names and places to protect my privacy and that of a few friends who also live close to the green world and treasure their seclusion.

So, why a collection of stories? Because some truths can be conveyed in story far better than the language of the reasoning mind. The heart may perceive where mere logic cannot, and in such perceptions we discover the true *knowing* of a thing.

The book covers our third and fourth years at the Hollow. It is laid out according to the sacred year, each month getting a chapter. In some very green-minded parts of the elder world, the year began with the commencement of the time of darkness and cold, so the book begins with October and progresses through to the end of the harvest season the following September. But living close to the land has taught us to think of the year in terms of seasons, not months or dates on a calendar.

We tend to think of the year as "gardening season" or "the season for Lughnasadh celebrating." The High Days of the sacred year feel more to us like potent little focused seasons, so I have given each a chapter, too. Every two chapters there is a Traditional Living essay. These essays are the closest the book offers in the way of how-tos. They aren't directly magical or spiritual, but they offer instructions on activities you can do that will certainly draw you closer to the spiritual and enchanting power of Nature. The activities vary widely, from learning how to make your own hard bubbly cider from scratch for celebrating the High Days to developing an understanding of the natural world through nighttime hikes.

So as you begin to journey through a year with us Hollow folk in the coming pages, it is my hope that you, dear reader, will take from these tales and essays inspiration and find your own means to keep the green world close in your life. You don't have to launch off deep into the wilds as we have done, but you do have to go out your door. The trees and grass, the animals and brooks and sea, and earth and sky have much to teach any who look to them. There is magic and wonder beyond your door, and it is happy to enrich you if you walk its Way.

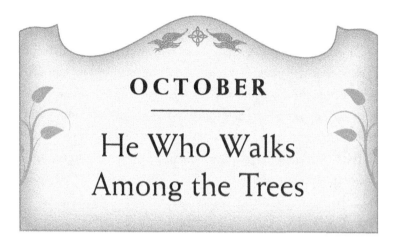

OCTOBER

He Who Walks Among the Trees

It was yet the morning twilight and I made my way through a forest of great maples, careful to keep silent, slow so as to remain unseen. The sky was whitening with the dawn, but within the forest, night still prevailed. It was tricky going. Everywhere there were natural obstacles: exposed stone, fallen branches, ancient logs half returned to the earth. A moment's inattention would lead to a noisy tumble and ruin the hunting here for the day.

The deer season had come. For a woodsman, this was a time of heady excitement. The Hunt is an ancient ritual, as old as life. For a follower of the old shamanic ways, it is a sacred time. The deer are the symbols not only of the Green Man but of the Cailleach (CAH*lock), the Old Lady of the Wood. The Hunt, if done right, is a spiritual thing—a time to bind the spirit to the land and draw sustenance from the wild. It is a time to give, as well. Nova Scotia has a thriving deer population and, sadly, there are not enough wild predators to keep their numbers in check. Deer are, beyond a doubt, beautiful, whether one speaks of the graceful doe or the mighty stag, but their numbers increase rapidly in a lush environment such as this country. If left unchecked, they will quickly reproduce to the point that the meadows and woods can no longer support them, especially when the hard months of a long winter descend. There are few sights sadder and more painful than trekking over a mountain ridge upon a late February day and finding the emaciated carcasses of deer that have starved. And if their numbers get too high, the suffering goes beyond those that merely starve to death. Those that survive till spring will be weakened by nutritional deprivation. Disease and parasites spread. A slow and painful process of lingering death begins. In light of these things, I had made the decision that the responsible thing to do was to hunt: never for sport, but for the spirit of the Old Ways and the health of the sacred deer. And I had to admit, I reveled in the Hunt. It wasn't the kill; that part I adamantly did not enjoy. It was the Hunt itself. It was a good reason to spend the coming days immersed in the green, stalking silently through woods and meadows, honing my tracking skills as I sought for spoor, applying my hard-won skill with the longbow. And the nights at camp were as exhilarating as the days—evenings round the campfire, eating trail rations of bread and goat cheese and drinking tea heated in a kettle over the coals. The brisk fall air possessed a keen bite, just enough to sharpen the mind and senses. The autumn stars offered a tapestry of sparkling wonder. Owls haunted the distant trees, their calls echoing through the great forest, hinting of mystery and wonder. The season of the Hunt, by day's wandering or night's fire, was a sacred time, magical and ancient and full of mystery.

I had scouted this country many times before and knew the way well. Without incident or unwanted sound, I made my way between ancient rock maples. A hundred yards to the north was a glade that was really more of a briar patch of raspberry canes and rose hips. Off to the south in the distance, the hardwoods gave way to a wood of young evergreens. I reached a point where the land dipped to form a ravine, barely more than a seasonal drainage for spring melt water. I turned north there and followed the ravine for several hundred yards, skirting the glade. A fallen log marked the point where I knew I should head east again, and I clambered out of the ravine, slipped through another fifty yards of mixed birch and maple, and came to a grassy break. It was not very big, only an acre or two. At its center was a stand of spruce, paper birch, and rock maple, like an island of woods within the forest. Near the edge of those trees I had set up a stand a month earlier. I made my way to it, withdrew my back quiver and tied it to a rope, along with my longbow and daypack. Then I climbed the sixteen-foot ladder to the chair braced against the old maple's trunk and hauled my gear up with the rope. I fastened the quiver and pack to supports and lay the longbow across my lap. I withdrew a thermos and had a cup of tea as I waited in silence for the sunrise.

The sky went through its wondrous morning transformation, becoming first magenta, then acquiring hues of ruby and gold. These faded into a moment's whiteness that swiftly darkened to azure. There was not a cloud to be seen. The dawn rays spilled out of the east over the forest, illuming the ancient wood's canopy of greenery. Maple predominated, and among the green was the barest scatter of crimson, the first leaves turning with the coming of the chill nights of autumn. It was yet early in the month, but every day I came out here there was more color in the leaves. The maples grew ever more crimson; the birches took on hues of butter. The raspberry at the edge of the forest became rusty, and the scattered blueberry beyond, in more open country, turned the Earth the color of fresh blood. Autumn would soon bring on the sleeping of the land, but not before a last vibrant burst of life expressing itself with magnificent color to rival any firework display.

But the Hunt passed slowly, there in the tree, and it was a challenge to remain still and quiet as a branch as the hours crawled by. My tea was soon gone, and I set the thermos back into its pack. To pass the time, I checked and rechecked my gear, making sure my bracer—an essential piece of archer's gear that armors the forearm against the lash of the bowstring when it is released—was firmly positioned and would not inhibit movement. I checked to make sure I had quick access to my quiver, ensuring I could reach the arrows with a minimum of movement. I felt the bowstring, making sure it was well waxed and seated in the stave's notches. And between these rituals, I observed the wildlife.

One of the beauties of hunting the primitive way, with a traditional longbow, is it forces you to become one with the land. A good archer learns to blend into the Earth so entirely that not even the forest creatures know he is there. I watched a squirrel who inhabited a neighboring tree emerge from his nest and steal wild apples from the pile I had left in the glade to draw deer. Not long after, a porcupine who had forgotten that the rising sun meant it was his bedtime shambled through the glade and expressed some curiosity over the apples though he didn't take any. Songbirds of every color hopped among the branches and over the earth, eating grubs and wild seed in the soil. I heard the roosterlike crowing of a pheasant and soon saw him emerge from the brush just east of me. The male pheasants of Nova Scotia are indescribably beautiful, resplendent with iridescent color—like peacocks of the north. He wandered among the raspberry canes, pecking here and there at the earth in the manner of domestic poultry. As I watched his antics, I was sure that the species must have some none-too-distant relationship to the common farm chicken.

But over the next few minutes, a remarkable thing happened. One by one, the creatures faded. The squirrel returned to his nest. The pheasant went in silence back into the eastern scrub. The songbirds vanished into the deep wood. The woods seemed to become silent and empty. The sun had risen higher, and I felt the first warm beams fall across me as it topped the trees. The only sound of life, just then, was the distant cry of a raven. Otherwise, all was silent. It had happened with such liquid subtlety that I hadn't noticed till just now. I looked around, not alarmed but thinking it very peculiar.

Then I became aware of a noise, like a rushing wind approaching out of the south. It sounded like it was skimming just over the tops of the trees. It was a peculiar wind, though. I did not see the treetops sway with it, nor hear their leaves rattle. And as I thought about it, I realized it sounded not so much like a wind but as if something huge raced through the air. And it was moving fast in my direction. But what kind of bird could be so large that I could hear it approaching from the distant treetops long before I could even see it. Again in the distance, a raven cawed. *Could it be a raven?* I wondered. No raven of this world could be large enough to displace that much air. It sounded like a small airplane, or a mythic dragon, was coursing low over the trees. In wonder, I strained to see what was coming. But just before I thought whatever it was would emerge from beyond the trees at the edge of the glade, it seemed to veer away. Suddenly it was gone, and the forest was silent once again.

I watched the trees at the southern edge of the glade keenly, struggling to make sense of what might have caused the sound. Minutes passed, and I took note that still the forest remained silent. I began to feel uneasy. Not fearful so much as *not alone.* I began to feel, more and more, as if I was being observed. I could not have said by what.

If I am a mystic, as some have said, then I am unusual for the breed, for I am not quick to believe in encounters with the paranormal. Even though I have been privileged to witness paranormal events several times in my life, I remain, by nature, a dubious person. My motto is: I want to believe, but you'll have to show me why I should. So it wasn't long before my innately skeptical nature began to write off the event. *A freak wind,* I told myself. *Perhaps a whole murder of ravens flying low, and they broke off just before they would have emerged over the treetops.* That seemed most likely and I reached into my pack for a water bottle. My throat had gone dry in the crisp air.

No sooner had I grasped the bottle than I heard a sharp rush of air again, as if the huge *whatever* had come back and was rushing straight for my treetop. I let go the bottle and it dropped back into the pack. I leaned forward, looking between the branches that sequestered me, gazing into the sky in the direction of the rushing sound. The sky was clear as a bell. I had an excellent view of the sky east, south, and west. Nothing!

The human ear is a remarkable feat of natural engineering. One hears a lot of talk about how dogs and cats can hear above the range of humans, and bats even higher. Animals like whales can hear lower into the sound spectrum than we can, too. And all that may be so, but humans have a discernment of hearing that is unrivaled. We can identify a single out of tune flute among all the instruments of an orchestra. We can distinguish melody and countermelody in fantastic complexity. We can feel sympathetic emotions with the timbre of another person's voice. And we have extraordinary directional hearing. With no effort, a human can tell instantly within two degrees precisely what direction a sound is coming from. I knew this, so I knew I should be able to pinpoint and see whatever was coming. It was clear, the light was perfect and I could hear it clearly. But there was simply nothing to be seen.

Automatically, my eyes tracked where my ears told me it should be. Sound travels slower than light so I glanced ahead. *Nothing!* It raced toward my tree and suddenly passed directly over my position. It sounded like it had come very close, just barely over the top of my tree. The rushing sigh of its passage indicated some huge creature—a great eagle perhaps. I stood in the deer stand and peered around behind the trunk, up through the thin canopy of branches, trying to spot it as it moved away, but I could see nothing even though I could clearly hear the rush of its departure. And then, as quickly as it had come, it was gone.

I gave up scanning the sky after a few minutes and carefully took a seat again. I was a good sixteen feet off the ground, not so high up but a long fall nevertheless. Soon the forest became active again. Mr. Squirrel went back to stealing apples from the pile. Songbirds took to singing in the trees again. Later on, a couple partridges emerged from the woods, pecking around the stumps of trees. I watched them and took note of other things, too. A patch of honey mushrooms that I might gather on my way out. A bit of bent willow where a buck had earlier rubbed his antlers. A faint hint of game trail a bit west. But as my forest-accustomed senses took note of these things, my mind wandered over probable and improbable explanations of what had just occurred. Perhaps it was some kind of strange wind, highly localized, that had just blown by. I quickly ruled that out. It would have moved the boughs of the trees, and I was sure it would have sounded much more like a wind and less like the close passage of some great flying creature.

But if it were some great flying creature, then what? I ran through a mental list of possibilities. Huge owls live in this forest: among them are horned, barred, and barn owls. But not only was it the wrong time of day for owls, but owls made virtually no sound in flight. They were night hunters, and in the night, sound is everything. Nature had equipped them with feathers that were not the most efficient for flight, but were as soft and quiet as cat's paws over velvet.

If not owls, then any number of large birds was possible. The forest was populated by various eagles, hawks, falcons, and ravens. At this time of year, other sizeable birds would be about, too, namely wild geese and ducks. Ravens, I could quickly rule out. They were noisy birds and I would almost certainly have heard a raven's commotion in flight. The other birds, well, they would all have been plainly visible against the sky.

Fantastic ideas entered my mind. Perhaps it was some otherworldly creature. A spirit. An elemental of the air in the form of wind. Even the ancient aboriginal god Raven came to mind. In the end, I had to make peace with the fact that I didn't know, though in truth the idea of something otherworldly appeared to make more sense than something corporeal. The fact was, it had been huge enough to displace a significant amount of air, had passed like a rushing wind, and it was invisible.

The day wore on uneventfully toward noon and as the sun rose higher it became hot, despite the lateness of the year. I had brought rations in my pack, but I had been hunting several days already and I decided a hot meal was in order. A friend owned a cabin only a mile through the forest. He almost never used the place and I looked after it for him, so had the privilege of using it whenever the mood struck. Using the rope, I lowered my bow and quiver to the ground and climbed down. It was a pleasant hike through the forest, though it went slowly as I was careful to stay quiet. I didn't want to accidentally spook any deer in the area.

Not far from the cabin, I stumbled upon a doe feeding in a thicket of scrub near where the hardwoods merged into evergreens. I drew and knocked an arrow, but opted not to shoot. Though she was only about fifteen yards away, an easy shot, there was scrub between us. Arrows are easily diverted by such detritus, and I did not want to risk a shot that would not result in a quick, clean kill. That would be cruel and dishonor myself and show a lack of respect to the Green Man and the Cailleach, to whom the deer are sacred. I replaced the arrow as the deer slowly turned and loped away. Perhaps I would come across her later, but the presence of a doe meant larger bucks were probably in the area, too, and I'd rather get one of them. I was in no rush.

The cabin in the Old Wood lies sequestered in cool green shadow.
Even though it is late in the year, it has been warm and
the leaves and foliage have barely begun to change.

In another ten minutes I reached the cabin. The day before, I had left water and some supplies there. Using the propane stove, I made a pot of tea. As it steeped, I dug into the supplies. Some of Daphne's hard goat cheese, some homemade hardtack, some half-frozen stew (it had been frozen when I left it yesterday). I drank a good liter of water as the stew cooked, and refilled my water bottle. And when the food was good and hot, I sat down at the little wooden table with a splendid view into the forest and enjoyed the meal. The cheese was aged and pungent. The chicken stew was hardy and the crumbled hardtack made it even thicker. All in all, it was simple and good—like many of the best things in life. And when I finished the repast, I broke into another part of the little cache I had left the day before, a cool ale from a batch I had brewed back in spring. Full and my thirst slaked, I lay down on a bunk for a nap.

I woke about two hours later feeling a little groggy, but refreshed. A cup of reheated tea soon did away with the grogginess and as the afternoon drew on, I slipped my puukko into its belt loop. It is a hefty seventeen-inch knife somewhat like the famous American bowie but of Scandinavian origin and without a guard. It's something between a woodsman's knife, a short sword, and a hatchet—an all-purpose tool as useful for cutting firewood as skinning game or removing a splinter. I slung the quiver over my back and restrung my longbow. I began the hike back through the forest to the glade where my deer stand awaited.

Back in the stand, the timeless ritual of the Hunt resumed. It is a slow ritual in which the hunter gets all kinds of aches from sitting stone still and mouse quiet for hours on end, blending mind and body into the background of the forest. To pass the time, I glanced at a few pages of a novel, trusting to my ears to alert me if a deer approached. I nibbled on homemade gorp, a mixture of dried fruit, nuts, and chocolate. I had refilled my thermos at the cabin and now finished off the tea. And I resumed the routine of quietly checking and rechecking gear. When a deer finally came, all must be smooth and silent and swift: I'd only get one shot and a moment to make it.

But the afternoon waned toward twilight and, aside from the doe I had seen and passed on near midday, the woods were quiet. However, I am a stubborn hunter and remained in the stand till the very last of the light.

It's hard to tell when the sun sets when you're deep in the forest, especially if you live atop a mountain. Ridges and the forest canopy play tricks with the light. In some places it can seem like it's night while plenty of light still remains in the sky. So I ignored the darkening woods and watched the sky for an indication of when I should call it a day. The hue of the sky darkened, transitioning from azure to deep ocean blue. When the west took on a florid magenta, I took that as a clue that the sun had either just set or was just upon the horizon. Time to go. No deer, but I was relieved to call it a day nonetheless. I'd been at it a while and needed a break. Hunting is intense work for the body and hard on the mind for keeping keen senses. It leaves you feeling tired inside, like you might feel after consuming a deep book. Once again I lowered all my equipment to the ground and then climbed down.

When I reached the ground, I realized I had miscalculated the light. Halfway up in the tree I had more access to the sky and it had seemed brighter, but on the ground it was so dark I almost had to feel around to find my gear. I hitched my pack around my waist, slung the quiver over my back, and grabbed the bow. It was getting dark fast. I had a pair of small flashlights, but I preferred not to use them. I preferred to rely on my own senses as much as possible.

I made my way south across the glade into the ancient forest. There, surrounded by the great trees, it suddenly seemed like I had left twilight behind and entered a world of night. Shadow stood against deeper shadow and I went slowly for several minutes, picking my way among a familiar game trail and letting my eyes adjust to the deeper darkness. Within a few minutes, I found I could see well enough in the fading twilight and figured I could make it all the way back to the cabin without a flashlight. I reached the edge of the ravine and glanced down to pick my way over a tangle of fallen branches. I looked up and a wave of adrenaline washed over me like ice water. Not thirty paces ahead stood the Horned One, or a being just like him. He was huge, twelve feet tall, and a spread of glorious antlers emerge from his brow. He was bare chested from the waist up; his waist narrow but with broad shoulders. From the waist down it appeared he wore britches, but it could have been fur. I could not make out his feet in the forest shadows. He stood stone still and regarded me, as I stood frozen regarding him, and silence reigned between us.

Then I blinked and the vision was gone. All that lay in that direction were the great trees. Perhaps what I had seen was no more than the standing trunk of a tree long dead that rose out of the ground halfway down the ravine. When I thought hard about it, that seemed most likely. Yet, when I thought harder about it, it seemed most unlikely. The vision had felt so real. The Green Man, horned and fey and wild. Or, at least, a green man. Here in these very woods. I didn't know if I should smile and feel comforted or feel very nervous. I had always sought to live in harmony with Earth and keep the Old Ways, and so honor the Green Man and the old gods. But the Green Man is not necessarily a friend of mortals at the best of times. If I had really seen *him*, was it a good omen or bad? If it was him and not just a trick of my eyes in the half-light, I could not imagine that I had done anything to offend him. Then an odd thought came to mind: *Maybe it was no omen at all. Maybe I was just so immersed in the wood's magic that I was catching glimpses of otherworldly things.* Old Celtic lore and shamanic legend spoke of this. Persons who drew very close to nature's spirits began to see things differently. It was like an acquired second sight. But I didn't feel sighted.

Nothing to do but carry on, I decided. And as I made the decision that rational, dubious side of my nature took precedence again. *Probably just a trick of the light combined with an unconscious yearning. Don't be daft.*

I had not gone ten more paces when, just down the shallow ravine, I saw a shadowy form walking. In some ways it looked like the huge Green Man I had just encountered, but this one was no taller than an ordinary man. The sight took me completely by surprise and I froze, my mouth dropping into an O of wonder. Antlers were upon his brow, but he was different in build and carriage, slenderer and more upright. And it didn't seem as though he were bare chested, but it was hard to say just what he looked like. It was really more like seeing a shadow walking, but upright and in three dimensions. The moment had a dreamlike quality, yet it was also vividly, intensely real. I felt that if I touched that image it would be as substantial as any forest creature I had encountered, any tree I currently walked among. So I stood there in silence, watching, and the shadowy figure simply walked past, never making a sound. And then it too was gone. It wasn't like it had vanished. It was more like it had simply dissolved into the deepening forest shadows. "Wonders," I murmured, my voice barely over a whisper.

Something crackled upon the dry leaves of the forest duff to my left, and close. I admit it, I was on edge at this point. I wasn't exactly afraid, but when one encounters the absolutely unexpected, no matter how wondrous, it gets one's guard up. I've lived in the wilderness much of my life. I've been charged by three grizzly bears, one black bear, five moose, and one berserk beaver. My reactions to surprise are probably somewhat similar to those of a soldier whose seen combat. I whipped my arm over my back, drew an arrow from my quiver, and nocked it to the string. In barely two seconds, I had turned to point a drawn bow at the threat . . . and found myself aiming a bladed arrow at a porcupine scrabbling about at the base of a slender birch. I released a tense breath that I had not even realized I was holding, that in retrospect I think I might have held since I saw the great Green Man a minute before.

I felt silly and whispered at the small creature, "Go spook someone else, okay?" The little porcupine acted as though I didn't exist and continued to scrabble about the base of the tree, looking for something in the soil far more interesting than me. I half smiled, feeling silly for letting the little creature spook me like that. Then a full smile forced its way into my expression. And then I felt a great burst of mirth come over me. I couldn't help myself. I didn't want to disturb the sacred silence of the wood, but a spring of laughter bubbled up in me. I released the draw on the bow and replaced the arrow, laughing as I did so. I laughed so hard and so long I staggered and had to lean against a tree till it passed, and when the laughter departed, I felt good. I felt clean. I felt right with the wood. I felt ... I don't know how to express it quite right ... but I felt approved of. And I felt as if the presence was waiting for something.

Now it seemed right to break the silence I had guarded so carefully all through the day, and into the darkling forest I spoke. "I get it, it's your wood. Look, I don't have a gun. I'm not that kind of hunter. I'm not going to kill for something as stupid as sport. I respect your wood, and I'm trying to live in balance with the land and all the creatures of this place. But I am here with a bow, so as to hunt in the Old Way, in harmony with the land. I am here for a deer, for meat for my family for the winter, and because there are too many this year. They will starve if they aren't thinned. You know it, and so do I. But I swear, I won't shoot unless I can make the kill clean and quick." The doe I had seen earlier came unexpectedly to mind. It would have been an easy shot but for a little scrub between us. Still, I could have taken the shot. Almost certainly I'd have hit it, but I had turned it down because of the small chance a twig might have deflected the arrow and I would only have injured the creature, causing it to suffer needlessly. Understanding came with the thought, and I said, "I think you tested me earlier with that doe through the thicket. And I think you've been trying to scare me out, and I was just too thick to get the message. I'll go if you want, but if you don't mind, I would like to hunt here. I will respect your land. I swear it."

There was no reply but the creatures of the night waking with the coming dark, announced with the hooting of a distant owl and the cry of some far off night bird I did not recognize. So I just stood there in silence, listening, waiting. And there was only silence in return. But now things felt right. I hadn't thought of it the past couple days; I'd been so consumed with the Hunt. But now that I put my mind to it, I recognized that up till now things just hadn't felt like they should. I couldn't say just what those things were. It wasn't like there had been anything bad or wrong. It was more like some part of me felt like I just shouldn't be here. But suddenly that feeling was gone. Everything in the forest suddenly felt right.

I nodded. I think understanding passed between that horned spirit and me. I resumed the long walk back to the cabin. A hot dinner and a fire awaited, as well as a good book and a much-needed sound night's sleep. And there was a lot to think about.

Over the coming seasons I had many wondrous experiences in that place. I came to calling that region of the forest the Old Wood. It was an old growth forest, but that wasn't really why. It was because old things dwelt there: things full of time and stories and enchantment. Not far from the glade, I found the remnants of an ancient cabin that must have dated back to the first colonial days, and there were hidden rock walls through the wood, the kind the original Gaelic settlers used to build. Later in spring, I encountered a region where all the wood's foliage had turned a brilliant sunny hue and hiking through there felt like walking amidst caverns of gold. At another time, I became perhaps the only person in Nova Scotia to be charged by a black bear in a century, though in the end it turned out the bear wasn't really charging me. It was more, let us say...a misunderstanding, and I had stumbled upon two bears having a disagreement over dinner. And many times I took my daughters up there to teach them the ways of the wood: where to find wild berries and herbs, how to spot tracks hidden in the forest loam, or sometimes just to listen to the dawn songs of the coyote pack that haunted the area. Always we went gently upon the land and always, thereafter, we felt welcomed.

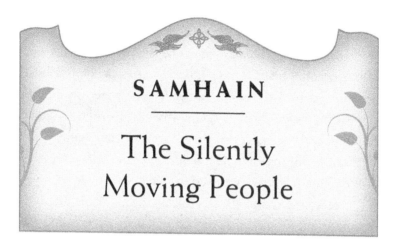

SAMHAIN

The Silently Moving People

Frissons. All my life, whenever the time of Samhain comes, I get fris-sons—that sense of tingling that travels up the spine and into the shoul-ders and neck, light as cat's paws, thrilling as faerie mischief. As a boy, I grew up on a secluded farm in the Louisiana bayou country among French-speaking Cajuns who *remembered* the Old Ways. In that shady, lush world, they said the meadows harbored ghosts that have lingered since the Civil War, and the forests contained primal spirits like the phantom lights we called *feux follets*. (The term means literally "fire sprite" but could better be translated to the "fool lights" or "swamp lads." No one knows if they are ghosts or fey spirits or something other. They are much like the will-o'-the-wisp of English legends.) And when Samhain was close, and the fragrant Deep Southern air held a pleasant nip and the sun held low and gave the land a burnished hue, you could feel the magical tension in the air. Enchantment flowed. Spirits yearned to wander. You just knew witches were out there, boiling magical potions in cauldrons while the voduns would cry out to their strange loa spirits. For we bayou folk, these things weren't just mementos out of Grimm's Fairy Tales. These things were our world. Everyone knew someone who had seen the *feux follets*. Folks had real fear of being turned into zombies by a bokor. I myself had seen, when I was twelve and out catfishing, the water on the opposite bank of a narrow bayou channel suddenly begin to writhe and stir, culminating with something like a snake made of water emerging from it and thrashing around for over a minute before slipping back into the murky depths. We Cajun folk knew we lived in an enchanted world.

So the season of Samhain has always brought me frissons. Not of fear, mind you. Of anticipation. Of delicious excitement. It is the time enchantment is most potent. It is when the veil that divides the green world from the Otherworld grows most thin and things may slip through and touch us, and occasionally it is said a mortal stumbles through that very veil into the Otherworld. The Scots folk that came to Nova Scotia centuries ago found a country of rolling hills, low mountains, and great old forests, primal and not far different from the British Isles a millennium ago. In those fey, dark woods they encountered beings much like the Good Folk of their homeland. Or perhaps the faerie spirits came across the ocean with them. In any event, it was enough to inspire many of the Gaelic settlers to hang onto their faerie faith, setting out food and drink by twilight on faerie plates, being wary to avoid mushroom circles while wandering the wildwoods. The Scots were so sure of the faerie presence in this land that they once called the forest *Coille n'an Sithchean* (pronounced COLE NON SHEE*ahn), which means "forest of the faerie folk." I have wandered the highland woods far and wide on horse and foot, and I know they are the abode of otherworldly things. And so, many years after my childhood in Louisiana, and far, far away from those mysterious bayous, Samhain still brings me frissons.

Living close to the land, Samhain has become very special to my family. It is the time for bonfires and long, pensive nights beneath chill stars meditating upon ancient mysteries. But because it also occurs at the end of late harvest and in the time of the Hunt, we also perceive it as a time of celebrating abundance, and we show our thanks by setting out the faerie plates—little offerings to the spirits that look after the Hollow and keep our animals and gardens so well. In the old lore, the thorn tree is especially sacred to the faerie folk and so we go into the forests at this time and seek out thorn trees and harvest their berries, some to make jam but many to plant around our meadows to become parts of the hedges that protect the horses and goats, feed the little wild creatures that share our land, and make sacred spaces all at once. And we have many happy harvest dinners in late October, but the best comes upon Samhain itself. Last Samhain we had guests from far and near share a dinner all of the produce of our gardens, and then we went to Hedge Witch Hill to gather for a great bonfire around which giant pumpkins stood sentinel while we toasted the evening with the ancient custard-like beverage *fuarag* (FU*rak), told tales, and bade the Green Man a fine sleep as the summer ended and the Celtic New Year began.

But let us look back to another Samhain, one just before we discovered Twa Corbies Hollow, but which also took place in this enchanted highland forest in the heart of the New World's Celtic lands, in a sequestered little farmhouse deep in the woods that was our home when we first arrived. It was there the frissons were strongest . . .

We were new here, both to the province and the nation of Canada. Though Daphne is Canadian, we had lived most of our adult lives in Alaska so even she felt like a stranger to the country. And though the friendly Nova Scotians made us feel welcomed, we were still acclimating to local life. Despite our years in the Alaskan bush, I had spent the last several years in Anchorage, studying counseling psychology in grad school, and we had become somewhat habituated to the *work-Work-WORK* culture that seems to predominate the west side of North America in both the USA and Canada. But life here was different. The tempo was slow and patient, based around the timeless pace of tradition and family. Folk worked hard, honest jobs, but they were content to set that work aside at the end of the day and immerse themselves in their lives and their ceilidhs (KAY*lees), gatherings where they told stories, played the music of *Auld Scotland* on ubiquitous fiddles, kitchen pipes (small bagpipes with voices soft enough to play indoors), and pianos. No one had much money, but life was good. It was beautiful. We had, in fact, chosen to come here for the way of life.

And I, more than any of us, needed it. I was soul-sick at the time. For a couple years after graduating, I had worked on the Kenai Peninsula, falling into extremely difficult work providing therapy to very disturbed criminals. Counseling is hard on the spirit. To do it well, you have to really immerse yourself in the client's psyche. While difficult enough when the client is a decent person suffering trauma or depression, it's painful beyond bearing when the client is a sexual predator telling you about raping children and cats. And with the mad work pace of Alaska, there was little time to stop and heal between sessions. So, I had worn down inside, reached a point where I hated the profession, was indifferent, anxious, and angry all the time. Alaska has a history of burning out therapists, and the clinic I was working for had an especially bad reputation. I stuck with it for twice as long as my predecessors, hoping that through the work I might make the world a better place, but it had drained me to the very soul. I look back on that time and realize I was almost a broken person.

When we arrived in Nova Scotia, I couldn't work for almost a year and a half while my immigration was processed. My wife was Canadian, so she was the only breadwinner. I felt bad about not being able to contribute financially, but in retrospect it was for the best. I needed that time to heal. I spent much of it with our daughters, then eight and thirteen. (This was a couple years before we bought Twa Corbies Hollow.) I had a fiddle and spent a lot of time teaching myself how to play. I did what I could to cook and keep up the ancient farmhouse we were then renting. And I spent a lot of time just wandering the endless woods, coming to know the land, and though I didn't know it at the time, its magic was slowly making me whole again.

By the time of our first October in Nova Scotia, we had resided in the province nearly a year. And one sunny afternoon, when the sugar maples sported leaves of blazing colors so dry they crackled in the breeze, Natalia and I had gone for a long walk through the endless Sithchean Wood behind the house while her older sister Arielle and Daphne stayed home to bake cookies.

The forest was mostly birch and maple, with the odd pine and white spruce, thorn, and apple. It was well into autumn and a sharp one at that, and the foliage beneath the trees had died away. The landscape rolled in endless hills, leading to plateaus to the west and low mountains further north. Samhain was just around the corner and the land felt Halloween-ish as we meandered through it, with fallen leaves crunching under our feet and the echoing calls of the island's numerous great ravens. And as we walked the lovely, drowsing wood, we spoke of small things. Her favorite cookies at a family bakery in the tiny village a dozen miles away. A small dispute she had had with her sister earlier in the day. Her first stumbling attempts to play the three-quarter–sized fiddle I had bought her. Hopes for chicken and dumplings for dinner. The warm, little things

. make family conversation so endearing. And then she said the most curious thing I had ever heard.

"... and you know those two children, with the blond, blond hair? The girl wears an apron that looks like it's from a long time ago, and the boy wears black pants and a white shirt. They passed by the window and I went out to play with them, but I couldn't find them."

I stopped and regarded her a long moment. I had seen them, too, several times back in high summer, casually strolling past the window in the middle of the day. They both had white-blond hair that shone like platinum in the sun and they looked so alike that I was sure they were brother and sister. But the most curious thing about them was their manner of dress. The girl wore a smock and apron; the boy dark trousers and a loose button-up shirt. The style resembled that of early nineteenth-century garb, a child's Sunday best. And each time I'd seen them, I'd darted outside to say hi, but they were never to be seen once I'd gotten outdoors.

The farmhouse was ancient and remote, deep in the forest near a huge inland lake. The next habitations were unworked farms a mile or two up and down the road in either direction, and there were large meadows between us and the woods. There was no way for the white-haired children to get to the woods or out of sight down the long country road in the mere moments it took me to dash out. And so in time I came to think of them as something other than entirely of this world, though they had looked so utterly, entirely real whenever they passed by the window on those summer afternoons, the sunshine gleaming in their locks, their peculiar garb of another century a stark contrast to the green meadow surrounding the old house. I didn't want to frighten Daphne or my daughters, and I wasn't sure what to make of the children in any case, so I had never mentioned them. And yet Natalia was now telling me she had seen them, too, and on more than one occasion. She went on...

"I'd like to play with them, but I don't know where they go."

I knelt down to one knee so we were at eye level. "Tell me more abou them. What did they look like, exactly? Tell me about what they were wearing."

She described the white-blond hair, and how they looked so similar she thought they were brother and sister. "The clothes were old-fashioned, Dad. Really old. Like the Mennonites we saw out west. I see them passing the living room window sometimes. I don't know where they go. I can never find them."

I put a hand on her shoulder, thinking carefully about what to say next. I didn't want to frighten Natalia. Honestly, lots of people are terrified of ghosts and sprites, but in my experience there is a lot more to be afraid of from plain old people. Why should otherworldly things wish us any harm? I think most people fear the preternatural in the same way children fear the dark—out of simple fear of the unknown. Still, otherworldly things should be respected. "Sweetie, I don't think you can play with those children."

She cocked her head and regarded me, puzzled. "Why not? They look about my age."

"Natalia, I don't think they're ordinary children. I'm surprised you saw them. I've seen them, too, and I thought I was the only one. I've looked for them, too, and when I go outside I can never find them. I used to think maybe they dashed off into the trees, but even if they could get there before I got outside—which is doubtful—I'd have heard them moving through the brush."

She looked away a moment, considering, then said. "What do you think they are?"

I shrugged. Ghosts? The Good Folk? Since coming here and spending so much time with the Gaelic-speaking Scots, I had learned they call the faeries the Sith (SHEE) and it doesn't mean faeries as in little elves in hollow hills, as is often mistakenly believed thanks to the influence of fantasy-genre fiction, though it's easy enough to see how the

ding developed because a hollow hill is called a *sidhe*, and
⸴ pronounced *shee*, and it is said that sometimes faeries live in
may ghosts and even gods. No, *Sith* means "the silently mov-
⸴le," and to the Scots, the faeries are a people in their own right,
⸴n not quite of this world, and not likely to be seen or heard unless
wish to be. And certainly these two children, who had seemed as
⸴l as stone when we saw them through the window on sunny after-
⸴oons had never made a sound when they passed, and vanished like
smoke in wind when we looked for them. I told Natalia seriously, "I
don't even know if they're really children."

Around us the day was perfectly calm, the woods perfectly still.
This late into autumn, not even songbirds skipped among the branches,
though here and there the odd squirrel or chipmunk darted among the
roots and branches, stocking up for the coming winter. Natalia glanced
into the woods on either side of the narrow trail and said, "Do you
think they were ghosts?" I thought about it, then shook my head. Call
it instinct, but when I'd seen them they looked too content and solid to
be the lost spirits ghosts are typically thought to be. She half smiled,
wonder in her eyes, and asked, "Do you think they were faeries?"

Again, I shrugged. "I don't know, sweetie. But the Scots folk around
here believe these woods are haunted by faeries. So do the Mi'kmaq, who
call them the Megumoowesoo. And, you know, the Acadians do, too,
and call them *les feys*." I spoke fair French by dint of my Cajun ancestry
and I had spoken with the Acadians on many occasions, up around the
village of Cheticamp. They seemed to like that I was Cajun, seeing me
as one their lost cousins who were exiled to Louisiana when the English
took Nova Scotia so many centuries ago, and so I had been privileged
to sit in on some of their kitchen parties which were, like ceilidhs, full of
music and old stories. "It seems everyone who lives around here believes
there is magic in these woods. That's why it used to be called Coille n'an
Sithchean—the faerie woods. It's like it's between the worlds."

"I like that," she said. "*Faerie woods*," she pronounced, testing the wor
and deciding they fit the landscape.

We walked deeper into the forest, following the trail which long
ago had been a farmer's path for harvesting firewood and maple syrup.
Around us the great old sugar maples rose into the sky, their limbs be-
decked in dry gold leaves and upraised, as if praying for the return of the
summer sun. Often we passed birches, and now and then a rowan tree or
a thorn, and here and there a lonesome oak. As we went, I shared faerie
lore with her. "The Celts used to write in an alphabet called the Ogham,
you know. And it was magical because each letter had a special tree or
shrub attached to it, and each of those shrubs and trees are important to
the spirits." I pointed at a thorn we were passing. "Thorn trees are especially precious to the Good Folk. Should you ever stumble into a thorn or
need to harvest its berries, make your apologies and show your respect."

The trail twisted and wound more steeply uphill, toward the vast pla-
teau a couple hundred feet above. Where the trail turned, a springhead
brought water to the surface, but the ground around it was relatively
flat and had turned soupy. Willows grew around the wet patch. "Willow
loves water," I told her. "Wherever you see them, the ground is sweet and
good for gardening, if it's not too wet. But it's an eerie tree. It is said at
night some willows uproot themselves and wander around."

Natalia eyed the willows suspiciously and asked, "Are they unseelie?"

I shrugged. "When you think about it, *unseelie* means unfriendly toward
Man. But I don't take that to mean unseelie is necessarily evil. Humans tear
down whole forests and drain entire wetlands. They kill entire species and
run machines that leave poisons everywhere. When you think about what
people do to Earth, we earn that enmity. But I honestly believe that if you
are the exception to the rule, if you live in respect of the Earth and show
consideration for the spirits, you have little to fear from any otherworldly
thing."

,lanced toward the sky. The sun was not yet so low, but
.t worked with the great old trees to make the forest darker
:ar blue sky said it should be. Still, it couldn't be more than an
,undown, two hours till full dark. "We should head back," I said.
:alia nodded but did not move. "I wish magic were real," she said,
ng very pensive.

"Well, of course it is," I replied. "We've been talking about all kinds
i magical things. The trees. The legends of the faerie wood. The
white-haired children."

"I know," she replied. "But I mean I wish I could see magic. It's almost
Halloween. I wish I could cast spells like a faerie." Then she lifted her
hand, held it out and made an odd, flicking motion, as if she were waving
a wand, and cried out, "Faerie magic! Be real!"

In that moment, it happened. A small thing. A great thing. A little,
big thing neither of us will ever forget. To the right, just off the trail,
a small twig not quite a foot long flew up off the ground, arced high
overhead, and fell to the soft earth just at our feet. Natalia and I both
saw the whole thing and glanced at each other in mutual astonishment.
It was as if something had picked up the twig and thrown it to us just
as she cried out the words. We stared into the forest. Autumn's chill
had caused the undergrowth of ferns to die back and the leaves of the
understory had long since fallen. It was easy to see a good way into the
trees, and the stick had launched at us from only seven or eight yards
away. Clearly, nothing and no one was there.

Natalia picked up the stick, turning it over and over in her hands as
if to assure herself it was real.

Without a word, we stepped off the trail to examine where the twig
had come from. There were no tracks. There was no one hiding behind
the trunks. We could find no rational cause for that twig to have tossed
itself off the ground and land in front of us.

"Magic," whispered Natalia.

I thought of the white-blond children. *The silently moving people.* Had they been walking along with us, listening to our mortal conversation? Had they taken a liking to us and given us a small sign to show magic was real, like Natalia had so wanted?

"Faerie pranks," I whispered to Natalia.

Faerie pranks, indeed. It was nearly Samhain, after all. The veil between the worlds was especially thin. We stood there, regarding the depths of the forest in the deepening shades of twilight, frissons working up and down our spines. But they weren't of fear; they were of wonder.

Since coming to the Hollow, we have enjoyed many wonderful Samhains. The girls trick-or-treated in the tiny village a few miles down the path, and we've had nights of blazing bonfires and friends and rites and hot colcannon and cold cider after. There is an ancient graveyard not far away and we have left little gifts for the dead and felt their gratitude. And sometimes we have taken guests camping and ceilidhing in the woods when the fickle autumn weather permitted. But that day near Samhain, years ago when we first came to this magical forest...and that simple walk with my dear little daughter when the silently moving people first reached out to us and started my own healing of the soul with the certainty that their magic was real...it was the best Samhain ever.

Natalia poses one Samhain morning with a pair of
giant pumpkins destined to become incredible
Jack-o'-lanterns at the celebratory bonfire.

Traditional Living

Making Fuarag: An Ancient Scots Divinatory Beverage

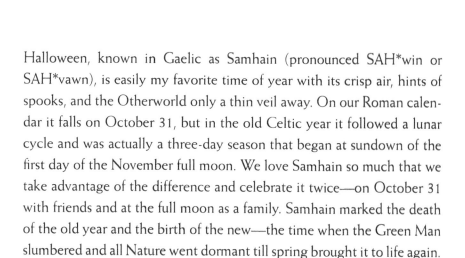

Halloween, known in Gaelic as Samhain (pronounced SAH*win or SAH*vawn), is easily my favorite time of year with its crisp air, hints of spooks, and the Otherworld only a thin veil away. On our Roman calendar it falls on October 31, but in the old Celtic year it followed a lunar cycle and was actually a three-day season that began at sundown of the first day of the November full moon. We love Samhain so much that we take advantage of the difference and celebrate it twice—on October 31 with friends and at the full moon as a family. Samhain marked the death of the old year and the birth of the new—the time when the Green Man slumbered and all Nature went dormant till spring brought it to life again.

Fuarag is a traditional Samhain recipe out of the
ancient Gaelic world, almost forgotten except in
the most remoter reaches of Nova Scotia.

The Gaels had a lovely divinatory practice associated with this season which has all but died out in Scotland but is still remembered in
some of the remoter regions of Nova Scotia and its adjoining isle of
Cape Breton to this very day. It is the consuming of fuarag. In part, it is
a way of toasting the harvest. But when combined with a few common
trinkets, it becomes a divinatory game, like breaking the turkey's wish-
bone. Fuarag divination is done for fun; I don't think it was ever meant
to be taken too seriously.

Fuarag is very simple to make, but its taste is full of the richness of
the harvest. In old times when it was drunk in the north of Scotland, it
was a stout beverage blended with oats, thinned with Scotch and water,
and flavored with honey and spices. But over time, tastes have changed

and fuarag tends to be made thicker and less alcoholic than in the distant past. Now it is more a rich custard than a drink. Throw in a coin, button, a pebble, and a ring to play the divination game.

For those persons who may worry about the alcohol content, I'd say there is little need. While the oats and cream carry the Scotch flavor well, the blend is much weaker than your typical cough syrup. It's more like a brandy cake though in soft, custard form.

There are many ways to make this ancient recipe, but the very simple one below is my favorite, and serves up to six:

½ cup fine oatmeal

1¼ cups fresh heavy cream

3 tbs honey

3 tbs Scotch whiskey

The charms (optional): A small coin,
     a ring, a smooth pebble, and a button

1. Toast the oatmeal in a skillet or under a broiler
   till it is golden brown.

2. Whip the cream till very stiff.

3. Stir the honey, Scotch, and charms into the cream.
   Do not stir in the oatmeal. (Of course, you can leave
   the charms out if you just want to enjoy the fuarag.)

4. Place layers of cream and toasted oatmeal in a large
   glass bowl and set in a fridge to cool for an hour.

5. To serve traditionally, give everyone a large wooden
   spoon and let them dip out a heap for themselves.

Whoever finds the coin shall come into wealth. Whoever finds the ring shall find true love. Whoever finds the pebble shall gain his hopes. Whoever finds the button, alas, shall fall into poverty.

Fuarag is like a creamy smooth custard and a belt of Scotch all at once. In other words, it's wonderful! And when you have it you'll taste something the ancient Gaels knew and loved, and relive an Old World custom of the magic of this mostly otherworldly season.

NOVEMBER

Little Spirits

If you don't tend wild apple trees, they will follow a biennial cycle: a year of superb harvest and a year of poor harvest, at least in these parts. Wild apple trees are also very common around Nova Scotia. Near the Hollow there are many. You are as likely to find them deep in the forest as standing in the midst of meadows or growing in hedges. Some wild apple trees yield sweet, good apples; others only give bitter, small, and scabby apples. Around the Hollow quite a few excellent wild apple trees grow. I have a feeling that the denizens of the Hollow in the nineteenth and early twentieth centuries were very reliant on those trees.

At the edge of the green spruces of the Elfwood, Grandfather Apple
greets the dawn with the first ripening fruits of the late harvest.

One could force the wild trees to give better yields. A potion of manure tea scattered over the soil beneath the outer circumference of a tree's
branches (where the feeder roots are) will provide the tree with the extra
nutrition it would need to fruit every year, but we have never done that.
The foremost reason is we prefer to let things follow their natural course.
Every organic gardener quickly learns that Nature knows far better than
we how to go about her business. So we let Nature manage the wild things.

This was a year of plentiful apples. A warm June followed by a mild
summer and very late autumn frost had been very kind to the trees. From
the crabapple tree down by the wild grapes at the abandoned homestead to the wild apples around the Hollow and in the Elfwood, the
trees were heavy with fruit. And not just any fruit, but perhaps the finest we had ever harvested. The apples were big, firm, and nectar sweet.

From a single scraggly tree at the edge of the woods just off our lands, we picked some four hundred pounds. From the small trees that grew out in the horse meadow and at the edge of the Elfwood, we picked a couple hundred more pounds of small, sweet apples. All were excellent, and Daphne and the girls busied themselves making apple pies, jellies, and fruit leathers. But of all the trees, the prized one was down by the pond at the edge of the brook. The tree grew just up the hillside from the pond, less than a hundred feet from the cottage. It had a perfect southern exposure on rich, black, rocky soil that was acidic enough to grow blueberries, too. This is the kind of ground apple trees love best. An artesian spring nourished its roots, and ensconcing spruces took the brunt of the occasional mountaintop tempests. This perfectly situated, ancient apple tree was huge as apple trees go, nearly thirty feet tall and just as wide—so big and aged I always thought of it as Grandfather Apple. Its branches spread so broad the girls had built a clubhouse in their shade. And each autumn, even on slow years, it yielded hundreds of pounds of huge golden apples of surpassing sweetness, with just the right amount of tart. We looked forward to its wondrous yields with an especial zeal. Why? Because from those apples we could make one of the finest beverages ever created by humankind: cider!

There are several kinds of cider. Soft cider is the juice of pressed apples, and it is oh-so-much fairer than the filtered, watery, clear stuff that comes canned and jugged in grocery stores. The good stuff ... well, you typically have to buy it at a farmers' market or make it yourself. If you're lucky, there might be a nearby apple farm where you can get the stuff freshly pressed, and if that is the case, avail yourself of the opportunity. I guarantee you won't regret it. The good stuff is thick and opaque, rich with fruit protein and even bits of pulp that are released with the pressing process. Hold up a glass of it into the sun and try to look through it. The light will reveal the traditional caramel color of cider, but it will be nearly opaque. Sip it! It is the gods' own ambrosia. There are few pleasures so fine as sipping fresh-pressed apple cider upon a crisp autumn day.

The other kind is hard cider. It takes two basic forms. One is the bubbly, alcoholic drink with the potency of champagne (if homemade). It is a little tricky to make but none too hard once one gets the knack. The best is made simply by pouring soft cider in a primary fermenter for a week or so with a bit of brewer's yeast and honey or sugar, then racking it into a carboy for another few weeks till the sediment settles. Then a small bit of sugar or honey syrup is added to the batch and it is bottled and left alone for a month or two. It will build up pressure in the bottles, rendering it bubbly.

The other hard cider is much like wine. You sweeten the cider a bit and let it go through an extended fermentation process, let it settle and clarify, then bottle the contents sans bubbles. This version is sometimes referred to as cider wine. When done right, it keeps for years. And it can be transformed into apple brandy (a.k.a. applejack) easily enough by dropping a gallon or two in a deep freezer or just leaving it out upon an icy winter night. The next day, what isn't frozen is brandy. It's very handy for making tinctures as well as sipping.

If you would like to try making either version of this ancient beverage for yourself, detailed instructions are on page 293 in the Traditional Living section, Harvest Cider.

The very best cider is made from only the sweetest, most perfect apples. The sweeter the apples, the less additional sugar has to be added, resulting in a more perfect brew bursting with unadulterated apple flavor. Thus, the apples of the great old tree down by the spring were a real prize. Other trees' apples could become pies and tarts, pastries and jellies, or just get stowed down in the root cellar. Grandfather Apple's perfect fruits were slated for cider!

But summer lingered on and on, and though it is a dapper gentleman and always welcome upon this cold mountaintop, it persisted right through the usual harvest season in late September, keeping the frosts at bay with southwesterly breezes. It's best not to harvest apples until they've been through at least one hard frost because it is the frost that tells the dreamy-slow arboreal minds of trees that Earth is soon to sleep, and they make a final magnificent effort to put sugar into the fruit. But the warm weather held and held, so the ripened apples lingered long upon the branch, but at last, near mid-November, we had three successive nights of hard frosts and it was finally time to harvest the apples from the old tree out by the spring.

Normally, because apple trees yield so much, I would just drive the tractor to the tree and we'd fill up the loader bucket. It can hold about five hundred pounds. But the hillside was too steep to get the tractor down there. We'd have to load the apples into milk crates and carry them back up the steep hill to the cottage. It would be hard manual labor. And because it was a big tree, we'd have to use special fruit pickers. These are small baskets with dull hooks mounted on eight-foot and sixteen-foot poles used to snag the apples and twist them off the branches. The apples fall into the little basket beneath the hooks so they don't get bruised. They are essential for getting the fruit off the higher branches where it grows thickest and arguably best.

So one fine Friday morning after the third hard frost, just days after the November full moon (the lunar Samhain), Arielle (then sixteen), eleven-year-old Natalia, and Daphne and I went down the hillside to the old tree shortly after breakfast. We only had one fruit picker and I used it to pass the apples down to Arielle, who crated them. Meanwhile, Daphne and Natalia gathered all the reachable apples and also inspected the windfallen fruits to find those that were useable. It was hard work, as most things are in farming, but it was good work. The air was brisk, just cool enough to make one want to stay busy. Partly rotten or worm-eaten apples were all over the ground, getting trampled as we worked, and soon the air filled with the fragrance of apples. Wild mint grew at

the edge of the tree, and though it was desiccated with autumn it still released bursts of fragrance whenever it was stepped on. Across the brook,
a pair of ravens landed in a tall, slender birch and cawed back and forth,
as if discussing the merits of our work. I saluted them, as seemed only
appropriate. After all, our homestead was named for them. Twa Corbies
Hollow is *auld* Scots-English for "Two Ravens Hollow." And I was pleased
to see them. Ravens are omens of transformation and in aboriginal myth
good luck and the animal form of the beneficent god Raven.

"Talk to them, Dad!" said Natalia as she watched them through the
young spruce that grew just beyond the edge of Grandfather Apple's
circumference of branches.

I paused in my work and cawed to them. In Alaska, where great ravens are plentiful, I had become fascinated with the birds after learning
of their extraordinary intelligence. It turns out ravens can count to at least
eight, and they have a range of hundreds of calls that some suspect is an
avian language. They can imitate human speech like a macaw. And they
mate for life. I had once seen a raven stand guard for weeks over her mate
that had been killed by a car beside a road. Every day I would go check
on the raven, and ask the Green Man to drive her off that she might carry
on with her life. I was afraid she would stay perched in that tree mourning her lost mate till she starved. Then one day, I suppose, my request
was answered. I walked past the tree and the raven was gone. Strangely,
so was the dead raven at its base. Ravens had intrigued me so much that
I had devoted a lot of time to learning their calls. I became very good at
imitating them, and in Alaska I used to be able to call them back or send
them away, or even get them to circle, but the ravens of Nova Scotia
don't quite respond to my calls the same way. It makes me think they do
have a language, and I just haven't been able to learn the local dialect yet.

The moment I called to them, the raven pair ceased their chatter
and looked in our direction, cocking their heads curiously, making Natalia giggle. "They're probably thinking," I told her, "'Hey! Does that

guy look like a raven to you?' And the other one is saying, 'What on Earth is he trying to say? I can't understand a word of that gibberish. Sure sounds like a raven, though.'" Natalia and I shared a chuckle.

Soon the ravens had enough of my senseless chatter and took to the air, circling a moment then flying off northwest, cawing incessantly as they flew. Daphne smiled impishly and said, "Guess they didn't like your accent."

It is amazing how fast you can pick a *lot* of apples. I had to stop my harvesting task every few minutes to run crates and bags up to the cottage. Despite the brisk air, I soon had a fine sweat going. No matter, I don't consider it good hard work unless it's accompanied by a good sweat. At noon, we knocked off for lunch and it was only then that we realized we were stocked with more than enough apples. Baskets and crates stood on the front deck and two big piles of apples besides. Hundreds of pounds. We had a nice lunch of spicy beans and barley with chard from the garden on the side, and took an hour after to relax with tea and light reading. Early in the afternoon, I got onto the next part of the task—making cider!

Daphne helped me bring the enormous cider press out of the wood-shop and we set it up on some level ground just in front of the east deck. The press is a grand, old, fully functional antique. I believe it came from Italy. I don't know for certain, but I do know it was used long ago by an Italian gentleman for pressing grapes. He made his own wine by the barrelful. How we came upon it is a bittersweet tale of strange fate, but it is personal to me. I'll just say it was a gift from the wife of a good friend who passed away. I never even knew my friend had had such a press, and his wife never knew how desperately, and over how many years, Daphne and I had sought for one. She just knew Daphne and I lived simple, back-to-the-land lives and thought her husband would have been happy to have us receive it. For us, it was an utter godsend because up till then, the only way we could press apples was to crush them in plastic buckets, which is terribly wasteful.

When we received it, it had been stained and a bit rusty, but we had lovingly restored it and brought it back to life. I struggled at first with using it because it reminded me so much of my friend. But one day another friend said, "I bet every time you and your wife use it, it makes Bob smile." That warmed my heart and from then on I was at peace with making use of the gift.

The press was massive and weighed over a hundred pounds. It was so big it could crush a bushel of apples at once. I've never tried to max its capacity, but I am sure it could manage a hundred pounds at a time. Daphne set a capture bucket beneath the press rim's lip and I began working it. It was hard work. The press basically screwed a hefty plate down onto the apples. Working it was a matter of sheer muscle power, walking round and round the basket in order to push the massive bar that screwed the plate down. As the pulp was crushed, juice trickled across the plate, off the lip, and into the collector bucket. It was a slow process, and often it was necessary to pause for as much as an hour to give the pressure time to work.

Daphne dumped the juice from the smaller capture bucket into hefty five-gallon buckets and sealed them between pourings as fresh air is never good for juice. The pressing process took the better part of that day and the next, but by its end we had some twenty gallons of cider. The whole yard smelled like apples, and the fragrance even permeated the cottage. Some of that juice we would use fresh or trade, but most would become cider wine and hard bubbly cider.

The next morning, we sent the girls out to feed the horses and livestock, and Daphne and I went promptly back to work on the juice. Even when it's cool, cider cannot wait. Of the juice slated for soft cider, the majority went right into a deep freezer so it could keep until we were ready for it. Twelve gallons were divided into two equal batches and set to fermenting. One batch would become bubbly hard cider, the other cider wine. The wines would be aged in the root cellar for a couple years, but the bubbly cider could be drunk as soon as the fermentation and priming had completed, in about two or three months. A few bottles of the cider wine would even be cold distilled into apple brandy, then mixed with honey and elderberries to be used as an effective cough remedy.

So, the apples were harvested. We used what we could right away and stowed the rest whole down in the root cellar where it would keep for months. The entire cottage smelled like apples and spices. To us, it smelled like autumn, and even in deep winter those apples would bring us back to thoughts of warmer days and harvest bounty. And down by the spring Grandfather Apple still carried many heavy fruit upon his aged boughs. There they would stay, regardless of whether we could use them or not. In fact, we made it a point never to harvest all the fruit from any of the apple trees except the youngest, if it looked like the weight of the fruit might damage delicate new branches.

It was late one November morning that Natalia and I found ourselves out wandering along the south side of the land. Snow had come and gone several times but never stuck. Still, the days were sharp with cold and the leaves had all vanished from the hardwoods. A lucent sky allowed sunbeams to pour between the boughs of the trees. They played over the forest floor like light swimming at the bottom of a pool, and whenever one touched us, it gave as a gift a momentary hint of warmth.

Earlier we had brought the Belgian horses to the corral where I had trimmed their hooves. Farrier work is, like so many things on a homestead, heavy labor, and we had decided to take a break after. We had left them in the corral each with a half bale of sweet hay and decided to take an easy walk down into the heart of the Hollow where the Rusalka Brook flows. We talked idly as we ambled, in no rush to get to anyplace, just enjoying the beauty of autumn—always my favorite time of year. Around us a great

Acadian forest of maples, birches, and the occasional rowan stretched bare branches skyward like skeletal sprites. Along the way, I pointed out animal spoor: bear, coyote, porcupine, ermine, and deer tracks, and explained how to distinguish each sign, tell how fast the animal had been going, and what it had been eating. Natalia had her longbow with her and occasionally took a shot at a stump just for the fun of it.

When we got back to Twa Corbies Hollow, we took the secret shortcut up to the cottage, cutting off the dirt path through a dense hedge of woods and hopping steppingstones over the brook, which bubbled and chortled cheerily on this perfect day. But rather than heading straight up to the cottage for hot tea, as we had both been contemplating, we followed our feet to the pond and the extension of spruce woods that surrounded the cottage like the protective embrace of the Elfwood, and soon we found ourselves at the base of Grandfather Apple.

There were new windfallen apples upon the ground and in the tree perhaps a hundred pounds of fruit remained, some beginning to take on the desiccated look of winter apples. I drew my puukko, which is hefty knife almost long enough to qualify as a short sword, a tool with a hundred uses around the homestead, and began hacking back the spruce boughs that were encroaching upon the tree's circumference of branches so the aggressive spruces could not choke the precious sunlight from the old tree. As I did, Natalia picked her way among the fallen fruit, scrutinizing them. She knew most of these were serviceable apples. They had fallen after the days had dropped below freezing and the fruit, even on the ground, had not been bothered by worms, insects, or rot. They were, by all accounts, perfectly good apples.

"I don't understand," she said after a bit.

I was on the opposite side of the trunk, at the edge of the thick spruces, hacking hard at a tangle of branches and had not heard her clearly. "Come again?" I called.

"You always tell us never waste," she said. "You kill a deer and we have to use every part. We make leather from the skin. We make decorations and tools of the antlers. We grind the scrap into sausage and feed the tripe to the barn cat. But this is our best apple tree and there's so much fruit left on it. It's just going to waste."

The puukko's blade had spruce sap on it now. I would have to clean it off later with alcohol or turpentine, whatever would dissolve the gummy stuff away. I didn't want to resheath it with the sticky sap on the blade, so I punched it forward into a tree trunk and left it in place. I walked over to Natalia, glanced up into the branches and pointed at an apple dangling lowest, where it could be seen clearest. "That's what we give back to the Apple Man, sweetie."

She nodded. She knew about the Apple Man. He is a creature of legend who tends apple trees. I suspect that he looks after other fruiting plants, too—a domestic sprite of the fields like the goblin and *glaistig* (GWAWSH*chik: a complex female faerie figure, usually a nocturnal household helper and shepherdess of flocks though some later legends say she is malevolent). Nova Scotia maintains a faerie faith, faint but still living. It had been brought to this land by those old Gaels who came here so many centuries ago and took to this land as passionately as they took to their craggy highlands and wooded glens in Scotland. Indeed, the name Nova Scotia translates literally to *New Scotland*. And we'd all seen enough hints of wondersto know that marvelous things existed in the surrounding woods.

"But who knows if he takes it," Natalia said, looking at all the fruit hanging high in the boughs.

The remaining fruit were all too high to simply pluck, so I leaned over, grabbed a thick branch and gave it a good shake. Shooting a seventy-pound longbow, tossing forty-pound hay bales into the loft, and splitting cords of firewood puts a lot of strength into a body and I was able to shake several apples loose. I tracked one's descent and pointed at it. "Grab that, Natalia."

She picked it up and handed it to me. I turned it around so she could see all sides. Here and there were little dark holes punched into its flesh. "Here the birds ate," I said and pointed out the holes. "See, their beaks pierced the skin at these points." I tossed the apple aside and looked over the ground beneath the tree. It took only moments to find a chewed fruit. I held it up and showed her the tiny teeth marks. "Look at these. Here a field mouse has been nibbling. And these larger marks are from a squirrel, maybe a chipmunk."

Natalia regarded the gnawed apple and pursed her lips. She looked from the apple up to me and said, "Yeah, but that's wildlife. They can get apples from any tree in the woods."

I nodded. That was true.

She went on. "How do we know if the Apple Man ever even takes an apple?"

That was a really good question, a challenging question, and there is nothing wrong with challenging one's faith now and then. It makes one think. It keeps one on one's spiritual toes. It ensures you know why you believe, and avoids the pitfalls of blind faith.

Natalia and I took a seat at the edge of Grandfather Apple's circumference in the entry of the rickety clubhouse she and her sister built a couple years ago. I thought about my friend, the faerie artist Mark Potts, who did the cover art for my last book, which had depicted an Apple Man. Back when we were planning that piece, we emailed back and forth quite a bit and in one of those emails he had surprised me by telling me he had once seen an Apple Man in the British countryside. But Natalia had a point. We ourselves had never seen an Apple Man, yet we left a significant portion of our apple harvest for him every autumn. How did we know we weren't just wasting those apples? And how to explain something so deep to a child in early adolescence?

"Well, here's the folklore answer," I told her. "The one straight out of the faerie myths. Some say that the Good Folk take the essence out of the food that is left for them, its nutritive, energizing force. It's said that if a person ate that food, he could eat his fill and still starve. For my part, I think that's nonsense. I suspect the idea arose in ancient times when people starved no matter how much they ate due to illnesses like intestinal parasites."

"Ew!" she mewed.

I went on. "The other myth is that the faerie folk take the offerings whole and true. And I think sometimes that does happen. We've all seen amazing things around here. The lights in the woods. The blond-haired children. And the food we set out on the faerie plates always disappears, though who's to say if faeries or wildlife nicked it, eh?"

Natalia smiled and nodded. I put an arm around her shoulders as we talked. She was a good kid: open-minded but not gullible. She would believe ... if there was reason to believe. I liked that about her. "Sweetie, I don't honestly know if the faerie folk take the food on the faerie plates or if the Apple Man takes any of these apples. In fact, some would say they're just spirits and couldn't affect the material world, anyway. But I know you and I both don't believe that. Remember the stick that launched itself at us when you wanted to see magic? What I think is that in some places the veil between the worlds is thin, and in those places, maybe spirits can become more real. And maybe this is such a place." I shrugged and added, "It's only my theory, though. I can't prove it. But I do know we have loved this land and respected its spirits. And in return, the land has been good to us. It gives, we give back—things go full circle. That's probably how the customs like leaving faerie plates and apples for the Apple Man got started, when you think about it. The circle of giving ... what could be more natural? It's the way of Nature. Last year's plant died at autumn and this year's seed grew upon the nutrients it left behind, and next year's plant will grow upon this one.

"So maybe it's not even so important whether an Apple Man actually takes any of the apples. It's just important that we share what Nature has shared with us. As you can see, the apples don't go to waste, that's for sure." I grinned and added, "But the truth is I suspect the Apple Man does occasionally slip by and nicks one for himself. Hey, they're good apples!" I poked her shoulder teasingly, as if to emphasize the point, and she giggled. "But I think the Apple Man is quite happy to have the furred and feathered forest folk have most of the bounty. That's as good as leaving apples for the Apple Man."

"So ... we share to show we appreciate what Nature shares with us," she said, starting to see the point.

"Exactly," I told her emphatically. "You ever notice how much milk our goats produce and how much food our gardens yield? This is not the richest land, but it takes good care of us. Think about it. The forest is full of raccoons and everyone around here loses whole gardens to them, but we don't even fence our gardens and the raccoons never touch them. Behind the Hollow, the deer gather in droves every summer, but they don't touch our fruit trees. Not a one! Coyote packs run in the forest, yet we never close the barn and they never go after a goat. We love this land. We love its spirits. Ultimately, the Good Folk know and they look after us. Get and give in return—the circle of Nature."

She smiled. No. She glowed. It was a good feeling, knowing Earth's own little spirits were looking out for us. And all they asked of us was a little respect, but we had gone further. We had endeavored to be their friends. It was a relationship returned in kind.

I stood up, going practical again. One can never sit around too long when life is dictated by the turning of the seasons and the cycles of the land. I grabbed the puukko's hilt and pulled it from the trunk. "Well, I have to get up to the cottage and clean this up before the sap makes it rust. Maybe after we can play croquet."

Natalia's stomach rumbled. "I wonder what Mom is making for lunch," she said.

I chuckled and replied, "I bet it'll be something good. Let me guess ... Apple pie. Apple cider. Apple bread. Apple dumplings. Venison roasted in apples. Mmm!"

"Ha! Ha!" she blurted, and we raced up the hill to the cottage doors.

DECEMBER

Cottage Magic

The myths of December are intended to turn our thoughts toward home, and I don't think where we live is ever homier than in the month of December. This is a time of cottage magic, though Daphne might call it motherly magic. At this time, her unceasing labors come to fruition. Herbs are strung from the rafters in the arctic entry over the nineteenth century–style, wood-fired cook stove, and late-harvested onions dangle from the stairway to the third level. Colorful jars of jams and jellies line every windowsill in the immense kitchen and the craft room. Dried, twisted stalks of corn and boughs of spruce decorate the walls at any given moment. Everywhere in the immense old cottage, the air is rich with the fragrance of baking bread, simmering stew, and warm cookies along with a mélange of fragrances from the hanging herbs drying in the gentle heat of the wood stove.

Arielle and Natalia are as active in creating the cottage atmosphere as Daphne, and at this time of year a festive spirit permeates their deeds. They get a break from homeschool and Natalia makes garlands of popcorn and tiny spruce cones and festoons them about the pillar in the living room and the rail at the stairwell that leads down to the library. She also has a knack for natural art and creates images from seashells gathered at the beaches that are never far off in Nova Scotia. Using bits of sea glass, dried seaweed, and tiny shells, she glues them together on stones flattened and smoothed by the ever rolling waves to create images of woodland creatures and seabirds.

A bitter cold winter evening settles over the cottage,
but the smell of woodsmoke promises warmth and a hot dinner.

Arielle, not to be outdone, contributes her own cottage magic. Arielle is a mistress of the oven, and from our stores of goat milk (which freezes well), homegrown eggs, and flour, she creates a variety of pastries, pies, and cakes to add warmth to the dark month of December when the solstice brings the shortest of winter days.

Even I, the irrecusable outdoorsman, am brought closer to home. In the depths of December, the saddle is stowed, the livestock stalled, the gardens tilled and put to rest, and the longbow set aside except for daily practice at our archery range. (To keep one's skill in traditional archery, which is a purely instinctual art, practice must happen several times a week, rain, snow, or shine.) The horses are turned loose in the pastures to play as they will and sleep under the trees while they grow their thick winter coats. My outdoor work is now close to home: splitting the firewood and clearing snow from the paths. My other tasks become indoor work. Chief among them is sausage making. The autumn's turkeys have been butchered, and I will use some of the deboned meat, along with venison, bear, and whatever else we have to make a variety of sausages. Some will go straight into the freezers, but a goodly portion will be sent for a time down to the ancient smokehouse, more for flavor than preservation. The little smokehouse is not fifty feet from the cottage, at the edge of the Elfwood, and when the breeze blows in from the south, the cottage fills with mouthwatering fragrances of alder-smoked meat.

Of course, for most people in North America, December is the height of the holiday season, as both Christmas and New Year's Eve fall in this month. Sadly, for many people this means a time of extraordinary stress as people feel compelled to create of their homes an artificial "perfect" holiday environment, and they immerse themselves in a materialistic orgy that culminates, for many, in a tangle of regretted bills. In my work as a psychotherapist, I see many people struggling with "holiday stress" and the aftermath of spending from November to February.

But in the Hollow we follow a more primal lunar/seasonal calendar, and for us the height of the High Days came and went two months ago with Samhain. In that three-day "time between times," the Green Man fell into his deathlike slumber and winter waxed with the rise of the Holly King. But here on the verge of the darkest part of the year we also celebrate a holiday out of old Germanic tradition, one that traces its origins deep into pagan prehistory and appears throughout Europe, as far east as Poland, as far north as Sweden, and as far west as England. This is the time of Yule, a celebration, in particular, of Odhinn, often misunderstood as a god of war, but who is in truth more a god of the uncanny and arcane things that are the stuff of eldritch lore, and a friend to brave, hardworking folk. Odhinn is so strongly associated with Yule that he is known among Germanic and Scandinavian peoples as *Jólnir*, the "Yule Figure." He valued wisdom so highly that he sacrificed one of his own eyes to obtain it, and his guidance is sought at this time to ensure a peaceful, bountiful coming year.

Yule also has strong associations with ancestor veneration that goes back as far as the Stone Age. In modern Western cultures, ancestor veneration is strongly associated with death and is misconstrued with horror and devilry, and such misconceptions are epitomized in the gaudy crop of horror movies that appear each summer and around Halloween. But if one examines ancestor veneration among Eastern contemporary cultures, such as in Japan where it is an integral part of Shinto, and among surviving primitive indigenous cultures, such as the aboriginals of Australia and North America, which maintain contact with the spirits of the dead through shamanism, we quickly perceive that there is no evil in these practices. After all, why would the dead who have been friends and loved ones in life seek to harm us in death? No, ancestor veneration is a healing, respectful practice in which those who have perished are remembered and honored among the living. We make them feel welcome and ask they remember us in the Otherworld, and we ask them to bless our living days with goodness. There are many ancestral spirits of both Gaels and aboriginals in this ancient land, and in the Hollow we do our best to do right by them.

With all that in mind, Yule was an important time for us. And Yule eve was always filled with excitement. Fun, fine foods, and generous but not decadent presents were planned for the next two days, and many magical traditions would be woven into each event.

We woke before dawn and had a delicious breakfast of pancakes with syrup made of blackberries we had gathered from the forest late in autumn. The sky was a clear azure and though snow had fallen earlier in the year, nothing yet had really stuck and there was only a film of white over the ground. In meadows with good southerly exposures, the bright yellow grass of last season was still visible. In the Highland Meadow, the horses capered and we even planned to let the goats out of the barn so they could romp in the Firefly Meadow. Cookies and cakes that smelled as good as they looked were heaped on the table and set along every kitchen windowsill. In the sink, Daphne had an enormous turkey thawing. Toward evening she would stuff it with a Cajun dish that I would make called *riz sale* (dirty rice), glaze it with honey, and then start it slowly baking.

Later in the day there would be games. The goats' meadow was yet clear of snow due to its direct southern exposure and we would play Frisbee. Toward nightfall we'd play board games. Once it was full dark, we would build a huge fire outdoors and burn a Yule log to warm the faeries, let the god of Yule know we remembered the meaning of the season, and request a safe, happy upcoming growing season with good crops. But first there were some needful chores. I wanted to cut and split a good week's worth of firewood, and Daphne wanted to thaw some milk and make cheese. So over breakfast we made our plans, and Daphne and I purposefully neglected to mention what we knew would be an absolutely essential part for the girls, especially little Natalia. I summed up: "So, you'll make cheese, I'll cut wood. We'll play games later and tomorrow, presents and the Yule feast!"

"Yep, that sounds like the sum of it," Daphne said, sipping primly from her teacup.

"Yes, ma'am. I guess we're right on top of things, then. Nothing else to do but relax." I leaned back in my chair as if to say the matter was settled.

"But what about the Yule tree?" Natalia demanded.

We were all gathered at the kitchen table and I had been nursing a large mug of Russian Earl Grey after the pancakes. I feigned indifference and said, "What about it?"

Natalia astutely observed, "We still haven't cut one, and Yule is almost here!"

Daphne told her, "Oh, yeah, that's right. Well, Daddy and I decided that since we're surrounded by a whole forest of trees, we could just look at them instead."

Natalia gaped, her mouth forming a horrified O. "You mean you're not going to cut a Yule tree?"

I shook my head. "Why bother? There are lots in the Elfwood all around us. And we don't even need to decorate them. They already have pretty needles and cones."

Natalia's mouth worked but nothing came out. Arielle picks up fast on any opportunity to tease her younger sibling, and said, "And by leaving the tree outdoors, we don't even have to bother digging the decorations out of storage."

Natalia glowered at Arielle, then saw Daphne and me nodding as if Arielle's suggestion was a good point. She regarded us as if she had suddenly realized we weren't her real family but a gathering of doppelgangers.

"Just think," I said, "with all the time we'll save, I can get a lot more wood split today."

"And I can make an extra round of cheese," Daphne piped in.

"You will not!" Natalia said with a stomp, literally putting her foot down. "We have to have a Yule tree!"

"Why?" Daphne asked.

She sputtered a moment, then declared the most obvious, best reason. "Because it's the Old Way!"

Wow! Out of the mouths of babes. And she was dead right, of course. It was part of the tradition of honoring Odhinn in midwinter. Some things need no further explanation than that.

Pretending to reluctantly concede, I moaned, "Fine, fine, we'll go march into the cold forest and cut down a Yule tree when we could be in the warm kitchen sipping hot chocolate."

Daphne knew I really loved getting the Yule tree each winter with Natalia and thought it might distract me from the practical essentials. Daphne's always been very good at keeping focused.

"There is still half the firewood to split and stack," she said by way of gentle reminder.

I nodded. "Okay, okay. Everything in its season. I'll split a little wood. After, Natalia and I will go get the tree, and I'll do more firewood in the afternoon."

I like to write first thing in the morning, and I never feel right unless I've penned at least a few pages before I get my day going, so for the next two hours I sat in the library, nursing another cup of tea while tapping away at the keyboard. When the old grandfather clock struck nine, I took a quick shower then dressed for the outdoors. There might not be much snow on the ground yet, but it was unseasonably cold, and an easterly wind was just starting to blow in, a sure sign winter weather was working its way down out of the north.

I stopped at the woodshop and snagged my chainsaw and maul, and then went onto the woodpile almost a hundred yards east of the cottage. For the next two hours, I cut the eight-foot logs down to eighteen-inch lengths, then split them by hand with the eight-pound maul. Splitting the hardwood was brutally hard work, and soon I had stripped out of the coat and was sweating bullets in the light sweater I wore underneath despite the subfreezing weather. The electric fence doesn't work well in winter when the ground freezes, and the goats had figured it out. They escaped at one point, and I saw the girls dash past to chase them back into their meadow. They had passed close by and I yelled a reminder to stay well clear when I was using the chainsaw and the maul. They replied they knew without turning as they passed.

By eleven I had a nice pile of wood split. In winter we kept the tractor in an old cabin that I had converted into a garage by removing its floor and a portion of a wall. I fired it up and used the large bucket loader to carry the firewood down to the French doors of the lowest level of the cottage. Daphne hauled in a goodly portion of it to stow in the furnace room, where the dry heat from the large wood stove would cure the wood of any remaining moisture before we burned it. Arielle and Natalia returned from chasing the silly goats back into their meadow and stacked the rest of the firewood under the wraparound deck where it would be safe from getting wet by icy rains or thawing snows that could freeze the firewood into an enormous solid block.

There are few jobs to match the physical endurance and strength required to split wood by hand, and I came into the house near noon spent and famished. Daphne and Arielle had been indulging their creative cooking interests, and there was a hearty stew of sweet late-season turnips, venison, and autumn onions, with homemade cinnamon rolls for dessert. As we sat at the table, the wind began to whistle outside, and a sheet of gray cloud blew in out of the east, riding high in the sky but descending until the cloud cover was just over the top of the mountain.

Arielle observed, "I think it's going to be a big storm." She was right. The welkin was already spitting the first flakes of snow. Not the fat, fluffy flakes that promise a dramatic but brief snowfall, but the little pellets that promise a full-scale blizzard. And the wind was still building out of the east, meaning the storm was still gathering strength.

From the table I glanced at the thermometer mounted just beyond the kitchen window. In the last couple hours, the temperature had plummeted from 25 degrees F to 10. "I think the snow is here to stay," I said.

We go by an organic calendar, just as ancient peoples did. For us, the seasons don't arrive when some number on a calendar says they do. They start when the weather feels like the season. And for us, winter really begins when it becomes wintry. But Natalia, who has always been very sensitive to the portents of the natural world, said, "Winter is showing up for Yule. That must mean it'll be a bad winter."

"That sounds right," I agreed, and sipped at a glass of sweet hot apple cider. I didn't mind. The homestead was virtually self-sufficient. We heated with wood. We had ages worth of food dried, smoked, canned, and otherwise stored in the root cellar and in deep freezers. And should the power fail, we could produce light from lanterns and candles easily enough, and I could get enough electricity to continue my writing by connecting a powerful inverter to the tractor so that it doubled as a generator. And we could get pure water year-round from the spring whose fountainhead was not one hundred feet from the cottage just down in the west corner of the Firefly Meadow. Truth was, if the whole world stopped, we might not notice for weeks. All that self-reliance felt good, but mostly I loved the way winter made the world still and close.

I finished the cider and stood up. "Well, we better get after that Yule tree. The snow's getting thicker."

Natalia stood up, too. "I want to come!"

"I wouldn't have it any other way," I replied honestly. "I'll need you to help me find the right tree."

We marched to the north meadow, about a ten-minute walk, but from the time we left the cottage to the time we arrived, the wind had increased to a steady howl, and the snow had increased from a steady fall to a stinging white fierceness that was nearly opaque. The ground, which could be seen only an hour ago, was already under a foot of snowfall as the wild mountain winds grabbed snow destined for the lowlands and packed it onto the Hollow in the form of drifts. We were accustomed to it: we get some wild winters on this mountain so far in the north, but the speed in which the storm had evolved from a mere promise of weather to an angry blizzard was alarming. From the edge of the meadow, which is a new forest of spruce with scattered birch and brambles, we couldn't even see the trees any longer, and for a moment I contemplated turning around. I decided against it, though. Natalia would be heartbroken if we couldn't get a tree and I figured even if conditions should become a total white-out, we couldn't possibly get lost. All we had to do to find our way back was go downhill. That would eventually lead us to the fences, and when we fetched up against one we could follow it back to the cottage. But I sternly warned Natalia not to go more than two arm lengths from me. If she should lose her way, I'd never be able to track her in this weather. The snow would cover her footprints in moments.

We made our way up the slope of the north meadow and I veered by instinct into the thickest part of the young spruce forest. The trees appeared like dark shadows in the flying white haze. These were all wild trees—none had been trimmed and raised to become a Yule tree. Picking a good one could be tricky. Often, they were full from some angles but scraggly from others. But I realized the snow would actually help us choose a good tree. It provided a starkly contrasting background and we could use it to quickly tell which trees were fullest by noting how opaque their silhouettes were against the white backdrop. I pointed this out to Natalia and we set to tree-hunting. In half an hour we found several that we agreed might be good. I asked her to pick out her favorite. She pointed to a tall, well-rounded one. I used my puukko to chop back the lowest branches so I could reach the trunk, then a small Swedish saw to cut it down. It took another ten minutes.

In the time it took us to go up the hill and find and cut down a tree, the wind had become considerably stronger. It blew a good fifty knots steady now, a regular winter gale. We were wearing medium arctic gear when we left the house, so we weren't cold, except for where the wind and snow stung our exposed faces and tried to get into our eyes. Now and then we had to turn away from the wind and let our thick hoods shield us from the elements until we could feel the blood return to our cheeks. I hefted the tree by the trunk and started hauling it out. At least the new snow made a good, smooth surface to drag it over. Willowisp had come with us and, blessed with canine senses (or senselessness), seemed oblivious to the weather and completely certain of his bearings. He ran round and round us, into thickets and out again, chasing rabbits or his imagination. Now and then he bounded up in front of me, look-ing purposefully from me to the tree as if he thought it was a great stick I would toss off for him to fetch—had I heaved it up a couple feet the powerful wind would have carried it tumbling away downhill and the goofy Australian Shepherd would have done his best to wrestle it into submission and drag it back to us.

We started downhill. Every now and then Natalia would look up and around. "What are you doing?" I shouted above the wind.

"Isn't it Wild Hunt weather?" she called back.

Good point. I looked around, but all that could be seen was a bel-lowing whiteness. I shouted back, "I think it's too stormy even for them." We continued on our way.

The snow was stinging Natalia, though, and I had her walk close in front of me so I could shield her from the wind with my body. It wasn't much, but it was the best I could do. Sure enough, before we reached the bottom of the meadow, the storm had increased to the point we couldn't see fifty feet. But we followed gravity the rest of the way downhill and found the fence. We followed it to the path beside the barn and in a few minutes more were back at the cottage. Daphne, who in my opinion has the intuition of the mother goddess, was waiting for us with hot chocolate and a plate of warm-from-the-oven cookies.

The blizzard was intense and blasted through the rest of the day and well into the night, though the snow had decreased to the point where one could at least see by sundown. In the evening, the girls went to go feed the goats and chickens and make sure their stalls had plenty of warm bedding and sweet hay. While they were out, I split more firewood, making sure we were set for several days just in case the storm persisted. But the wild turn of the weather had cast aside our Yule eve plans. There could be no games in the goats' meadow and no Yule fire in the chimenea. But as I am sure our ancestors learned to live by the Earth's moods, so we adapted.

At the woodpile I split one log in half and hauled it into the woodshop. I drilled three small holes in it and pressed candles into the holes. A rowan tree grew just a few dozen yards off the cottage near the brook and I gathered some of the remaining berries from it. They were dark and dried, but close enough to the effect I was after. To add more color, I added some bits of spruce bough. This became our makeshift Yule log. We would burn the candles through the evening and when the girls went to bed the Yule log would be burned when I tossed it into the wood stove.

The girls finished their tasks about the same time I finished mine and I set up the small ornament on the coffee table in the living room near the Yule tree's place. We had a fine dinner of stew and pie, played some board games, all the while the Yule ornament's candles burning, reminding us what this time of year was about. Then we gathered in the living room with hot cider and I read a tale from the Norse folk myths. Natalia has an especial love of the old lore and loves reading Grimm's original fairy tales, my collection of faerie lore, and she's delighted by the various books in the library on Norse folklore. Afterward, Daphne and Arielle went to the kitchen to prepare the turkey, which would go in the oven tonight to slow bake. While they were out, Natalia and I threw on coats and walked out to the covered back deck. It was time to wassail: call the blessing upon the apple trees for a good harvest next year. I lifted my glass of cider in the direction of Grandfather Apple down by the spring and toasted its good health. Natalia joined me in the toast, then we leaned against the rail and watched the snow fall. The wind was howling through the forest, but it was blowing in from the east and we were on the west side of the cottage, sheltered from most of its force.

I looked up into the dark night. You couldn't see a thing except the snow streaking past the lighted windows. "It really is a night for the Wild Hunt," I told Natalia, thinking of her comment up on the hill. "How did you know about them?"

She explained she'd read about them in a book in our library. I smiled. She was clever, and always routing through the dusty old tomes down there. Every month I had to remind her to bring whatever books she'd borrowed back to the shelves.

"You know what they are, the Wild Hunt?" I asked her.

She said, "I read they're spirits of the dead. Or faeries. Or little gods. They go hunting travelers on wild winter nights."

I nodded. "Yeah, that's what the old myths say. I wonder why Odhinn would do that."

Natalia mused a bit, then said, "Odhinn's good, so he wouldn't do it just to be mean. Maybe it's to keep people where it's warm."

I wasn't sure, but it made sense, and I nodded. How many people venture out in deadly weather like this, only to pay the price? In Alaska I'd seen people die of exposure for going out when they should have stayed in. Even here in gentler Nova Scotia it happened from time to time. A belief in something like the Wild Hunt in elder times might have served to deter the recklessly intrepid from venturing too far when winter was at its worse.

Natalia said, "Let's go in. Mom's making whiskey balls." That's a kind of small round pastry made with a little whiskey for flavor. Its texture is a lot like cookie dough, and it has chopped nuts and dried cherries in it, and is doused in powdered sugar. We went back inside and everyone gathered in the kitchen and talked over cookies and more hot cider until the girls couldn't keep their eyes open anymore. But it was a holiday night and we let them stay up late. The whole kitchen was filling with the delicious scent of a roasting stuffed turkey.

Finally, they drifted up to their bedrooms and Daphne turned the oven down to give the turkey a long slow bake. She would have to get up again at three a.m. to baste it. I watched her go down to our bedroom then wandered about the house turning things off and making sure we were well battened down should the storm become more furious in the night. The Yule tree had been decorated with popcorn garlands, many of the girls' woven ornaments and hard-baked, painted cookies, and some blown-glass miniatures and candy canes. The decorations shone in the last light of the Yule log. Presents were wrapped under it for the girls. Giving presents wasn't a Yule tradition, per se, but we would not deny the girls the excitement of the season that most other kids get to experience. The candles had just about burned down to nothing and I blew them out. I stood up, holding the log and said, low voiced, "So, old One Eye, why, on a night when we remember your wisdom and goodness would something like the Wild Hunt ride?" In response, only the storm wind howled. I carried the log down to the wood stove and threw it in. I wished it could have been done earlier when we were all bright and awake to see it, in a big fire in the chimenea, but the weather had its own plans.

The next morning the girls were up extra early, as can be expected of kids anticipating presents under a tree. Daphne and I got up and we all exchanged gifts. The girls got some new clothes and books. Natalia got a new board game. The girls gave their mother cards and I got a blanket sporting wolf imagery. Nothing was very expensive, but it was all very dear. And when the gifts were all handed out we gathered up the wrapping paper, carefully folding it for reuse next year. Then Daphne and Arielle started breakfast while I stoked the fire and Natalia finished tidying the living room.

The storm had abated during the night, leaving a snow-covered landscape and slate skies. It was cold and all the wintry gray made it look even colder. But in the hearth room, the fire crackled in the huge old wood stove. Upstairs in the kitchen, Daphne and Arielle chattered happily. Natalia was quiet, but sound travels well in this solid old house and I'd heard her settle onto the couch on the level overhead. Doubtless already delving into one of her new books.

Odhinn had been remembered in our happiness and in our deeds. The apple trees were wassailed, so with Old One-Eye's blessing and the help of the Green Man we'd see a good crop of fruit next year. And the cottage was full of the warm routines that make it not just a dwelling, but a home. I felt Yule was honored properly.

I walked out of the furnace room, having rearranged the firewood, just about the time that Daphne called for us to come have breakfast. I could smell a buttery porridge of hot grain cereal and my mouth watered. "Be there in a moment," I called back. The teakettle began to sing, and I heard her go tend to it. I walked over to the big windows in the French doors in the library and looked out. Now there were little bits of blue peeping through the sheet of clouds, like the merry wink of a prankish but good-natured god. I couldn't help but think of Odhinn and his one good eye, and I smiled. I slipped on my high boots and stepped outside, no coat on. The winter air bit at my bare arms, but it felt good after the last ten minutes in the over-warm hearth room.

I stood on the stone entry just beyond the French doors and looked around. Icicles hung from the cottage. All the trees were frosted in white. And as I contemplated the beautiful wintry landscape, the warm cottage at my back, and the people I loved within, I thought back to Natalia scanning yesterday's storming sky for the Wild Hunt. They say they are faerie spirits, and spirits of the dead, and even Odhinn himself. "So why do they ride stormy skies at this time of year?" I mused to myself. And I realized Natalia had gotten it right. *To remind us where it's warm.*

I took a deep breath. It smelled of cold spruce and the freshness of new snow. It felt inviting and I was tempted to wander. But today I belonged inside. Daphne and the girls had taken this old dwelling and brought it alive with a heaping dose of cottage magic, some of the best magic, and it was the right place to be on a day like today.

Traditional Living

*Animal Talk, or The Adventures
of a Little Lady and a Big Goat*

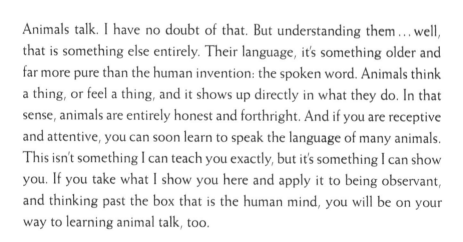

Animals talk. I have no doubt of that. But understanding them ... well, that is something else entirely. Their language, it's something older and far more pure than the human invention: the spoken word. Animals think a thing, or feel a thing, and it shows up directly in what they do. In that sense, animals are entirely honest and forthright. And if you are receptive and attentive, you can soon learn to speak the language of many animals. This isn't something I can teach you exactly, but it's something I can show you. If you take what I show you here and apply it to being observant, and thinking past the box that is the human mind, you will be on your way to learning animal talk, too.

Father Goose has been hovering over his young gosling
for an hour, regarding it closely as it played and rested.
The language is clear: paternal pride and devotion.

Early this autumn, I was hiking down the southerly path back of the
Hollow, down into the very heart of this mountain valley that is a region
of old growth Acadian forest. As I went, a raven flew over. The motion
caught my eye, and just as I glanced up, it dropped something it had
been carrying in its claws. The object fell not fifty feet away at the base
of a large old birch, but it had happened so fast I had had no chance to

see what it was. But the raven wanted it back. It circled sharply around and alighted atop of the old tree, eyeing me cautiously. There are lots of ravens in these parts, and they aren't exactly fearful of humans, but I knew it wasn't going to come down out of that tree to retrieve its treasure until I moved on.

But I have always been fascinated by ravens and wanted to see what was of such interest to it, so out of curiosity I meandered over to the base of the tree. The raven glowered at me as I approached, and when I was only yards from its treasure it must have presumed I meant to steal it. It launched skyward, thrashing the air indignantly with its wings, cawing in the sharpest, most affronted way I have ever heard a raven manage. What it was saying was clear: *Mine! Angry! Thief!*

When I realized how I had offended the bird, I promptly stepped away in hopes the raven would see me leaving and return to retrieve its treasure, but it flew straight away, never looking back, cawing sharp curses at me until it vanished far over the forest. Out of respect, I never went back to the tree to see what had fallen. The raven had obviously valued it, and I felt bad for having ruined its day.

Animals not only talk through what they do, but they also leave messages upon the Earth, if you know how to read them. On our frequent Nature walks, we encounter all sorts of spoor and there is language in those telltales. One morning Arielle and I took a winter hike after a snowfall the night before. We were traveling along some trails deep in a partially wooded area that had long, long ago been a homestead with wide meadows for livestock. It wasn't long before we came across the canine tracks of what could have been a mere domestic dog. But dogs don't have to worry about where their next meal is coming from, and their tracks swerve here and there as they investigate every little curiosity. These tracks went straight and businesslike—the clear sign of a wild canine. A coyote, in fact. The tracts were closely spaced, meaning the coyote had been in no hurry.

Just then, the tracks swerved left and there were a great many of them all around a single point. The tracks said the coyote had caught scent of something interesting and was investigating it. We investigated what appeared to be the central point of those tracks and found fresh rabbit droppings. The tracks then led up the trail a couple hundred yards more, but more widely spaced, meaning the coyote was eager and picking up its pace. We came to a point where the tracks became vastly spaced, with the forepaws imprinting the snow behind the rear paw prints—clear sign the coyote had caught sight of its quarry and lunched into a full run, and not much farther on the chase ended at red-stained snow where tufts of white fur marked the place where the coyote had caught a rabbit meal.

Such is the language of animals: honest and clear. They speak their language through what they do in the present, and they leave the traces of their language in their passage through the world. But it is another language, and to speak it you have to invest yourself in learning animal talk. Some may not believe me, but I don't think there is anything psychic about communicating with animals. It's a thing, rather, of the mind and heart. It takes an open mind, open enough to see beyond human preconceptions. It takes very sensitive empathy, because if you can tell what an animal is feeling, you're halfway to understanding what it is trying to say. But most of all, it takes keen observation. Speaking the language of animals makes you a student and scholar of the Green Man's world.

On farms it becomes very important to learn the language of domestic animals, and I've always felt you can tell the best, most humane farmers by how well they communicate with the creatures that share their land. Watching Daphne work with the goats is a joy, and occasionally amusing!

Puck the Buck decides to nibble willows on the way to the Firefly
Meadow, and he's telling Arielle he means to stay right there.

Nanny goats (goatkeepers prefer the term *does* these days) are typically placid, even demure. They're very maternal and happily spend all
day idling with their young. They will congregate under the shade of trees
at the height of day, chewing cud and making small noises like old biddies
gossiping at the ice cream social. And they enjoy human attention. They
will happily stand around to be petted or hold out their feet in a most
princess-like fashion for their pedicures when Daphne trims their hooves.

It is the girls' chore to milk the goats, so when the sun rises Daphne,
Arielle, and Natalia will go out to the barn and each milk a doe. The does
are always eager for this since they get a breakfast of oats and molasses
while up on the milking stand. Daphne is barely conscious of it, but she
has learned all the body language to get the does to go where she wants.

All she has to do is open a stall gate, take a step back, slightly spread her arms and gesture toward the milking stand, and the goat goes there. When the doe has been milked, it returns to its stall, guided in the same fashion, while the next doe takes her turn. In this way Daphne will soon have all the goats milked.

Then she'll open all their stalls and let them out, along with the Puck the Buck. The does know the morning routine and happily trot out toward the Firefly Meadow. Usually the mornings go smoothly and Daphne will walk along with the goats who will occasionally glance toward her as if to be sure they are doing the right thing. Goats naturally suffer an attention disorder, though, and if one spots a tuft of clover on the opposite side of the path, or espies some summer blossoms she hasn't yet sampled, she'll turn aside to check it out. Without a thought, Daphne will circle the goat and simply stand in the direction it was heading. The doe will notice Daphne as if for the first time, then glance back at her friends, and you can see her putting thoughts together: *Oh yeah, we're going to the meadow. Silly me!* Then she'll dash back toward the flock and in a few moments the lot of them are safely in the meadow.

But the billy goat named Puck (billies are referred to as bucks these days) is four now and in his prime, a hundred and fifty pounds of stout muscle, dwarven beard, and curved horn. By and large, he likes to pass his day in the meadow with the does, but here is the frank truth: billy goats are sexist. Now and then he seems to take note that Daphne is female and for no other reason than he won't take directions from a *people-doe,* he will disobey her. Often I've been out tending the gardens or mending fences, only to overhear Daphne shouting—and occasionally resorting to swearing—at the stubborn old goat who is clearly preparing to square off with her. Puck the Sexist Buck is well aware Daphne does not have the raw strength to overpower him and he just seems to need to rub it in now and then. He will walk to the other side of the path and just stand about, daring Daphne to try to put him in the

Firefly Meadow. When Daphne approaches he'll get up on his hind legs and shake his shaggy head around to emphasize the size and curl of his impressive rack of horns. You can just hear what he is thinking in that simple goat mind of his: *Uh, uh! I ain't taking no orders from no girl. See these big horns? These mean I'm a buck, and I don't have to listen to you!*

It doesn't help that Daphne, a remarkably capable woman in so many ways, is very much—and in her own words—a girly-girl. She responds to Puck in all the quintessential girly ways. The hand goes on the hip. The toes tap. The foot stomps. The lips pout. The finger wags in time with the ponytail. And Puck, the consummate chauvinist like all bucks, remains a stubborn old goat.

Sometimes, when Puck seems to feel he's made his point, he'll turn and trot into the Firefly Meadow on his own, as if he just needed to remind Daphne he is only going there because he wants to, not because *a girl told him to.* But sometimes he'll get especially ornery and lower his head as if to charge her. He's never actually bucked Daphne. Either he's not mean, or maybe he just knows I'd barbecue him if he did! But Daphne, for her part, can be equally stubborn and she doesn't like to give up. And she, understandably, doesn't like being bullied by a sexist goat. I hate to intervene because it is important that Puck learns to respect Daphne, since she is for all intents and purposes the shepherdess, but a couple times I have had to. On those two occasions I took a no-nonsense approach and simply walked straight up to Puck, and the moment he lowered his horns at me I just grabbed one and hauled him without preamble into the meadow. That was my animal talk for: *You're not the biggest buck around here, so behave, buddy boy!* Puck understood that language well and now stops the shenanigans right quick if he sees me coming to deal with him, but he still likes to get on Daphne's nerves now and then.

It was our older daughter, Arielle, who has a very keen sense of animal talk, who figured out the problem was cultural. She knew that it made no sense for Puck to resist going into the Firefly Meadow, since he clearly enjoyed his time with the does. Then she figured out that in Puck's proud but simple goat mind being driven into the meadow by people-does was the same as losing face in front of his wives. Arielle started the practice of simply leaving the gate to the meadow open on her way to the barn and then leading out the does first, right after milking. When the does were all in their meadow, Daphne would open Puck's stall and simply stand aside. With no people-does telling him what to do, he invariably went straight for the meadow and let himself through the gate, chest puffed out and head high. *Ha! Ha! I'm the big buck! No does tell me what to do!* Whatever, the girls gave him his pride and we suppose every goat deserves it. But ultimately, it was learning to talk Goat that made everything work out for the best.

Realizing the does and kids have all gone ahead of him
into the Firefly Meadow, Puck the Buck dashes
through the gate with no further prompting.

Animals speak a pure language. The first step in learning it is being observant. The only mistake you can make is anthropomorphizing animals. Animals are not people. They don't think like us at all. See the green world through their eyes and animal talk will come.

JANUARY

Stay Home Time

There are wild spirits in January, and don't let anyone tell you different. They ride the wicked northeast winds that blow down from a pewter sky. They whisper in the forest and upon the high meadows where people seldom roam. They gurgle within the depths of streams whose bright surfaces have long since darkened with thick winter ice. The wild spirits are fey and largely indifferent to Man, but that is not to say they are un-friendly. They are elementals of Nature, personifications of the essence of winter. Some myths say such spirits don't possess any real ego or per-sonality, like the Penates and Lares of Roman myth, but they certainly have a goal. They push through the highland forest and drive the snow deep into every ravine. They blast it off the ridges so that the hilltops might be bare but for a thin rime of ice after a blizzard. They bank the snow against the windward side of hills and valleys. In the Hollow they even try to push winter into the barn and coops so that the animals feel its bite. The horses' stalls become lopsided as stale bedding freezes to the ground faster than we can clean it. The goats grow shaggy coats but on the bitterest nights they still shiver in their stalls. The chickens huddle together in their snug coop for warmth, then peck at one another because they do not care for the crowding. And any person unlucky enough to lose his way in the countryside may well succumb to the cold's bite if not adequately prepared. The wild elemental spirits herd the winds of winter; they mean to press their demesne everywhere. The land will change because of it. The Earth will fold and groan like great gunshots as the frost heaves. Great stones on heights will become dislodged and tumble when the ice slides down. Trees may split wide under the tremendous force of freezing sap. And if animals or persons are hurt by the forces of the cold, it is not as if the winter elementals meant it, it simply is, for it is a fact that the time of ice must come. It is a spiraling power as irrevocable as a standing mountain and all must respect it.

But while winter descends with powerful elemental force over the highlands, and some even whisper the Wild Hunt rides the backwoods ways, searching out foolish wandering souls and damsel faeries known as moss maidens, all is warm and secure at the cottage, for we have been preparing for winter's onslaught since late summer. Cords of firewood have been stacked neatly beneath the raised deck on the west side of the cottage. The root cellar and deep freezers are full to capacity. Whatever the weather does, even if we were snowed in for months, we can feel secure despite the fury of winter.

But while we may feel secure, the wild weather is a stark reminder that in the distant past this was a worrisome time of year for our ancestors. The Gauls of ancient France called this month *Anagantios*—Stay Home Time. By this time snows were deep, ice was treacherous, and to wander far from hearth and home was to invite misfortune. What's more, with winter only half behind, the folk of old were becoming keenly aware of their food stores. If the stores fell short, they faced many hungry days before spring and possibly death by starvation, so they would unearth their casks of grain and tally the remainder. If the stocks were meager, there would be desperate supplications to the gods to make a quick end to winter so that growing and hunting and gathering could recommence. If there was no shortage, there would be celebration. Great balefires would be built, celebratory dishes prepared, guests hosted, and song and story shared in plenty.

This year, with a bountiful harvest from our own gardens and more than enough meat laid in, our larders were full and we too would celebrate. Soon we would invite guests up for a night of feasting and camaraderie. But first, I had to attend to another important tradition of yesteryear—it was time to finish the brewing that had started in November with the pressing of the apple cider.

In ancient Europe, around Gaul, Britain, the Germanic regions and lands north, some traditional beverages of celebration were ale, mead, and hard cider. We make all of them, but the apple was long a sacred fruit, which only makes sense given the apple's central role as a food source. It is a main crop on the homestead as well, and given that we cultivate our own trees and press our own juice—basically making cider from the ground up—it holds a special place in my heart, and is my beverage of choice for day-to-day use and celebration of the High Days.

But in those most ancient days, the people couldn't make their brews keep. They didn't know much about sterilization and had only a limited ability to keep the beverages from air, which will spoil any fermented drink. So they did their fermentations quickly—a process modern brewers refer to as making *small* beverages—and drank the results fresh. Small brews are passable, though they are weak, sweet, and cloudy.

At the cottage, we're a little more advanced. We have the means to sterilize our equipment and seal the finished product airtight so it will keep for years. Thus, we rarely ever make small brews. What we make are, if I dare brag a bit, some of the finest organic ciders and meads, grape and fruit wines you will find. And today it was at last time to bottle the ciders we had pressed back in November.

It was a good thing the final phase came during Stay Home Time. Among other things, it was very cold. A lot of fresh foods get stored in the cottage and during warmer months we might have been troubled by tiny fruit flies. If even one of the almost too-small-too-see bugs got someplace it shouldn't, it could ruin a whole batch of cider. But more to the point, bottling is meticulous and time-consuming. The cider has to be carefully racked from the carboys where it has aged back into primary fermenters to separate it from the silty dregs produced during fermentation. This is a careful process of siphoning that takes two people, patience, practice, and steady hands. Once the racking is done, the cider has to be promptly bottled and sealed to protect it from oxygen. And it goes slow because there must always be meticulous attention to sterilization.

We began this January's racking on the first Friday of the month. The carboys were sitting on a table in the small craft room beside the huge kitchen. They were made of heavy glass and each weighed about sixty pounds when full. The first to be racked would be the stuff slated to become hard bubbly cider, for we never used preservatives and it kept the least amount of time.

Daphne prepared the kitchen by clearing away all her food preparation equipment and wiping down everything with a spray of water and vinegar to sterilize surfaces. While she did that, I hauled crates of bottles up from the storage area near the root cellar. Then we selected sixty-six bottles and sterilized them in a mild bleach-water solution and rinsed them in first scalding, then ice-cold water until every vestige of bleach odor was gone. Then she placed these in neat rows on the floor while I sterilized the racking tubes and collected the bottle capper, sterilized the caps, and prepared a syrup of sugar water. About the time I was done with all that, she had all the bottles in place and I set an empty, sterile fermenter bucket under the carboy.

She joined me in the craft room, and I removed the airlock from the carboy. The room immediately filled with an overwhelming fragrance of ripe apples and a fainter scent of fresh baking bread—the fragrances that indicate a good fermentation. I could tell already it would be a good batch. I dipped a wine thief (a rigid narrow tube with a hole at each end) into the carboy, then covered the top end with my thumb and withdrew it. It held the liquid like a straw when one end is capped. I placed the wine thief over my mouth and let my thumb up to sample the brew. The cider dribbled into my mouth. It was good, but flat, not too dry, and bursting with apple flavor. Daphne stood beside me and I winked at her and held the wine thief near her mouth. She tipped her head up and I let the rest dribble into her mouth.

"Yum!" she declared. "But where are the bubbles?"

I winked and said, "They'll be here in a few weeks." It had indeed been a good year for apples. The long summer and late hard frosts of autumn had made them very sugary and flavorful. I flicked the wine thief so the last drop dribbled onto her forehead.

"Hey!" she barked, but I kissed it off playfully.

Then we set to work. I inserted a long, rigid plastic tube into the carboy. It has an upturned bottom to prevent the silty sediment from being siphoned out along with the cider. Attached to the siphon is a long, narrow flexible tube, and I sucked on it a moment, drawing up the cider. Then I passed the end to Daphne. She held it with steady hands, for any movement in this most delicate part of the process would stir up the sediment. While she held her end over the empty fermenter, I guided the rigid tube down deep into the carboy and the liquid was slowly transferred. When we were done, there was a half inch of sediment rich waste cider at the bottom of the carboy. I always hated that it went to waste, but there was nothing for it. At least I'd gotten skilled enough at brewing over the years that I only needed to rack brews twice to get them fully clarified, because each racking can waste up to a half liter.

When it was all done, the eight-gallon bucket that was the primary fermenter held just under six gallons of crystal clear cider. The sugar syrup I had mixed in a small pot was ready, and I poured a single cup into the bucket and used a long stainless steel spoon to gently but thoroughly dissolve it. The sugar would *prime* the cider, feeding the remaining yeast just enough to work a little more. The byproduct of the yeast's action, gaseous ether and carbon dioxide, would pressurize the beverage right in the capped bottles.

When the sugar was dissolved, I lifted the primary fermenter and brought it to the kitchen table where we began bottling, using another siphon with a special bottling fixture to transfer the liquid into dozens of recycled beer bottles. I knelt to the neatly lined up bottles on the floor and one by one filled all sixty-six until the bucket was completely empty. The whole racking and bottling process took close to four hours.

I got up and stretched, and Daphne knelt over the empty fermenter bucket and sniffed. It smelled wonderful, like a whole forest of apple trees heavy with fruit, and brought back thoughts of autumn—one of the beauties of finishing the brewing during Stay Home Time. Then she glanced toward the wasted dregs in the carboy, almost muddy with silt. "I wish I could figure out a recipe for the dregs," she lamented, but the only use we knew was to toss them in the compost piles.

But brewed beverages and air don't play well together. There was no time to mourn the lost dregs. As soon as I'd worked the stiffness out of my legs, I knelt on the floor again and started capping the bottles. Daphne quickly boxed the capped bottles so they were out of my way, which allowed me to go even faster. That minimized the cider's exposure to air, improving its quality. With her help, capping took just over five minutes. When it was done, we had six gallons of bubbly hard cider in sixty-six single serving bottles, which she carted back to the craft room. We would let them age in there where it was just under room temperature for several more weeks, during which time the cider would become as bubbly as champagne. In the meantime, there were more carboys in the craft room to attend: cider wine, grape wine, mead, and ale, all of which would need to go through a similar racking process, though the wines would not receive the sugar syrup priming as they are served flat. But racking and bottling is hard on the joints. It takes a lot of bending over and staying very still, so we would only do one batch a day. It was time to knock off, get dinner going, and maybe play a board game with the girls before dark when the animals would have to be fed and tended. Beyond the kitchen window another snowstorm was kicking up, spitting the first pellets that indicated a lot more snow to come.

A selection of homemade vintages down in our wine cellar.
Ales and bubbly ciders are just beyond in the root cellar.

A few weeks later I sampled the bubbly cider. It was perfect, and I moved the crates down to the root cellar where the dark and cool air would help preserve it. Homemade bubbly cider is not like store-bought varieties. Made the Old Way, it is as strong as any wine because the fermentation does not stop until the yeast has used up all the sugars in the juice. Without a milligram of sulfur dioxide or potassium sorbate (common wine preservatives), it will keep for many months, maybe more than a year. I can't say exactly because it's never lasted more than a year around here. We serve it regularly at meals and to guests. The girls get some, too, which I feel is important. Not only is a glass of cider or wine good for the blood, but I've always felt that if one doesn't make alcohol taboo, then kids will not think drinking makes them adults. Thus, we have always offered them a bit of whatever we're having at mealtimes (as my own French parents had often offered me), and so having it is nothing special to them. And half the time they decline.

But now that the cider was ready, there were some magical-spiritual purposes I had in mind for a little of it. One was a way of honoring the Apple Man, whose work is so crucial to the Hollow, from a tradition that comes out of Cornwall. Traditionally, the apple farmers and their laborers will go to the apple grove with cakes soaked in cider and place them upon an apple tree's branches, and recite a simple incantation for a full harvest the following year. Then they will dance around the tree.

We don't exactly farm apples. In Nova Scotia they practically grow like weeds. But the Apple Man seems to make sure the trees around the Hollow are especially prolific and sweet.

I went out alone near dusk, and the frigid sky was a deep indigo. I had in my coat pocket a scone Arielle had baked earlier in the day. I went to the best of our trees, old Grandfather Apple down by the spring. There, I cut open the soft scone. It smelled wonderfully of fresh whole-wheat flour and kitchen goodness. I laid the halves on the lowest branch of the old apple and opened a bottle of the cider with my Leatherman. I pressed indents in the scones, then poured some of the cider over the bread, slowly so it could be soaked up. Then I lifted the bottle and toasted the Apple Man:

> *To your health, Apple Man,*
> *And to the health of the apple trees,*
> *And to the good of Earth,*
> *And health to my wife, my family, and me.*

Then for Earth I poured a bit more of the cider over the ground, though the frozen soil could hardly soak it up. It didn't matter; it was the gesture that was important. But the simple incantation was done. I did it alone. I could have brought Daphne and the girls out with me, but it didn't feel right. I've always felt our Apple Man was a shy soul. Doing this alone was best, I felt sure.

From there I walked the short distance over to the smoker, not far from Grandfather Apple. Regular use through the winter had left a neat trail worn into the snow, and the warmth of the smoker's ancient wood stove melted a circumference of ground around it. I checked the stove and restocked it with a mix of greenwood and seasoned alder, both of which would make cool but flavorful smoke. Then I lifted the sidewall off the four by six-foot smoker and examined the meats. Half-done turkeys were taking on the color of warm mahogany and deer hams that had been cut to the size of small roasts and marinated in a spicy brine were dark and smelled wonderful. These were done. Not having thought to bring anything to collect the hams, I broke a stick of spruce from a nearby tree and speared two of the roasts, and used it to carry the meat up to the kitchen where Daphne could work her magic on it.

Up at the cottage, the girls were preparing another tradition of the harsh winter month of January, a fine dinner of the harvest surplus for guests who would be arriving later in the day. I went around to the north side of the cottage to the chimenea. It had been buried halfway in snow, but earlier in the day I had used the tractor to plow the snow away from it. I piled wood in the chimenea, starting with kindling of twigs from a windfallen birch branch and finishing with some substantial logs. By the time it was ready, the sun was upon the horizon, though the graying sky did not make for shadows. It was extraordinarily cold; a perfect time for the winter balefire. I set a match to the kindling and it caught quickly. In minutes the infant flame grew into a small campfire and continued to grow as the heat built strength and began to lap at the big logs at the top of the heap. I stepped back from the building fire, and just about the moment full dark arrived, it had evolved into a bonfire, with flames climbing all the way to the top of the chimenea's pipe and thrusting above. I had a small package of powdered metals and I tossed it into the fire, and in a moment it turned an otherworldly green. Overhead, the brightest winter stars were struggling to shine through the thin cloud haze, and the girls came outside to watch the eerie fire burn with me. Daphne and I stood beside one another, our arms around each other, content.

The balefire was an ancient, simple magic: a bright, hot fire lit in the depths of winter to call back the spirit of summer. It was a very magical fire, and its oddly green light played over the bare birch boughs and cast dancing shadows among the evergreen spruce of the surrounding Elfwood. The play of fire and shadow moved me, called to me, and as I regarded it, my mind seemed to cast back to some long forgotten ancestral memory: a warrior carrying a spear and dancing round a great bonfire with his clan members. I felt the warrior's heart pulsing in my chest, felt the hardwood shaft of the spear in my hands, the heft of the obsidian spearhead. I could hear the laughter of the clan's children also dancing round the fire, and sense the presence of my woman beyond the dancing warriors. The experience was vivid, and with it my heart yearned for an elder, eldritch time beyond the reach of history.

But then the guests arrived, friends who carpooled from a small town almost an hour away. They marveled at the emerald fire. The sky had cleared and the cold stars shone bright in the dark. On such clear nights the temperature drops sharply. Soon the ladies went inside with the girls. Outside, I had set aside several bottles of the cider and handed them out to the two men who stayed with me by the fire. We toasted the reaching of midwinter and chatted there at the edge of the Elfwood, with the flame, beginning now to return to its normal color, casting swimming shadows among the trees. We told stories of the previous year: men's stories of travelling adventures and outdoor rambles and hunts. We laughed at memories of our children's antics and remarked on the graces of our ladies. And now and then from within the cottage's kitchen we could hear the ladies' laughter as they told women's tales, and through the window I snatched glances of them puttering about the kitchen, and the girls helping with the midwinter feast's preparations.

The two men got to chattering about something to do with business, a subject of little interest to me, and my mind wandered. I took another swallow of the dry cider and glanced into the wintry forest. Hundreds of square miles of woodlands surrounded the cottage, a beautiful country of rolling hills, wild low mountains, and endless mystery. It was full of wild January spirits, and don't let anyone tell you different. But there was no malice in them; they were merely forces of Nature seeing to the balance of life, even when all goes dormant in the frozen depths of Anagantios. And if the Wild Hunt was out there, I was not worried. It was Stay Home Time, and that sounded good to me. We had a warm hearth, a solid roof. The bottling part of brewing time had come and gone, and there were fine beverages to share with our guests. The fragrance of smoked venison emerged from the kitchen, and a magical fire blazed before me while laughter bubbled from my friends and family—my clan—as we shared talk and tales. At this time of year, all the magic we needed was in the people and land we held most dear.

IMBOLG

Promises of Imbolg

When the wind is in the west and the bite of snow is yet hard in the air, and the days, though waxing, have yet to bring any warmth, winter has been long and hard and it can seem like it will never be over. It was upon just such a February day that my wife, our daughters, and I found ourselves in the barn going through the endless rites of winter passage on a farm.

Our daughters, Arielle and Natalia, were sharing sweet hay among the three horses, and Daphne was in the feed stall mixing grains, molasses, and vegetable oil to create high-calorie feeds. During the cold season, the barn animals burn a lot of energy just staying warm in this severe climate, and a little oil and molasses in their feed go a long way toward helping them keep the inner fires glowing. I was climbing around the loft, trying to get a sense of how much hay remained. It would be as many as a hundred days before we could count on the meadows to feed the animals again, so we needed to ensure we had at least three hundred and fifty bales remaining.

Twa Corbies Hollow is named for a silly yet eerie folk song about two Scots ravens deciding how they would devour a dead English knight they had stumbled upon. The Hollow is in a shallow valley atop a low mountain deep in the Nova Scotia highlands and encompasses many rolling acres of meadows, forests, breaks, ponds, and springs, and also boasts an enormous century-and-a-half-old cottage, a cabin, a smokehouse, and other artifacts of yesteryear. And like nearly every structure in the Hollow, the barn is a living, functioning bit of history.

Many decades ago when the original homesteaders were still using horses to do a lot of their labor and every cottage kept its own livestock, it was necessary to have a good tight barn, and ours is large and spacious. It has its faults, though, like the slowly decaying shingles that line the outer walls and require endless maintenance—slated to be replaced one day with long-lasting red steel siding—but it has some remarkable qualities, too, not least of which are the foot-thick timbers of solid maple from which it is constructed. When I bought the homestead, I had thought of tearing down and replacing the old barn with a roomier, airier modern design but after seeing those timbers, I decided that with work it would probably outlast me, so I decided to simply refurbish it even though that is probably more labor intensive.

So I was climbing among the bales, a job that is both fun and prickly because occasionally they will roll, tumbling you down among other bales, and had counted off about two hundred when I heard my younger daughter, Natalia, cry out. "Oh, Mom! Mom! The doe doesn't look well."

Daphne left the food stall, and I vaulted over the edge of the loft and slid down a rope to the main floor behind the horses, then slipped under a beam that closed off the third of the barn given over to our dairy goats. As I arrived, I heard Daphne telling Natalia, "She's fine. It looks like she's about to have a baby goat."

Goats are amazing creatures. They require very little ground and will eat most anything green. They make use of country that would otherwise produce nothing. They are rugged and do well in cold heights like our Hollow. All in all, they require very little maintenance. But now and then a birth can get complicated, so we all dropped our tasks and made ready to help the doe bring her kid into the world. Natalia and Arielle were sent back to the cottage to get clean towels and heated water. Daphne went back to the feed room and got an iodine mix. I went into the stall and watched the birthing process, being alert for any signs of a breach. If a breach occurred, we'd need to straighten out the baby. The cottage is about two hundred yards from the barn, so it was a good fifteen minutes before the girls returned with the items we requested. We didn't really think we would need much of it, except perhaps a little water to help clean the mother afterward, but it was better to be prepared.

Then the long wait began. Outside, the sky, which had started that morning bright and relatively cloudless, was doing something Nova Scotia is famous for—it was rapidly transforming into a mess. As the doe walked slowly around her stall, shifting her weight as she anticipated the birth, grim clouds thickened across the welkin. Soon all the bright azure of the morning was blotted out and the clouds thickened and thickened until they seemed more like looming smoke. The inside of the barn became almost as dark as if it were night rather than three hours after sunrise. The Hollow is not on a very high mountain as mountains go, only about fifteen hundred feet elevation at the highest point, but it is high enough that in this maritime climate, the clouds often roll right through us rather than over us. The gray cloudbank glided lower and lower until, with a shudder of ghastly cold air, it covered all the land with an icy fog that warned of a looming, treacherous snow.

Daphne and the girls stood just outside the stall, and I knelt one knee on a thick tuft of straw near the doe. "Can you get her something to drink?" Daphne asked Natalia. We did not leave standing water in the stalls at this time of year because should a goat upset the containers and manage to get itself wet, it would likely catch its death. Natalia is a great kid, but like many kids is not too fond of getting special chores, but without a complaint or even a hesitation she got a one-gallon bucket and carried it to the spout at the far side of the barn, passing the two great Belgian horses contentedly chewing hay in the large midsection, and half-filled it with water. She carried it back, pausing a moment to pet the quarter horse, who has her own stall near the midsection. "Here, Dad," she told me, offering me the bucket.

"Come in, sweetie," I said to her.

Cautiously curious, the small girl opened the stall gate and came through, shutting it behind her. The doe knew us well and was not troubled by the two humans in her space. Natalia walked over to the doe, petted her black curly fur. She set the bucket down and the doe took a sip of water. Natalia looked concerned and I told her, "She's fine, sweetie. She knows the baby is coming and she just has to wait for it, like us." Natalia nodded and let the goat finish her drink, then put the bucket outside the stall.

"I can see the head!" someone called. I think it was Arielle, but I had noticed it, too. It was so wonderful to see that all I can honestly say is I registered a voice making the statement, not whose it was.

Once the kid begins to come, it goes pretty quickly. In only a few minutes there was a shivering, wet baby goat lying on the straw. "It was a good birth," I pronounced. I had needed to do nothing to help the doe, and when Nature has her way like that, it is best.

Daphne went to the grain stall and returned with a little box of baking soda and some slightly warm water with a little apple cider vinegar in it, both revitalizing tonics for a new mother goat. She set a tablespoon of the baking soda on a board at the edge of the stall and placed the water just beside the gate, where the doe could lap at either as she chose, but at the moment the tired but happy mother was licking her baby clean.

"I think that went well," I said and started to stand up.

"I see another one!" Arielle blurted.

This time I did register it was Arielle who spoke. I turned, and sure enough, there appeared a little head, then a pair of tiny cloven hooves—another little kid making its way into the world. But like I said, once a birth begins it goes quickly and a few minutes later another perfect goat in miniature, about the size of a big tomcat, lay beside its sibling. Twins, they looked just alike. I checked them briefly and they looked fine and healthy. They were wet and shivering with the cold though, and it was tempting to help the mother dry them, maybe wrap them in warm old blankets, but we all knew better. They needed this baptism by cold to kick-start their bodies' own heaters and defenses. If we tried to dry or wrap the little ones, no matter how well meaning, we would have doomed them. As I said, often it is best to let Nature work her magic in her own way.

"What's the verdict?" said Daphne impishly.

"A little doe and a little buck," I told her, and my wife smiled.

The mother was doing fine and I decided my part in the morning's drama was done. Outside, wind had kicked up and the first wild flakes were sheeting almost sideways across the sky. Big wet flakes, but the wind was from the west and the temperature was dropping fast. Soon the big flakes would metamorphose into the tiny pellets that mark a long and deep snowfall.

Natalia went over to the great central doors, left wide open since the wind was coming from behind the barn and snow could not blow in, and looked out at the wild storm. At that moment Daphne flipped on the barn lights, and white light spilled into the flying ice and fog, revealing dervishes of wind kicking up whirlwinds of snow. The wind began to howl. Natalia sighed, her mood shifting from wonder and elation at the kids' birth to long-suffering resignation. "I don't think winter will ever be over," she exhaled.

The kids of Imbolg, sister on the left, brother on the right,
have been buddies from the start. Here, they relax in the
Firefly Meadow shortly after the last snow has broken.

I walked over to her and we stood together at the great opening for
a long while, looking out into the February morning, which only an hour
ago had appeared bright and full of the promise of imminent spring. I
put an arm over her small shoulders. "It's going to be milking time soon,"
I said. She looked at me curiously, wondering what that had to do with
another winter storm. "Soon we'll be making yogurt and homemade ice
cream, and Mom will be making cheese, and we can pick strawberries
and have summer picnics with cream tea."

I tilted my head back toward the doe, now standing at ease between
her new kids who were making their first uncertain attempts at her udder.
"See, even the baby goats know. This is the season of Imbolg. It starts
to seem like winter will never let go, but then the little goats come, new

babies of a new spring. And the milk comes with them. And like magic the new grass follows. And the warm sun. And playing in the brook and riding the horses and all the other things we love. But it all starts here, because 'in milk' is exactly what Imbolg means. The goats have their little ones and come into their milk again. Those babies let us know that sometime soon, maybe not today or tomorrow, but very soon, spring is sure to come."

Natalia smiled at that. I turned then to go back up into the loft. A farm has its seasonal rites of passage that must be honored, and that meant I still had hay bales to count. On the way I passed by my wife, Daphne, giving her a light pat on the shoulder and a kiss on the back of her neck, as I always did, then climbed back up into the loft to resume counting hay bales. Down in the goat stalls, Daphne was giving grain to Puck the Buck, the male goat who was now a proud new dad. Natalia promptly started a debate with her big sister about who was going to bring the towels back to the house.

I smiled and glanced from the high loft back through the great doors into the wild storm. I thought, "Go ahead and blow, Old Man Winter. Here it is warm and good, and just around the next turn spring waits to come. The goats have come into their milk and the promise of Imbolg is finally here."

Traditional Living

Growing the Earth: Creating Organic Gardens for Health and Spirit

If you have a patch of ground, you can keep a garden. Even a tiny garden, if well-tended, can yield an amazing amount of food. *Mother Earth News* magazine once ran an article about a suburban woman who planted a very small but well managed hundred-square-foot garden.[1] Her goal was to see just how much food could she could coax from that tiny plot, and the yield was worth $700. But the value of what she grew could not be measured merely by its monetary worth. The produce of her garden was GMO-free (there were no genetically modified components, an increasingly common aspect of the diets of persons in the industrialized world). There were no toxic, carcinogenic pesticides or herbicides in her

---

1. "Grow $700 of Food in 100 Square Feet," by Rosalind Creasy with Cathy Wilkinson Barash, ©2010. *Mother Earth News*.

produce, so she could feed her family free of worry over the long-term effects of the food. And the nutritional value of produce grown using organic methods is far superior to anything grown using industrial farming methods. Every vegetable produced in her garden had more vitamins and minerals per calorie. You can also factor in the exercise and sense of personal satisfaction that come with keeping a garden, which has long been recognized as psychologically and spiritually therapeutic. Working a garden adjusts your personal pace to that of Nature. The sun and rain work in their own way; the plants grow in their own time. Minerals and water, soil and light, dance a dance as old as time, and the gardener becomes an element of that interplay of pure Earth magic. I firmly believe a garden is a way of integrating the Green Man, not as an abstract concept but as something alive and present, there in the soil, over there in the stem, strong and sure in the ripening pod.

A single small garden can yield a great deal. This raised bed,
a mere six by twelve feet, provides two meals per week of
asparagus for our family of four through much of the summer.

If you want to create a garden of your own and have even a tiny yard with access to water and sun, it can be done. And it is worth the effort. If you desire herbs for healing or magic or the kitchen, a few dozen square feet will yield far more than you can use in a year. A few hundred square feet (a mere twenty by twenty feet) will keep a family of four in fresh produce all summer and a good part of the fall. But to make it flourish, take Nature's path and do not rush it, and don't let getting produce be your first goal. Aim to heal the land and love the soil and, trust me, your garden will reward you beyond your expectations.

Growing the Soil

The first thing you must do to create a garden is grow the soil. A few places, like the Louisiana bayou country where I was born, have naturally perfect soil: rich, black, sweet and loamy, full of compost and plant nutrients. But in most places the soil must be established before a garden can flourish, and forgetting this essential fact is a mistake even experienced gardeners often make. The soil is the life of the garden, and compost is what gives it life.

To start your garden, establish compost buckets or heaps the year before. Into these you may place coffee grindings and used tea, along with any uncooked vegetable matter from your kitchen. However, do not add raw seeds of any kind or they are likely to grow. Daphne once threw an old packet of seedcake seeds into the compost pile meant for her herb garden and we ended up weeding out the poisonous poppies all summer. Every now and then, as organic matter accumulates, scatter some established compost over the matter and stir it in with a hoe or pitchfork. This will introduce microbes that will speed the composting process.

If you're really ambitious, you can visit farms or horse stables and collect manure. For persons not used to rural life, that may sound pretty awful, but the manure of herbivores is little more than ground plant matter. Almost as soon as it dries it will crumble into dirt. Throw this in your compost heap and it will not only add necessary loamy mass, but it will impart valuable plant nutrition to your soil.

A lot of people like to use compost buckets, and I suppose if you live in town it might be more sightly. For my part, I prefer to lay my compost right over the ground so that worms and insects, small mammals and birds can get up in it. They will turn the compost over and over, breaking it down quickly and thoroughly.

I suggest you start your compost heap a year before you plan to garden so you can make lots. The more you can put in the ground, the better. When the compost is ready—and you can tell it's ready when it becomes crumbly, black and light and smells slightly sweet—use a tiller, pitchforks or shovels to thoroughly turn it into the ground where you will establish your garden.

Even with abundant compost, expect only modest yields from your garden the first year because it will take time for the soil to "come alive." In time, the soil will fill with thousands of earthworms, and birds will visit and turn it. Healthful bacteria will become active in the soil. If you live in the country, you may be lucky and have a family of hedgehogs move in. These and other small creatures can be very beneficial as they hunt down harmful grubs and other undesirables that would hurt your plants at the roots.

Also, from the very start you can sow some hardy squash like zucchini and summer squash into your compost heap (especially if it also has herbivore manure in it). The squash plants will speed up the breakdown of the organic matter, contribute nutrients to the soil, and give you some tasty vegetables in the short run. We add various squash and pumpkins to our compost heaps every year.

Be aware that you should never put anything cooked in your compost pile (though tea and coffee grindings are okay). Do not add meat or animal protein, including raw eggs, eggshells, or milk products. These things will eventually compost, but it takes a long time and in the short run they can introduce toxins. Also, never add tree matter, neither saw-dust nor woodchips nor even little twigs or pine needles. Such things take years to break down.

I have a saying I share with students of gardening: "It takes three years to create an organic garden. The first to start your soil. The second to nurture your soil. The third to mature your soil." It's really all about the soil. Nurture and love your soil and the rest often takes care of itself, but it takes patience. Of course, you can and should start planting seed the first year you actually break ground in the plot, and if the ground is half decent it will do okay, but do not expect bumper crops until year three when the soil has reached maturity.

Growing the Ecology

While your compost is aging, mark out the area where you want to establish your garden and go on out and turn the soil by hand or with a tiller at the beginning of your growing season (after the last danger of frost). Our gardens are very large so we use a small tractor for the job, except for the herb gardens and perennial beds, like the asparagus, which must be carefully worked by hand. When the soil is turned, seed it the first year with legumes such as snow peas and beans. You'll get some nice vegetables and the soil will be enriched by the action of the plants, which will put valuable nitrogen into the soil. (Legumes are one of the few plants that can actually draw nitrogen from the air and turn it into soil-borne nitrogen, essential for plant growth.) You can also add what is called green manure, which means spreading pasture seed of tiny legumes over your soil, letting the plants grow a few weeks, then hoeing them all down before they go to seed, thus increasing the fertility of your soil. This puts nutritious, bulky plant matter in the soil and draws in earthworms and essential beneficial bacteria. A healthy garden's soil is unbelievably teeming with life. Every handful should have earthworms in it. A single grain the size of the head of a pin should contain millions of beneficial bacteria.

Get a rake and slightly work the ground just around the outside of your plot. Then get a can of wildflower seed and scatter it over that area. Surround the plot with the seed if you can. The wildflowers will grow and summon helpful insects, and the garden desperately needs the insects. They move pollen, allowing your fruiting plants such as melons and tomatoes to be fertilized. They eat away at dead tissue. And predacious insects such as ladybugs and certain wasps prey on aphids and grubs that you cannot have in your garden.

Our faithful Australian Shepherd, Willowisp, patrols the edge of the garden. He's been trained not to enter it. The untidy looking area to the right of the image is an intentionally overgrown hedge that wraps round the entire garden. It is home to tens of thousands of beneficial insects that pollinate blossoms and prey on garden pests.

I cannot emphasize enough how important it is to create this insect ecology, and it is a step often overlooked by gardeners because, sadly, people tend to think of bugs as bad. When we first established our gardens, we worked night and day to control infestations of flea beetles eating the tender new leaves of beets, aphids attacking the fruit trees, and cutworms knocking down Brussels sprouts and cabbages. In the second year, we started scattering wildflower seed around the gardens and between the fruit trees. In the third year, droves of predator insects moved in and took out the pests for us. The flowers also brought in birds that preyed on problem insects as well as the nocturnal slugs. Since then we have rarely had to worry about managing bugs, except for occasionally taking out a lone cutworm or getting rid of post-rain slugs.

If you live in the country, in an area where there are hedgehogs, try to draw in a family of them by pulling an old log up near your gardens and leaving out little saucers of bread and honey at the base of the log. Hedgehogs make a few annoying little holes in the ground, but they get under the soil and eat undesirable grubs that would otherwise prey on your plants' root systems. It is a lucky gardener who draws in a hedgehog family.

You would do well to place some birdhouses of various sizes around your garden, too. Birds are beneficial to a garden in so many ways. They eat insects, and small ones, like hummingbirds, aid in pollination. Plus, they're beautiful, and there are few things more pleasant than gathering in the garden for an outdoor dinner while being serenaded by birdsong. I suggest not adding birdfeeders near the garden. It detracts them from their natural roles.

If you establish the ecology, chances are your garden will see to its own health. You may have to occasionally control some more tenacious problems like slugs. Diatomaceous earth (DE) is excellent for that. It is not a poison and so is completely organic with no short- or long-term after-effects. The stuff is made from dried out diatoms, ocean microbes with silicon exoskeletons ... in other words, natural microscopically fine glass. It looks like a very fine white powder and is light, like talcum powder. If slugs become a problem, sprinkle it at twilight in the areas they turn up. Spread it thinly, but make sure the plants and ground in the area receive complete coverage. As the slugs, or any insects, move over it, it will lacerate their bodies so that they cannot hold moisture, killing them by dehydration. Only worms and insects are vulnerable to the effects of DE; it is harmless to all other life forms. In fact, you can even feed it to pets and livestock in small quantities and it will safely deworm them. But bear in mind that in the garden it washes away easily. If it rains, it'll be gone into the ground in no time. (Don't worry, it won't kill the earthworms if it washes into the ground. As soon as it mixes into the soil, the concentration becomes too low for it to have any effect.) The only thing to remember is when you put out DE, it will kill any insects and worms that come into contact with it, even the ones you want in the garden, like ladybugs and honeybees, so you can't just use it all the time. Pick the time and place to apply it and as soon as the problem is eliminated, break out the hose and wash it away.

You might also assist your garden by visiting it at night and spraying any insects you encounter with a mixture of dish soap and water (use pure soap without scents or additives). Soap kills most bugs and is otherwise biodegradable and harmless. Generally, any bugs you see by night in the garden should not be there. However, when you get a good ecology going, even nighttime control will rarely be necessary.

If you find plants knocked down at the base of the stem, you have a cutworm problem. Cutworms only attack one plant per night, but they are frustrating because they are so wasteful. They bed down by day under the base of the roots of the plant they have killed the previous evening, so dig up the soil of the fallen plant around midday, find the grub, and kill it. Then in the evening place DE around the base of the neighboring plants to make sure any remaining cutworms yet to emerge meet a quick end. Your cutworm problem will be over in a couple days. Remember to wash away the DE the next day shortly after sunrise so it doesn't kill beneficial insects and worms. Cutworms don't move around much, so they are only a problem in new gardens.

Three Turns of the Soil

Before you actually plant your garden for the first time, you should turn your soil three times. The first time should be four weeks before the last frost of the season. Then again two weeks later. The third time should be the day before you plant. This has the effect of constantly breaking up the budding roots of weeds, making them too weak to compete with your desired plants for the first couple months. Remember, your desired plants are putting their growing energy into making food for you, so you have to make the job of growing easier for them. That is the task of the gardener.

Deep Bedding

When it's time to plant, don't use rows. That's an age-old recipe for weeds. Instead, try deep bedding.

Deep bedding is a method in which you sow seeds relatively close together, the same distance side to side and lengthwise down a broad bed instead of a row. You plant the seeds a little closer than the seed packet's instructions recommend (usually about 25 percent closer). The effect is that the plants have room to grow but create deep shadow under their slightly crowded leaves. This chokes out the weeds that would otherwise threaten to choke out your plants.

Create beds as long as the length of your garden and either four or six feet wide, with eighteen-inch walkways between each bed. Stack the soil onto the beds at least six inches deep, preferably nine inches. When you get your packets of seeds, they will have instructions on them on how far apart to sow the plants. For example, lettuce might read: "Sow seeds twelve inches apart in rows two feet wide." Ignore the instructions on how wide to make the rows—remember, you're not using rows. Look at the first part where it said, sow seeds twelve inches apart. That's all that matters. Deduct 25 percent of twelve inches, yielding nine inches. So, sow your seeds nine inches apart in your beds, lengthwise and breadthwise.

With your soil rich in compost and your garden's ecology established, the lettuce will grow strong and sure and soon be choking out weeds that would dare invade the space. Bear in mind you will have to do some weeding early on because it takes a few weeks for your plants to get big enough to shade the soil beneath them. But because you have weakened the weeds by repeatedly turning the soil, they will be far less of a problem.

Also, late in the summer you will have to do more weeding. Weeds grow fast and their seeds will find their way into your soil, mostly by way of wind and birds. By this time your plants will be so far along that the weeds can be dealt with in a fairly leisurely fashion and will represent no real threat to your plants unless you get some especially invasive species that requires aggressive pulling. But even the most aggressive species can be tamed by covering that region of the garden with a dark tarp for a year, choking out its sunlight.

Thousands of turnips occupy two four-foot-wide beds.
The close planting style makes for slightly smaller turnips,
but the leaves shade out competing weeds.

Growing the Spirits

Organic gardening is three things at once. It is a science in which you take a working knowledge of ecology and apply it to nurturing desirable plants. It is also an art, in which you develop an intuition of what is needed to create health in the land. But it is also a magical process which invites the presence of little spirits and even greater beings like the Green Man. The attraction of Nature spirits to gardens is noted in many mythologies. For example, there are the corn gods of the American aboriginals, the corn dolls representative of the goddess of ancient British peoples (though in Europe, corn refers to other grains), the Greek god of wine, and even faerie myths of beings like the Apple Man and the sprites of flower gardens. In my experience, gardens simply fare better when one is considerate of the land's spirits. And we fare better too, as if attending to the spirits of the land is good for the human soul. Not surprising. We are ourselves spiritual beings who are extensions of the soil.

In the Hollow, we do several things to honor the spirits in our gardens. We frequently plant things for no other reason than they are sacred to the Earth spirits. One year we planted a great many marigolds because medieval legends speak of them pleasing the faerie folk.

When we harvest, we always leave some behind as an offering to the spirits. A few tomatoes always remain on the bush. Some turnips always remain in the soil. Bits and bobs of other things invariably stay in the gardens, too. It's our way of giving something back to the spirits. In time, those offerings always vanish. Perhaps the land's spirits take the offerings. Perhaps the wild animals of the Elfwood eat them. Either is fine, for the animals, like the spirits, are part of Nature, and I doubt the spirits mind sharing with them. And if some of it merely withers on the plant, that too is fine. It will return to the Earth and become part of the strength of the soil in the coming year, and the spirit of our offering remains whole.

A beautiful wild pheasant has adopted us and for the past three years it has been venturing into our gardens come midsummer and persists till long after harvest, nibbling at this and that. It takes very little and it is a lovely creature of shimmering jewel feathers. We gladly let it have what it will, feeling that it is as much a part of the land as we strive to be. In sharing with it, we honor the wild creatures which are the ward of the Green Man.

The long and short of it is: do not neglect to make a place in a proper organic garden for the spirits and the land's creatures. They are as much a part of the ecology of a healthy garden as sun and rain and earthworms. And I have found that if honored and given a little place of their own, things in the garden just seem to go much, much better.

FEBRUARY

The Elfwood

Surrounding the cottage on all sides save east is the Elfwood. It was once part of the surrounding forest, a region of great trees predominated by maple but possessing an abundance of other varieties: silvery birches, rowans with fanning leaves and bright clusters of ruby berries, broad white spruce, spanning ash, and many more. But nearly two decades ago, long before we bought the homestead, much of that old forest had been cut down and carried away to be sold for lumber and firewood.

But Nova Scotia is a forest province, and untended land wants hard to return to woods. The year after the land was cut, saplings began to grow. Maple saplings that had been too small to be noticed by the loggers spread their tiny boughs into the newly opened expanse of sky.

Alders and willows, fast growers that may become bushes or trees, grew in dense thickets. Birds carried apples from nearby trees into the field, and the seeds worked their way into the soil and sprouted. But it would take many years for the saplings to grow into a mature forest once again. For a long time the land would remain open—the soil exposed to the sun.

But Nature is never wasteful, and she is quick to take advantage of any opportunity. The land, under the full sun, became ideal for various wild herbs and the brambles that grow ubiquitously in every untended meadow. By the end of the second year, the meadow became a thicket predominated by wild raspberry and blackberry. In rocky exposures where clusters of softwoods had grown and made the soil acidic, low-bush blueberry spread woody branches over the ground, sporting tiny leaves and looking very much like untended bonsai trees. Tall Jerusalem artichokes grew in small, scattered clusters, raising bright yellow sun-flower-like blossoms on two-yard stalks to the sky. In the future, some of those incredibly hardy plants would be dug up and transferred to the gardens around the cottage both for their sunny, late-season flowers and their small tubers, which have been likened to artichoke hearts, though I don't personally taste the resemblance.

Down by the brook a thick, dense hedge of hardwoods had been left and at their verge were many useful herbs. There were several kinds of mint. One offers a chocolaty flavor and another smells of both mint and orange if crushed underfoot. The mint is resilient and prolific and spreads everywhere. Upstream is watercress, a peppery herb full of vi-tamin C that is excellent for salads and sandwiches, or simply munch-ing raw. Stinging nettle, a superb green if carefully picked and steamed, is scattered here and there along with bright magenta fireweed, from which superb jams can be made. Numerous medicinal and magical herbs grow as well, from the simple bushy willows whose bark cures pain to the marsh marigolds that are said to impart the second sight.

And there is more, so much more. Something I love about the forests of the Maritimes is the incredible variety of its wild lands.

But none of that can be seen in February. Wild winter weather has been blustering over the highlands since Yule and the ground has long since frozen, allowing snowfall to accumulate. The highlands are in a snow belt, and on top of this mountain we get almost twice as much snow as the rest of the province. The fields and forest are covered so deeply that one cannot walk about without the aid of snowshoes, and even the trees, reduced to bare, leafless bones by autumn, are coated in a rime of ice. According to the ancient Gauls, this month was "ice time," and Nova Scotia is even colder and more rugged—no exposed place has escaped the power of the ice. The land is buried beneath winter's breath and all is pulled relentlessly down into the cold's stupor, to sleep with the Green Man.

In the cottage, we feel that pull toward dormancy, too. Even though the days are lengthening, the weariness of late winter pervades. Beyond the windows, the sky is almost always slate. Icicles as long as I am tall hang from the roof. The fire blazes in the wood stove to ward back the north wind's chill. We settle at this time. When we are not tending to the essentials of feeding the animals and changing whatever of their bedding that has not frozen to the floor, we stay indoors and play board games, read, drink tea, and talk. And we all have crafts to occupy us. Daphne knits and researches new cheese recipes. I plan my next year's writing projects and pick out tunes on my fiddle. Arielle experiments with baking recipes and draws. Natalia, ever artsy, creates images of wildlife from tiny seashells and stones she collected during summer at the beach. February may be ice time, but it is also together time, and we happily relax together and enjoy the family bonding.

Even so, we're all outdoorsy and whenever the weather relents, we're eager to get out. So it happened that one Saturday, about halfway into the month, I awoke to be greeted by a cerulean sky beyond the window. *Yes!* I thought as I leapt out of bed. Daphne was already up, and wafting down from the kitchen I could smell hash browns on the stove—last year's crop of potatoes finding a good use. I faced the image of the Green Man that hangs from the wall at the foot of the bed, bobbed my head respectfully, and then dashed off for a quick shower.

A half hour later, I sat at the table with Daphne. Arielle had gone out for a walk and Natalia was in the yard building a gigantic snow fort. The girls were planning a snowball war later, so it was just the two of us in the cottage for the moment. We sipped tea and discussed our plans for the day. A nice day in February is too rare to squander, so we decided to hike up to the cabin late in the afternoon and spend the night, just she and I. There are few pleasures so simply romantic as a night spent together in a cozy, rustic cabin, while winter wind soughs among the trees and a fire flickers and crackles beyond the mica window of a wood stove. Arielle was old enough to look after the cottage for an evening. But for right now, we thought it would be a good time to let the horses out of the barn for a bit. The ground was too icy to let them go far, but the barn had a small corral just in front and we could let them stretch their legs after so long cooped up in their stalls.

So we spent the morning out at the barn. The doors had been frozen in place, and I had to break the ice with a shovel then use the powerful tractor's bucket to doze the snow out of the way. We opened the doors and released the horses who dashed out as soon as we were out of the way. They ran in joyous circles around the little corral, exulting in the movement. It was amazing to see Aval, an enormous beast of Belgian stock, kicking his hind legs like a nimble spring colt. After running and kicking for a while, the horses rolled in the fresh snow, getting winter grime out of their coats and then settled into eating the sweet, fine hay of a pair of bales we put outside for them. They got so messy in winter that it was tempting to get a brush and groom them, but it is never a good idea to brush horses in winter. It removes essential oils that waterproof their coats and upsets the natural lay of guard hair and undercoat that insulates them. They would just have to keep looking messy till spring. Even so, it was fun to watch them, and when Aval walked over to the fence and turned himself sideways to me, inviting me to get up on his back, I couldn't resist. He is an enormous horse—one cannot simply "jump up" on Aval. I walked him over to the hay bale, stepped up on it and leapt, using my arms to heave myself up over his back. With no saddle and no reins, I let Aval just walk around the corral with me. The quarter horse, Sidhe Bheg (Shee Vek), whinnied jealously, and Acorn sidled up beside Aval, wanting a turn carrying me, too, but Aval stepped away from them, head held high, a proud prance in his step because he was the one to get to carry somebody today.

I let Aval carry me around till he decided he was more interested in nibbling at the hay and slid off his back. The horses needed to be watched because, with the snow so deep, they could easily step over the corral's fence if they took a mind to, but Daphne was in the barn by now, mixing grains for animal feed, so she could watch things. I went back to the cottage to see how the girls were faring. I found Natalia sitting dejectedly by her snow fort with an unused pile of snowballs. I asked her what had happened with the big snowball war and learned that the girls had squabbled over some little thing, as sisters are wont to do, and Arielle had gone off to make her own fun. I offered to have a snowball fight with Natalia, but she declined. Apparently, the argument had stolen the fun out of the idea. I tried to talk her into Frisbee or sledding, but she was too pouty to engage, so I went inside and in the kitchen began the complex conjuration of an ancient potion of legendary soothing power. It took several minutes to warm a base of moon-white liquid, and when it was hot I blended in an amber fluid as viscous as tree sap and dissolved into the blend an exotic brown powder of South American origin. As I worked, I could see through the window that Arielle had returned, but they still were not on speaking terms. Carefully I poured the steaming potion into three vessels, then I went to the door and called to the girls. "Hot chocolate! Come and get it!"

Hot chocolate is a potion that crosses all emotional borders and makes things right. The girls came inside, each pouting dramatically, but a few minutes after settling at the table and sipping their cocoa, which I had served with some cookies someone had baked and stored in the breadbox, they were on speaking terms again. That lasted till about five minutes after the cocoa was gone, then the topic of their argument came up again when Natalia lamented her unused snow fort. Apparently, they had had some disagreement about the rules of a snowball war, and when the argument began to resume I headed it off at the pass by interjecting: "Hey, let's go explore the Elfwood."

Both the girls looked at me, intrigued but dubious. The Elfwood was seven or eight times larger than the portion of our land that we used for livestock and the gardens, and we had barely explored it because getting about in it was very difficult. The thickets of young trees, hidden old stumps, half-buried boulders, and tall brambles made the land a treacherous obstacle course that could easily result in painful abrasions and sprained ankles. And at this time of year, the snow would be to my waist, almost chest high for the girls. It would be virtually impossible to navigate. But I knew something they didn't. In the past week there had been strong, dry winds, and when such conditions are just right, the snow can take on a hard-packed crust that even a grown man can walk on. I explained this and they decided to give it a try, so we deposited our cocoa mugs in the sink, put on our toughest high boots and thickest winter coats, and hiked up to the Hedge Witch Meadow and there turned west, following an old path into the Elfwood.

From the Hedge Witch Meadow, which lies almost a hundred yards north of the cottage, we hiked along the northern hedge to a large boulder at the corner that was easy to climb. I pressed down on the old barbwire fence while the girls clambered over. They were nimble and probably didn't need my help, but, hey! I'm their dad. It's my job to help them. When they had crossed, I stepped on the boulder, grabbed a low branch of birch just overhead, and hauled myself over the fence. On the other side of the hedge it was suddenly, radically different. The meadow had a tame feel, but the Elfwood, spanning west and north, looked impossibly tangled and wild. The raspberry and blackberry canes were everywhere, and the snow clung thickly to them, making the snowfall seem even deeper. An old game trail, little more than a thinning between thorny canes, led away from the fence. We followed its winding way westward, deeper into the tangled growth.

Scattered here and there were tall saplings, some as high as twenty feet. These were young alders and white birches, fast-growing trees that are quick to colonize open ground. I pointed out to the girls that both these varieties were friendly trees. Both have medicinal uses, and alder yields a pungent smoke that is excellent for smoking meats and cheeses, while white birch yields minty-sweet sap in spring and the under-bark and twig tips can serve as a food source. The bark can even be stretched over a frame to make a canoe.

We ventured farther west and through the saplings we saw a grove of tall, old trees standing like an island of the old forest. The grove was about an eighth of an acre, and was comprised of maples, willow, white spruce, and birch, and at its heart was a small springhead, now frozen, that fed a darkly shaded, shallow pondlet. Many similar stands dotted the land. Natalia pointed at the tall trees and said, "When the logger cut the forest all those years ago, why did he leave the stands?"

"Various reasons," I replied. "They provide starter stock to help the forest reseed itself. And wildlife use the groves for shelter. Birds nest in the branches. Deer feed in the clearing at morning and twilight and hide in the groves by day and night."

Arielle said bluntly, even a little bitterly, "I wish they'd never cut the forest."

"I wish it, too," I agreed, and Natalia also nodded. "There are so many people in the world now, and the forest cannot keep up with all the demands made on it. But it has been cut, and years later we bought the homestead, and now we're protecting it while it heals."

We walked into the grove. The trees were dense and the shadows deep, and we had to weave between the spruces whose boughs go all the way to the ground. We clambered over a large boulder and descended into a shadowed dip where the soft snow went almost to our chests before we forged our way out the other side. Everywhere around us were signs of busy wildlife. Tracks revealed where rabbits frequently darted into the grove to hide from falcons. At the base of an ancient maple was a large round dropping, riddled with tiny bones and short brown fur—the spoor of an owl that had devoured a mouse or meadow vole. Small, widely spaced paw prints with convex rear pads showed where a fox had dashed into the grove in pursuit of game. As we regarded the tracks from the icy shadows of the grove, I interpreted the tracks for the girls, although Natalia was learning the tracker's art quickly and often able to explain the spoor before I did.

We ventured through the small grove and, upon exiting the other side, took note of an especially large maple from which, one spring, we might draw sap. Currently, when spring came, we were tapping an ancient sugar bush down by the brook at the far edge of the Firefly Meadow where the goats graze.

On the other side, more of the Elfwood was revealed—brambly clearing with scattered thickets lying north. But to the west the land became more interesting and, even, inscrutable, for in that place the loggers must have become drunk because strange passages between young trees had been left. They almost formed a labyrinth in some places and were thick enough to give the illusion of a forest unless you were very close. Those trees were predominantly young white spruce, but there were also elms and willows, alders and silver birches, rowans, and even the rare thorn. They were the sacred trees of the Ogham, I thought wistfully, an ancient magical script of the Celts, similar in its way to the runes of the Norse.

The Ogham was a writing system which was symbolically attached to animals, months of the year, and, most notably, trees.

We continued hiking in the direction of the labyrinthine hedges, and as we went, I began telling the girls of the useful properties of the dormant foliage we passed. "Raspberry not only makes a fine fruit, but its young leaves make a lovely tea—an excellent substitute for black tea." Passing a willow, I said: "Willow trees feed wildlife and are especially favored by moose. Old Irish lore says that on some nights certain enchanted willows will walk about in the woods." Natalia had heard about this before and asked me if I had ever seen a walking willow. I shook my head and smiled, remarking that I would love to one day. A small rowan was obvious by its clusters of dark, half-dried ruby berries still clinging despite the frequent winter winds. "Birds eat rowan berries, and they are an important food source for them in winter," I told the girls, indicating the graceful, small-branched tree with a nod, "but, above all, the rowan is a seelie tree. Unfriendly spirits will not come under a rowan, and it's said its twigs and berries will ward away bad luck. That's why we keep a sprig of rowan in the house."

We entered the labyrinth. From somewhere down in the valley came the echoing, lonely cry of a hawk. I scanned the northwest skies and spied it circling high over the forest. It was hunting its day's supper. And from our vantage, we could see down to the brook that ran along the south boundary of the homestead. I pointed to a region where I had crossed many times in pursuit of deer. "I've seen marsh marigold down there," I told the girls. "If it's anything like other marigolds, faerie folk love that flower, and it's said that if you steep the blossoms and wash your eyes in the cold tea at dawn you will be able to see them."

At the mention of seeing faeries, Natalia said that sometimes, while playing at the edge of the Elfwood, she saw structures off down in the valley. "They look like an old barn and a cottage," she said, "but if you look hard at them, they vanish." We had all hiked deep into the forest in that direction many a time and knew there were no cottages or barns that way. There was no human habitation in those woods at all. We mused over whether she had seen the ghostly afterimage of an ancient homestead. Anything was possible in this magical country. The girls and I had all seen the white-haired children dressed in nineteenth-century garb over several months at the farmhouse we were renting in Cape Breton when we first came to Nova Scotia. And sometimes at nights I saw a slender woman in a long skirt and pale blouse standing about that old farmhouse's kitchen. Even Eldritch, our black cat, must have seen the apparitions because sometimes he dashed wildly about the house as if alternately chasing and fleeing something beyond human perception. Our cottage here in the Hollow did not seem as haunted, but the woods were. We all knew that from experience. "When the snow melts, we'll go explore over there," I told the girls. "Maybe we'll find the remnants of an old homestead." Arielle remarked there could be some antiques. That was quite possible. Useful and curious things were often found in these woods. I always kept my hopes up that one day we would come upon an old anvil, which would be immensely handy for a dozen tasks.

But our hike continued and momentarily we passed a twisted wild apple that still bore desiccated winter fruit. "Apples are not just food, but the fruits can be sliced up and put on the eye for ailments like pink eye." For some reason the girls thought that was funny and giggled. I went on. "And apples were sacred to the Celts and are prized by at least some spirits. If you cut them open, you'll see the core contains the outline of a pentacle. And, as you know, we always leave a few apples on the trees for the Apple Man who looks after the trees, and I also suspect the cider makes a favorite faerie offering, like for the faerie plates we put out near Samhain." The faerie plates are an old Gaelic tradition—little offerings of bread and cheese or fruit, a little milk or brew, left under sequestering trees for the friendly faerie folk that certainly bide near the cottage. They leave us signs of their work, like keeping the raccoons out of the cornstalks. Some of our neighbors have had their entire corn crops eaten bare by raccoons but never once have they even entered our gardens. I told the girls about one morning this past summer when their mother, who is open-minded but very grounded in the practical world, diffidently said to me over tea: "I know this is going to sound weird, but sometimes I see strange things in the forest and in the barn." I lifted my eyebrows and asked her to describe them, and she said, "They're like movement just at the corner of my eyes. They look like shadows darting into deeper shadows." I am a psychotherapist by profession, and the poor woman must have thought I would think she was losing her marbles, but I had smiled and reminded her of the little marvels we'd witnessed at the leased farmhouse up on the island. Besides, I already knew we had a barn bruanighe (more commonly called a brownie nowadays).

Not far ahead, I knew we would come upon an ancient stone wall laid down centuries ago by the original Scots settlers when they worked to clear this meadow for their sheep. Most of those early homesteads had vanished more than a hundred years ago when the rural folk were drawn to the fertile, more easily farmed grounds of the lowlands and to the new wealth of the urban centers. We passed through a thicket of tall, slender trees which I thought were ash, though it was hard to be sure because they lacked their summer leaves. The young trees grew so close we had to squeeze between their trunks. I remarked as we passed through: "I'll have to come back in summer with a Swedish saw and thin these out, otherwise they'll choke themselves to the point none will grow."

We reached the stone wall. Beyond lay the great old forest we call the Rusalka Wood. Those ancient trees . . . you can feel the press of time and secrets when you walk beneath their boughs. Natalia once hiked with me through there near twilight, looked up at what had to be the largest maple we'd ever stumbled across, and said, "We need to go home. I have to draw a picture." When we got back to the house, she went straight up to her room and drew for hours, then came down and presented an amazing image she called *My Liege*, portraying the forest trees bowing reverently to the great maple king. I've since had it framed.

We turned north at the stone wall and started up to the far boundary of the land, and from there began a circling trek back to the cottage. The snow was deep, but if we could find exposed spaces between the brambles we could walk on the crusty surface. Wherever the canes were thick, the snow was pocked with hollows, and when we had to pass over those places—which was often—we sank into crumbly snow to our chests, slowing our progress. But we came in time to a rise where the canes thinned and the wind had blown the snow away. Wild blueberry covered the Earth and between it were sulfur yellow and luminous red patches of lichen. We stopped and leaned against a bare boulder for a breather.

Natalia said, "Why do we call this part of our land the Elfwood? It's hardly woods at all. What makes it different from the rest of the forest?"

Good questions. Twa Corbies Hollow was large, a quarter mile in every direction, but it was a mere postage stamp in the vast hollow atop this mountain, and the hollow was only a tiny place in the immense forest of the highlands. And our little Elfwood was indeed barely woods, with its broad cutover areas dotted by scattered groves, its bizarre labyrinth, and the whole of it outlined by thick hedges and eerie rock walls. But as I looked about, I took note of the half-grown trees that were slowly filling in the clearings, and with pride I thought of how we made those young trees safe. We warded this land so it could heal. It was a sanctuary for wildlife and the land's spirits. "It's not really any different from the rest of the forest," I explained, "but it's ours, and we gave it back to the Green Man. We keep it safe so it can heal and regrow, and the spirits can make it their own, along with the wild creatures that share it with them. So it's like the sacred groves the druids kept long ago. *Elf* is just an old word for faerie or spirit, so these are the spirits' woods."

The girls looked around. Surrounding the great valley were ridges west and hills that rolled off to the east. It lent the Hollow a sense of extreme seclusion but also made one aware of how small this place was within the expansive mountain's demesne.

The Elfwood through the second-story study window.
A late winter wind has driven the snow from the trees.

"It's not much," observed Arielle.

I nodded. "Yeah, true enough," I said somberly. "It's small in the grand scheme of things. But if we each do a little bit to make the world a better place, it'll all add up, right?"

The girls nodded.

Natalia sighed, looked around at the endless snow and ice covering all the ground and riming all the trees, and her shoulders slumped. "I wish spring would come," she moaned for the millionth time. By this time of year we were all eager to see green grass again.

I pointed at a willow shrub. It had a fortuitous sheltered southern exposure and the furry tails of catkins had emerged from its branches. "See those catkins?" I told her. "They mean spring is on the way." That brought a smile.

We rose from the boulder and started the long hike back to the cottage, taking the interior way, walking atop another ancient wall of fieldstone for easier going. It led us along the north border of the land. Here, deep among the young trees, there were even more signs of active wildlife. We passed the remnants of a rabbit that had recently been a hawk or eagle's meal. We came upon the dark droppings of a coyote. A cluster of bushy willow shrubs with bobbed twigs indicated a winter feeding ground of whitetail deer or perhaps a rare moose. A small, deep hole beneath the partial shelter of a log was some creature's den. But the day was wearing on and the cold was biting, so we pressed harder for home.

It was more than halfway into the afternoon when we got back to the cottage. We came in like a chilled herd, reveling in the wood stove's dry heat, and kicked off boots and coats. Daphne has a strange maternal prescience, so when we arrived she already had milk warming on the stove for mugs of hot chocolate. Whatever she was concocting for dinner smelled wonderful, too. She had already stuffed a duffel with our sleeping bags and toiletries, and was ready for our night alone together up at the cabin. She served the hot chocolate and dished up some thick turkey stew for the girls. The rest she put in plastic containers for us to take to the cabin, along with bread and cheese for breakfast, and I threw in a bottle of home-brewed wine that had been aging in the root cellar since last year. The cabin was only a couple miles away in the Old Woods near the east ridge, and the girls had a radio to call us in the unlikely event of an emergency.

When the girls were done eating and instructions given for the evening—all that needed to be done was putting out grain and water for the animals—Daphne and I made ourselves ready to set off. The sun was just lowering in the west and we were just heading out when a thought came to mind. "Wait a minute," I said and dashed to the stairs to call Natalia. "Hey, Bubbles, come give me a hand, will you?"

Natalia came down the stairs. I took her into the kitchen and had her cut a little wedge of cheese and I cut a slice of bread from a loaf in the breadbox. I popped the top off a bottle of my home-brewed ale and poured a little into a tiny shot glass, then returned the cap to the bottle and replaced it in the fridge. We went out the back door and down the deck stairs, trudged through the deep snow to the very edge of the Elfwood. We pushed into the spruce trees, passing a small wind chime sounding like lazy, high-pitched bells in the mild breeze. A bit further in we entered a small clearing where half-buried in the snow was a ceramic mushroom that is hollowed out to look like the faerie houses that can be found in some Maine woods.

"Set the saucer down here," I told her and she put it down. I set down the little ale glass on the edge of the plate.

"It's the wrong time of year for faerie plates," she remarked. We usually put them out around Samhain and Bealtaine.

I shrugged. "Hmm, maybe. But this is the Elfwood. It's always a good time to let the spirits know that here they are welcomed, and that we are friends. Don't you think?"

Natalia smiled her half-impish, half-pixie smile and we went back inside, she to a novel, and me to join Daphne for our winter night up at the cabin.

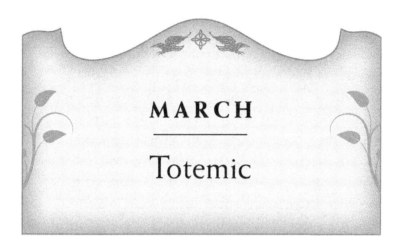

MARCH

Totemic

Arielle and I were down by the brook on the southeast corner of the homestead upon an icy, clear mid-spring day. The spring thaw had engorged the normally placid little brook, and its waters tumbled and pounded wildly upon the stones scattered among its bed. The spray had frozen wherever it touched leaf or twig and metamorphosed into a menagerie of icicles that hung from the branches of young trees and shrubs leaning out over the water. We were preparing to tap an ancient maple that was just beyond the fence surrounding the Firefly Meadow. The sun was shining, and it was just a couple degrees over freezing—a perfect day for sugaring. The sap would flow vigorously in such weather. And no sooner did I finish drilling a hole, angled slightly downward and about an inch into the tree, than clear, sweet sap began to run. It reminded me of the Green Man's blood, though it would do this great old tree no harm to accept a few taps—it was so large I could not wrap my arms around its circumference! In fact, the attention it had received over the last few years as a "sugar bush" had led to some essential doctoring when we had noticed it had some rot here and there and had done a bit of tree surgery to stop the infection. Otherwise, the old maple would not have made it much longer.

When the sap hole was ready, I stepped aside so Arielle could tap it. With a small hammer, she drove in a little nickel spigot with a hook attached to its tip. From this we hung a sap bucket sufficient to hold about a gallon. We hung five such buckets around the trunk and stepped back to survey the work. A tree such as this could produce much more, but we made it a point to take no more from Earth than we needed. On a day such as this, the tree might fill each of the buckets, and five gallons of maple sap were enough for us for a good week. We didn't actually produce syrup; we just wanted the sap. It is little known what a wonderful beverage spring sap is—like an ambrosia of the gods. And not just maple sap. We also tapped birches in spring, which produce a wonderful slightly sweet, minty sap.

Just then we heard Natalia running down the meadow. She was crying. I turned, about to ask what was the matter, but before I could speak she cried, "Dad! Something killed the kittens!" Just a moment ago, I had been happy as a lark and feeling proud of a good job done in harmony with the green world, but suddenly all that melted away. The kittens she was referring to were born of a stray cat that had adopted us late in the winter and moved into the barn. She became an excellent barn cat, keeping the mice out of the livestock's grain stores and stoats out of the chicken coop. We had planned to have her spayed, but she was already several weeks pregnant, so we figured we'd let her have the litter first. If you have a barn, you quickly learn that careless persons will often dump their unwanted kittens on you. We had developed a fair bit of experience finding homes for cuddly little kittens. But these kittens had been born just a week ago and were far from ready to leave their mother. I felt bad about the loss, but Natalia has an especial love of cats, and she was taking it hard.

I let her lead me back to the barn where the mother cat, whom we had taken to calling Bronwen, had been nursing the kittens. She had found a warm spot between some hay bales. "I came to feed the chickens and they were just gone," said Natalia between sobs.

I knelt by the bales and felt around. There was a little hair in the hay but no blood and no meaningful spoor of the kittens. I was certain a wild predator must have gotten them, most likely a stoat. Except that stoats usually kill more than they can eat and leave the surplus. But the forest was full of other predators: great ones like wildcats, bears, and enormous coyotes, though they never seemed interested in even crossing our farmed land. It was as if an unspoken pact had been created between them and us; they would respect our little cultivated area, and we would respect and nurture their forest. But there were even more numerous small predators in the forest: mink, martens, fishers, raccoons, foxes, and others, any of which might make a meal of a few tiny kittens. Normally, they respected the barn, too, but occasionally one stole in and killed a chicken or two. It was part of living in the wilds.

I dug around in the hay a bit more and found a tiny speck of blood and a bit of brown fluff. The kittens were all black and gray, so this was not their hair. It looked like something from the weasel family to me. I stood up. "I'm sorry, Natalia. I think a stoat got them."

Natalia nodded. She was trying to be brave. Like every farm kid, she knew death was a natural part of life. She'd found chickens killed by hawks and ermines. She'd seen me bring back deer from the forest and had even come hunting with me as I taught her how to use a longbow to carefully stalk and humanely take game. But this was different for her. She gets so attached to cats. Her voice catching on sobs she struggled to control, she said, "I want to find a home for Bronwen now."

I nodded sympathetically. "We could just have her spayed and let her be a barn cat. She seems to like being outdoors, and every barn needs a cat." Ours did, that was sure. We had found a home for our last barn cat last summer because he had gotten a bit old for the harsh winters of the highlands, and the moment he was moved out the mice had taken over. When Bronwen wandered onto our homestead one day and made herself at home in the barn, the mouse problem had gone away almost overnight. And no one could ever say our barn cats weren't well cared for. Every day, twice a day, they got fresh, warm goat milk and were fed a porridge of meat scraps and eggs.

Daily practice is required to perform well with the longbow,
whether shooting stumps in the forest or, as in this image,
a grain sack stuffed with plastic. These shots were placed
at thirty yards. My fist is on the target for scale.

But little Natalia shook her head. "She's too prissy for a barn. I want her to be a house cat."

I pursed my lips and nodded. I knew that was a hard decision for her to make. She was especially attached to Bronwen, who was indeed a very prissy cat—very poised and graceful, and who, among cats and people alike, could only be described as impeccably mannered. Daphne and I had even considered adopting her as another house cat, but we couldn't. We already had an adopted stray, plus Eldritch, plus a dog, and all the other animals to look after. So I nodded. "I'll contact some friends and put the word out that she's available." Bronwen was such an endearing cat that I was sure we'd find a home for her inside a month.

Later in the day I decided to go stump shooting. This is an essential traditional archer's exercise in which you wander the woods and shoot at stumps at various heights and distances. Shooting on a range will train you to aim, but it won't teach you to instinctively watch for obstacles—and any little twig or bramble can deflect an arrow—or to estimate distance and wind on the fly. Stump shooting is great for that. So I saddled Aval, slung my longbow and quiver over my shoulder, and rode him up to the Old Wood, the old growth forest a mile east of the cottage where my friend's cabin lies at the edge of a maple grove. Every time I walked in that wood, I had the peculiar sense that I was being watched. I did not sense a malevolent presence, just something keeping an eye on things. The Old Wood was alive—not just with trees and birds and terrestrial creatures—I felt in my heart it was full of enchantment. I never felt quite at ease there, but I loved that wood, too.

Aval and I are old friends, and we often pass warm days together
wandering the forests and meadows about the Hollow.

At the edge of the forest, I rode Aval into a growth of young spruce. A little hidden meadow was concealed within and because of its southern exposure, the snow was already gone from the open areas. I had a length of rope in a saddlebag and tied it between two trees, then tethered Aval to the rope with a short lead. That would allow him to graze without risk of tangling his legs. I strung my longbow, a stout stave of maple laminates with a seventy-pound draw weight, and slung a quiver over my back with eighteen field-tipped arrows in it. Then I made my way into the forest, slipping between gaps in the trees, heading toward the hardwoods that grew just a couple hundred yards beyond.

The snow was half gone and where the ground was exposed, the grass was all brown with fallen leaves everywhere, even among the spruce at the edge of the hardwood forest. I practiced moving across the landscape in silence, as I would as if stalking wild game, stepping only where the ground was moist and soft. If I broke a twig or crunched over dry leaves, I froze in place for a random count of moments. It is impossible to move through dense eastern forests without making a sound, so the trick is to blend into the background. Forests are always full of sound. The crack of a falling twig. The soughing of wind in the trees. The songs of birds. The tapping of woodpeckers. The rustle of small animals in the underbrush. So moving quietly means becoming just another random voice of the living woods. When I reached the hardwoods, mostly great old maples with the odd scattered willow, alder, and silvery birch, the trees opened out and movement became easier. Here there was melting snow and the duff on the forest floor was damp and soft. As long as I was careful to avoid stepping on twigs, I was soundless. Now and then I withdrew an arrow, set it to the bowstring, and took a shot at a fallen log or a broken stump. I was aiming for "barebow bull's-eyes," meaning to hit the target within six inches of my goal if fifteen yards or farther, and within two inches of my goal if less than that. The arrows hit the wood with loud *thwocks* that echoed through the forest, and I withdrew and reused them as I went.

Here and there I spotted spoor: the little round pellets of deer and slightly ovular pellets that looked like they were made of sawdust but are the leavings of rabbits. I came upon a bit of unmelted snow on the northern side of a great tree that was stained red with white fur scattered about. A quick glance at the tracks revealed clawed paws where the back pad made a concave chevron. Here a rabbit had been killed and eaten by a bobcat or lynx—and recently. It was a good year for rabbits and their tracks were everywhere. High rabbit populations would feed the predators that relied on them and spring would see the births of more small wildcats and foxes. A year or two later the predators would become too dense and eat back the rabbit population, whereupon many of the predators would starve over yonder winter. It's a natural cycle of rise and fall that takes roughly seven years.

The sun continued to move higher in the sky and once, when I glanced at it, I espied a huge horned owl sleeping high in a tree. I figured by the sun it was two hours till noon, and I would head back in an hour to be home for lunch. For now I continued working my way steadily east, deeper into the Old Wood. Natalia's sorrow came often to mind, but there was nothing to be done but give her time to grieve. Still, I felt bad for her and the kittens, and the feelings lingered.

Then, while rounding a huge, half-rotted log, I passed a single track in a small space where the Earth was bare and soft. A huge paw print was embedded there. It looked almost human, but bigger than my own foot, and I'm a big guy at a hair under six feet and two hundred pounds. Above the pad were the small dots of toes, going from little dot to large dot, but where the large dot of a human would have been on the inside of the foot, the creature's big toe was on the outside. And above each dot was a tiny indent indicating the large curving claws of a creature capable of scrabbling up trees. This was the paw print of a black bear—a very big black bear. I knelt and closely regarded the print. It was sharp and fine edged—fresh. It could have been made an hour ago or a day ago, but not much beyond that. So ... a bear was up out of hibernation a bit early, and would probably be hungry and ornery, looking for an easy meal. I stood up and glanced around warily, but there were no other signs of the bear. I wasn't particularly worried because eastern black bears learned a long time ago to avoid people. But I felt a momentary pang of fear for Aval, tied off as he was to his line in the clearing, but I quickly dismissed the thought. Aval was bred out of warhorses and weighed three-quarters of a ton and had rock-hard hooves like plates. He could stomp a small car flat. No bear in its right mind would attack a horse that big, so I continued into the forest, yet I could not escape the feeling that something ursine watched me.

There was a dense thicket to my right and I regarded it often, out of old, cautious habit from my days in the Alaskan wilds. I've been charged by grizzlies in the past, and the instinct to be leery of thickets where bears might lie in wait was still strong. But my rational mind knew no eastern bear would behave like that, and I chided myself for the fear. Even so, the image of a huge black bear in those shadowy evergreens, watching my every step, kept cropping up in my mind's eye. I could feel its gaze boring into me. I shook my head hard to break hold of the thought. "Nonsense!" I chided myself. "You're just feeling bad for Natalia and the kittens." To break the spell of a runaway imagination, I drew another arrow from my quiver, set it to the string, and sighted in at a golden patch of moss near the base of a tall tree twenty yards away. And it was then that I came out of my cogitations enough to really look around and see the place I had stumbled into.

In this little section of the forest, the snow was gone, completely gone, and gold reigned. Golden sunshine spilled in crystalline rays through breaks in the forest canopy. The ground was covered with lichen and moss and last autumn's fallen leaves, all of which retained a splendid buttery hue. Huge maples rose overhead, their boughs vaulting skyward, and between them smaller alders grew. The alders, sheltered from the fierce winter winds by the enormous maples, yet retained their autumn leaves, which glowed in the sunbeams like the translucent wings of dragonflies. All around on the forest floor and on fallen logs were desiccated mushrooms: corral, honey, and varieties I could not identify, and they were all gilded by the dazzling sunshine spilling over them. It was as if I had wandered into a sunbeam, or what a sunbeam would be like if it could take on material form. Suddenly I knew I had stumbled upon a place of such beauty that here the Otherworld must touch upon the green world. This was certainly a place of wild spirits. The soughing breeze felt like music, and despite the sadness that had pervaded since the morning's tragic discovery, my spirits lifted, brightening with the golden luminescence of the place. I threw my arms overhead and lifted my face skyward to the light and the wind's own composition, a melody to surpass mortal remembrance, and lost myself to an approaching, benevolent presence. Time suddenly had no meaning. Sorrow could not hold. The gods of the place were old and close, and it was only that moment that mattered. Without meaning to, I had stumbled into a place of power and found myself in the middle of what some have called a peak experience—a timeless moment of closeness to the numinous.

I stood there I don't know how long. It might have been only a moment, or the moment might have been much longer. But an instant came when I felt... well, the only way I know how to describe it is "in myself" again, and I slowly became aware of time and lowered my arms, looked around. It felt as if completion had been reached, but completion of what, I couldn't say. But there was no more apprehension over the bear, even though I had the sense that he was still watching. I walked back to Aval, brushing my hand upon trees and stalks of grasses as I passed, soaking in the place on every sensory level. And somehow I just knew everything would be all right, though I couldn't imagine how that could possibly come to pass.

But back at the cottage things were not all right. Natalia is a great kid, but she's prone to being headstrong and oversensitive (not unlike her father), and with the demise of the kittens her mood had turned foul. She was lipping at her sister and ignoring her mother and in general taking out her anger and hurt on her family. I had often reflected, as a psychotherapist, that it is an odd trait of humans that we take out our dark feelings on those we love most—the very ones who are closest to us and care for us most. I thought I knew why, though, for those are the persons who are safest when darkness makes us vulnerable. We know they will bear the brunt of our pain and see us through.

But Natalia had been at it awhile, and when I walked into the cottage after currying Aval and bringing him back to his pasture, the tension was thick enough to cut with a knife. Arielle and Natalia were sitting at the table over untouched bowls of soup scowling at one another, occasionally saying something to egg the other on. Daphne had given up trying to rein them in and was at the sink vigorously scrubbing the skins off potatoes. When I walked in she gave me a look that said, *Please help!* I took her aside and asked what was going on, and learned, to my surprise, that she didn't know what had set Natalia off. She hadn't been around the house when I left on Aval, and Arielle had been so upset about the kittens that she hadn't yet spoken to Daphne about it. And Natalia had said nothing, either. She had simply come storming into the cottage at lunch, defiant and sparks flying.

I blamed myself. I should have made sure Daphne knew what was going on before I left. When I explained about the kittens, Daphne's vexation faded. She also understood how attached Natalia became to cats. We discussed talking it over with Natalia but decided to wait till her mood cooled. When Natalia got like this, nothing we might say would register.

So I ate a bowl of stew and tried to put the tension out of my mind, then I went outside to split some firewood. The days were still cold and we would need to keep the wood stove going another month or two. After a couple hours, I had a quarter of a cord of hand-split wood to move down to the cottage, and while working on that project I noticed the raised deck, under which I was storing the wood, needed some maintenance. Nothing major, just a couple boards here and there had warped a little due to the cold, dry air and needed to be tapped down. I snagged a hammer from the woodshop and climbed up the outside stairs to the deck. To get at the boards, I had to move an antique wooden barrel. I set aside the hammer and leaned over the barrel to grasp it from either side of its open top and saw movement within its shadowy confines. I ducked my head lower, shielding my eyes from the sunlight, and, unbelievably, there were four sleeping kittens at the base of the barrel. A broad smile split my mouth and I stood up straight, chuckling gleefully and shouted, "Natalia! Come see, sweetie. I have a surprise for you!"

Natalia came sullenly outside and around to the southern deck. "What?" she asked, her voice flat-toned and insipid, probably expecting a pep talk she wasn't in the mood for.

"A surprise," I said again and pointed at the barrel.

She took a long-suffering breath that clearly said *I don't want to do this,* but walked over and looked into the barrel. Her entire aspect changed. She lit up. No, she radiated, and cried out, "The kittens!"

Daphne and Arielle heard and came out back to see what all the hubbub was about. We showed them the kittens and the girls laughed with delight. Daphne said, "The mother cat must have moved them."

The Green Man's luck was with these little strays,
so we found them a cozy place to grow up—inside a hen's
laying box, up safe off the ground in the snug barn.

I nodded. "Yeah, but she wouldn't have done that unless she felt they were threatened." Then I began to put the picture of what happened together in my head. Something had come for the kittens, probably one of the small but vicious stoats that occasionally took a chicken. The mother cat, Bronwen, had fought it and either killed or injured it. That explained the speck of blood and the bit of brown fluff in the straw where she had been keeping the litter. Then she had determined her young were not safe in the barn and brought them one-by-one someplace she knew no predators ever dared go, to the cottage, where she found a veritable fortress—from a cat's perspective—in the old barrel.

Everyone was overjoyed to see the little kittens doing well, and we decided to go the extra mile and keep them indoors till they were weaned. We cleared out a kennel that we use for a "chicken hospital" whenever poultry are injured and brought them inside. Natalia watched the barrel until Bronwen showed up to nurse her brood and carried her to the kennel, too, and we kept them all there warm and safe. Natalia volunteered for the task of feeding and watering them, and changing the litter daily. What can I say? She's a cat-girl.

When the kittens were mature enough, we found homes for them all, and even Bronwen found a nice lady in the village to adopt her. But we had become so attached to the little feline family that we couldn't say goodbye to all of them, so we kept one—a pure gray tomcat who became a spoiled house cat named Luthien who now keeps our aging black cat, Eldritch, company.

The old Norse believed there was a skein that held our fates, and on that day when the kittens were irretrievably lost, Natalia's heart was broken, and our spirits low, it just seemed as if too many things came together just right for the events to have been mere chance. There must have been a design woven into that skein. Still, the events of the day were such a beautiful and unlikely series of events that I have spent a great deal of time trying to make a deeper sense of them. And in the seasons that have passed since that day, I still cannot say that I fully understand what happened, but I feel I've reached some insights.

In my life, I have had an uncanny number of bear encounters. Three times I have been charged by grizzlies in Alaska. I have stumbled upon them many more times. One of the most beautiful experiences in my life was of tracking a black bear through the Chugach Forest south of Anchorage one fine summer afternoon, observing it unseen from just fifty feet away and downwind in a gorge with a beautiful crystal river flowing just beyond the towering softwoods. The wind concealed my scent and the river hid any sound I might have made. And I had a most unusual encounter with a pair of black bears one Nova Scotia autumn when I stumbled into a squabble they were having over some wild apples. Of course, I've spent a lot of my life in the wilds so I'm bound to come across one now and then, but I've encountered them so many times and in such unusual circumstances that an old hiking buddy once joked that if I had a Native name it would be Chased By Bears. He then went on to state that given my peculiar luck with the creatures, no bear would ever actually hurt me. It would probably just leap over me and eat whatever, or whoever, was beyond. Whatever the case, I seem to have an affinity with bears, and the gods know my wife has called me a surly old bear enough. But that day when the kittens vanished, I had felt such a peculiar closeness with the spirit of Bear in that golden place in the Old Wood.

In old aboriginal lore, one didn't always find their totem through a meditative journey—as is expected in modern shamanism. In the old days, it was not uncommon that a totem came to a seeker in the flesh. This often happened during a spirit quest into the wilds wherein a young warrior or an aspiring shaman wandered until a power creature found them, and the encounter was not without risk. Often it tried to kill the seeker, bringing on an initiatory crisis—a life and death challenge which, if overcome, would allow the seeker to make peace with the spirit of the animal and thus acquire it as a totem. I have never felt that one day I had a single transformative experience whereupon I acquired Bear Spirit as a totem, but I do feel that over the years, Bear and I have encountered one another enough that we have developed a mutual understanding, and have become, in a way, friends and allies.

Natalia, on the other hand, has been strongly drawn to cats since the beginning of her life. She just seems naturally aligned to the feline spirit. And after so many years living in the wilds, I have come to believe that when one naturally has a totem animal spirit, it will try to meet you—so watch out! Those meetings can be harrowing, even if you are ready.

I think that day Natalia's totem tried to meet her, and the trial of losing the kittens was her initiatory crisis. Her challenge was to face the loss of her beloved cats and make peace with the ordeal in order to move on spiritually. But Natalia did not quite yet have the maturity to deal with it and the ordeal overwhelmed her. And I think when I wandered into the forest and came upon the bear track and that magical place sequestered in the Old Wood, Bear was there and was sensitive to my paternal desire to protect my daughter and worked things out for those kittens to be okay so that Natalia could heal and be well enough to face her totem again at a time when she is better prepared.

Some might think that this is a harsh interpretation, I know. A totem risking a seeker's life and emotional well-being seems like too much in today's spiritually domesticated world, but keep in mind: the spirits do not change over time as we do. In fact, we do not change, either, not so much as we would like to think. Our level of technology might have changed, and our cultures might have altered, but in the heart of our psyches we are still the same early man and woman who first stood upright and looked out upon a green world with wonder. And so, what was appropriate for the spirits of yesterday's world remains so today. The initiatory crisis is an essential part of spiritual growth for anyone upon the shaman's path. It tests the seeker's capabilities and tempers what is there. It prepares the seeker to move on.

So, Cat Spirit tested Natalia and she was not ready, and in the forest I found my ally Bear Spirit, who sensed my concern and made it right. The story had a happy ending. But Cat Spirit will come again for Natalia someday, and perhaps at that time she, too, will pass her initiatory crisis and acquire her power animal. And that will be a good thing, for she is as in love with the green world as I am. I feel sure that she, too, will become a caretaker of Nature in her time and this can be a hard path. She will need a formidable ally, and Cat Spirit is clever and mighty despite her small size—perfect for little Natalia, for as Shakespeare wrote of Helena in *A Midsummer's Night's Dream*: "Though she is little, she is fierce."

Traditional Living

The Kitchen Witch's Secrets:
Herbs for Health and Hob

The Hollow possesses very large gardens, a vineyard of experimental arctic kiwi vines, and groves of young fruit trees along with old, established apple trees. I tend all the gardens save one, the raised beds that are devoted to Daphne's herbs. Daphne is an animal person and does wonderfully with the goats and chickens, but she will tell you herself she has a brown thumb. One year she mistakenly weeded up hundreds of garlic cloves that I had painstakingly planted throughout the beds because they are good companion plants and keep insect pests away. And, of course, they yield those wonderfully flavorful bulbs. But she had mistaken the young garlic shoots for weeds and pulled them. Another year she confused the growing instructions for rainbow chard, which directed to plant the seeds eight inches apart. She harvested

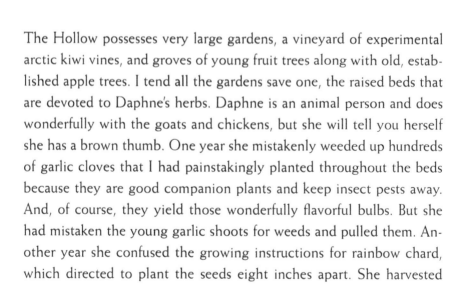

the entire bed of it at eight inches tall, less than half grown. And then there was the time she decided to prune an apple tree and cut back five years' growth ... well, you get the picture. She is so brown-thumbed that years ago we established a rule: she stays out of the vegetable gardens and away from the fruit trees. But for some reason, she and herbs get on well. They just seem to understand one another, and really well at that. Every year, from two modestly sized raised beds, she coaxes so many herbs from the soil that we must give and barter away half. There's no doubt about it—she's a natural herb witch. And here are Daphne's tips for growing abundant herbs for home, craft, and hearth, and some culinary and medicinal pointers, as well.

Of our four raised garden beds, Daphne uses only two for her herbs (the other two hold perennial asparagus and rhubarb). Each herb bed is about twelve feet long and four wide, providing a total of eighty-five square feet of growing space after you deduct the area used for borders and walkways. Herbs are typically small, loosely spaced plants and need a bit more tending for weeds as well as ongoing harvesting, so bisecting the gardens with little walkways makes it much easier to get low to the ground and tend the frequent work.

A late harvest season sampling of wild herbs and domestic produce, all bound for the passive solar dehydrator or simply to be prepped and hung until air cured during the cool late season days. From top left going clockwise: yarrow and pearly everlasting from forest glades (the former useful as a blood clotter, the latter useful in floral arrangements and as smoke for shamanic workings), summer and winter squash (the former is white, the latter orange), zucchini, Purple Chieftain potatoes, burdock (wild but growing in the gardens and useful as a blood purifier, a tea, and for its huge, nutritious tubers), Nova Scotia tomatoes, wild sumac berries and leaves from the forest (the berries are for making sauces and drinks, and the leaves are for smoking in herbal pipes during shamanic workings), and white onions along with broad beans still in the pods.

According to Daphne, anyone who has access to soil and sunlight can grow herbs. "If I can do it, anybody can." And does she ever! Any given year we are likely to get several pounds of cilantro, basil, and savory from the few square feet she allocates for each. If that doesn't sound like much, bear in mind that I am a full-blooded Cajun and grew up on my French-speaking grandparents' farm with regular meals of jambalaya, boudin, ecrevisses etouffes, seafood gumbo, saucisses chaudes, alligator sausage, and other dishes hot and spicy enough to melt the stewpot. To Cajuns, Mexican food is merely adequately spicy and East Indian cuisine is becoming daring. But when Cajuns say spice, we don't simply mean hot, we mean flavor. Hot is just hot, but oh so much more can be done with so many wonderful things to flavor food. Bottom line: Cajuns use a lot of herbs in their cooking. And even with such heavy use, a single harvest of Daphne's herbs provides upwards of two years' supply for our family of four. It begins to mildew after a year since we don't use preservatives, so we end up giving away and trading much of it. So, if you allocate a small section of your ground to growing herbs—say, a four-by-four foot plot—you can grow a variety for your family all year!

In terms of value, note that a tiny vial of savory at the grocery, perhaps three ounces, can cost $5. Ten dollars in seeds that you grow yourself can yield a thousand dollars' worth of herbs. The surplus can easily be traded, bartered, or turned into wonderful gifts.

Some herbs are tricky and take some experience. Thai basil, for example, tastes wonderful but is sensitive to moisture and warmth. Growing it means carefully monitoring your plants and watering as needed but being careful not to overwater, and having a warming cover (a cloche) on standby should the temperature threaten to drop. Daphne recommends beginning herb gardeners stick with resilient, hardy herbs. The initial success is not only encouraging but the grower will learn valuable lessons the first year that will make future plantings more likely to succeed. She suggests novices start off with parsley, thyme, chives, and savory. She also says you may want to rake some mint seed into your yard or flowerbeds. It will grow on its own and provide more mint tea leaves than you can ever hope to drink, but be careful. It is aggressive and invasive. Once you've established mint, it is there to stay.

Starting an Herb Garden

To start any garden ground, see the essay "Growing the Earth" on page 105, which is all about creating organic garden soil and a beneficial ecology. Your goal is to create soil that is loamy, dark, full of earthworms and beneficial microbes, and rich in plant nutrient and organic matter. This is the foundation for a productive garden. In the small space of an herb garden, it is easy to do and you can speed the process by purchasing a few low-cost sacks of composted earth if you desire.

Daphne recommends you plan for a plot at least four feet by four feet, and section out one part for perennials and the other for annuals. You may wish to add an additional two by four feet for self-seeding plants. Plenty of herbs will reseed themselves if you leave a few behind. You can mark the divisions of your plot by driving in small sticks or stakes and running string between them.

Cultivation of the Novice Herb Garden

Assuming you start with her recommended herbs, you will gain experience growing ordinary perennials, invasive herbs, biennials, self-reseeders, and annuals. All this experience can then be carried into cultivating a wider variety in coming years. Yes, we're talking years. Patience is essential to good gardening, and especially in regard to organic gardening.

Thyme is a noninvasive perennial shrub. Plant it in a corner of your new herb garden where it can remain for years undisturbed. We still have the first dozen thyme shrubs we planted several years ago. Make sure it has a little water and organic fertilizer and it'll reward you with abundant leaves for a long time.

Mint is an invasive perennial herb. The roots will weave themselves everywhere into the ground and you will never get it out because it can regrow from even the tiniest rootlet. I imagine you could kill it if you really wanted it gone by covering its growing area with a dark tarp and letting the tarp stand over the ground for two years. But unless you want to do something so radical, be sure to place mint someplace where you will be happy to have it. Once you put it in the ground, aggressively cut it back promptly whenever it grows beyond its area.

That said, mint will reward you in all kinds of ways. If you let it spread into your yard, cutting the grass will become a fragrant pleasure. It will yield more leaves than you can ever use for tea, and it is so hardy and vigorous you can start harvesting the leaves as soon as they have budded and continue all year. One of our favorite summer beverages is made by going to the mint thicket beside the house at first light and harvesting a handful of leaves (which takes about three seconds—just swipe your closed hand up a stem and strip all the leaves along the way). Throw the leaves in a gallon jar of cold water, add one cup of sugar or two-thirds cup of honey and let stand in the sun till late in the day. Ice and serve. It's an old Amish treat that probably dates back to the Old World and is just called mint water. The sweetener is optional.

There are many varieties of mint, too. Apple mint. Spearmint. Peppermint. The list goes on and on, each with its own subtle shades of flavors. Feral orange and chocolate mint grow up and down the brook and by our pond. Mint is very adaptive and will pretty much make itself at home anywhere it can get water and half-decent soil.

Despite mint's invasive tendencies, we think of it as a very friendly herb. It has so many uses and is both pretty and fragrant.

A good annual for the novice is savory. Make shallow dimples in the soil with your fingers and drop in the tiny seeds, cover with just an eighth inch of soil, and it will grow up to knee high. Daphne suggests you pinch the ends of the stems when they are about a foot high so the plant will put its energy into making flavorful leaves rather than evermore growth.

Savory is delicious cooked into beans, stews, and soups. It is a valuable herb and sells for a pretty penny at any grocery, yet it is so easy to grow and so prolific that a few square feet should yield a year's worth for a family of four, with some to spare.

Parsley is also an easy-to-grow annual, but you'll want to give it a permanent space because if you leave a few plants it'll easily reseed itself, providing trouble-free herbs year after year. If you think you know parsley from the dried stuff supermarkets offer in bottles, you don't know parsley. Try it fresh chopped into any dish. It lends a wonderful, sweetish pungency. Or try it mixed fresh and whole into salads for a whole new dimension in flavor. Parsley: it's not just for garnish anymore!

Chives, like parsley, are an annual that will happily reseed themselves, so also give them their own space. They are slightly invasive but easily managed. Just pull up any that you see growing someplace you don't want them. Fresh chive stalks lend an oniony tang to foods, and some varieties, if allowed to grow to the point they start to make seed, can be pulled up for their small bulbs. Simply grasp a bunch of them firmly at the base of the stalks and haul out of the soil. If the soil is firm, you might use a trowel to dig a couple inches under them and lift the trowel to break the ground as you pull. These mature chives will have whitish, blanched bases that are slightly swollen—not quite a real bulb. A moderately spicy and extremely flavorful alternative to onions, they are wonderful chopped and served in fresh salads.

Maintaining the Herb Garden

Because herbs are smallish plants and seldom spread broad leaves, they allow sunlight between their stalks. This allows for the growth of various weeds, so the herb garden will need more weeding than a vegetable garden. Also, because herbs are arguably weeds themselves (in fact, with a working knowledge of identifying wild plants and access to green places you can often find many herbs growing wild) it can be tricky identifying what is herb and what is weed. Pay extra attention to what your herbs look like at all stages of growth so you don't mistakenly pull them.

Herbs need additional nutrients each year. Rejuvenate the annuals section by raking in good, rich compost, which provides everything a plant needs. The perennials and self-reseeders cannot have their soil raked, but you can add organic, good-for-the-Earth nutrients with manure tea. This sounds horrid, I know, but remember, herbivore manure is basically just ground-up plant matter. If you can get a few pounds of herbivore dung (any local stable operation or livestock grower will usually be happy to let you have it), put it in a five-gallon container filled with water and stir. Let sit a day. Pour into a watering can and sprinkle over your herbs. Use lightly. It is very rich and can easily burn plants with too much nitrogen.

Add body to the self-reseeder and perennial soil by carefully sprinkling an inch or two of fluffy, black, well-rotted compost around the plants when they are a few inches high. Again, do not rake. You'll either damage root systems or push young seeds in too deep.

Keeping the Herbs

Herbs are only used a little at a time, and inevitably a well-tended herb garden will yield far more than you can use at once. You'll have to preserve it. We find the Old Ways work great and taste best.

The traditional way to keep many herbs is simply to bunch them by tying them together with a scrap of twine and hanging them someplace dry where the air can flow. This will shortly dehydrate the herbs and they will keep through the winter. And they look nice like that. I love to wake up on late summer mornings and drink tea in the kitchen with herb bunches hanging overhead and the whole place smelling of the garden's freshness. To make leafy herbs such as savory keep even longer, strip the leaves when they are dry, put them in jars, and seal.

Seeding herbs such as dill have to be bunched and dried in pillowcases because the seedpods will split as they dry, spilling the flavorful seeds. After a few weeks of drying, beat the plants in the pillowcases, then remove the plants and pour the seeds out of the case into small containers like baby food jars.

You can preserve your herbs' flavor even longer by making herbed vinegars and oils. These are remarkably simple and affordable to make at home, but exceedingly expensive when bought at your local grocery. Simply fill a jar with the herb of choice (don't pack it) and top it with oil or vinegar. Let it sit about one month. Daphne adds that she likes to remove the herbs from the steeped oils and vinegars and cook with them. The steeping process refines the herbs, making the flavors subtler and more sophisticated.

For magical and healing purposes, you can grind dried herbs into powders in a mortar. These can be burned in braziers on charcoal as incense or made into poultices by mixing them into lard. You can also make a tincture out of any herb in the same way you make herbal oils and vinegars. Be sure to use a potable alcohol, like rum, if the tincture is for ingestion.

I'm going to add my favorite useful plant to this list, even though it is not an herb in the usual sense: the elderberry. Elderberries grow from small trees or shrubs. I like to plant shrubby varieties on the outskirts of the gardens because they are easy to grow and adaptable, and like herbs, they have various uses.

Elderberries like a little shade and do best around hedges or forest edges that give them partial protection from the sun. They are prolific and often yield berries in the first year. The berries and blossoms have magical and spiritual significance, healing properties, and culinary uses. Some old folklore says that wine made from the berries was the unparalleled favorite of the faerie folk. The elderberry is such a useful plant that in the Middle Ages it was required that every household grow it for their personal upkeep. My favorite food uses are making elderberry cordials and jellies from the blossoms or berries. It not only tastes wonderful, but it is especially good, I believe, to leave a bit out for the spirits now and then. The elderberry, like the thorn and its berries, is sacred to the Good Folk.

One of the most useful things that can be done with elderberries is the making of cough syrup. You may have read that in recent years studies revealed that many of the cough remedies purveyed in pharmacies are no more effective than a placebo. That is to say they only work if you believe they will. Well, it was also established that good-old honey and lemon actually did help with coughs, but any elder wife from this traditional Gaelic land could have told you that. Yet with elderberries you can do better.

Simply make a rich tincture by crushing a half cupful of elderberries, pour into a small jar, and add a half cup of rum. (Actually, any hard liquor works for this, and we usually use a bit of our homemade apple brandy.) Seal the jar and let it steep a month. Then pour the rum into a larger jar (you can use the berry pulp to make candies or a lovely rum-berry pie). The rum is now an elderberry tincture, and this will be blended into a cough potion. Just measure the quantity of tincture (it will vary a little depending on how much rum the berry pulp soaked up) and add two measures more of honey. (It should be a 2:1 ratio of honey to tincture.) Stir until thoroughly blended. Simple as that. If you experience a cough, take a tablespoon and swallow slowly, a little at a time. It's terribly sweet and doesn't taste great—not like elderberry foods and drinks—but it's wonderful for beating a cough.

APRIL

The Fair Folk

March had brought a couple weeks' respite from the cold with a false spring. It had become very warm, melting had begun in earnest, and we'd even been able to get the horses out of the barn and start sugaring. But a little more than halfway into the month, winter made another bid at possessing the high country, and for a while it seemed like it would win. The snow quit falling abruptly at the beginning of April, and the days became lucent under an eager sun. Yet, winter still refused to yield the highlands. By mid-April, early afternoon temperatures reached into the low forties, but if so much as a cloud shadow passed over, the Hollow felt wintry in an instant. The snow kept melting and refreezing, which made for wicked ground. All the land became an ice rink, so slick you could have donned skates and glided over the bare hilltops, so slick the poor horses were stuck again in their stalls, even though the sun outside the barn looked full of spring. They were desperate to get out, but to let them run in those meadows was to invite a nasty fall that could lead to a broken leg, which is the death of a horse.

Likewise, the goats were getting cabin fever. We had plenty of fine, sweet hay for them from last season, but they were restless with inactivity. Domestic goats are homebodies and creatures of habit. They longed to go back to their familiar little meadow where they could idle all day among sweet clover and pass high noon gossiping in the shade of the old maple down by the brook. But there was no new clover, and the shade was frigid.

Sidhe Bheg yearns to get out of her stall, but we dare not let
her on that ground. Just below the snow is treacherous ice,
the product of numerous thaws and refreezes at this time of year.

Even the hardy chickens were stuck in their coop. There was no good in letting them out. The Earth they longed to scratch in search of last year's seed and fine, fat insects was still frozen only a finger's breadth beneath the surface. The chickens would merely have been a tempting target for hungry eagles and falcons. Normally, the highland's aerial predators would never bother adult chickens (though an owl might try to steal one staying out too late), but at this time of year food was in short supply everywhere, and every creature did what it had to in order to survive.

So the Hollow passed the April days under a midday sun that hinted of spring but could never really muster it. Despite the promise of Imbolg, the land seemed in stasis, the trees bare and austere while the Green Man continued to doze far deep in the Earth. The girls and I worked extra hard day in and day out. Water had to be lugged over slippery ground from the brook to the chicken coop in the Firefly Meadow. It was a struggle to keep the barn serviceable because the old bedding would thaw long enough to make a mess, then promptly re-freeze in place. And, in addition, we were getting near the end of the supply of ready firewood under the deck, so I had to cut and split more every few days, and then it had to be dragged to the cottage in a small sled because the tractor, despite having four-wheel drive, couldn't safely navigate the icy but otherwise gentle slope around the south side to the French doors that led through the library to the furnace room.

While all this was going on, we were also looking after a year-old doe who was due for her first kidding and was running quite late. Since a new doe's first delivery is the one that's likely to be tricky, we had to make frequent trips to the barn to check up on her.

On this day, the girls and Daphne did the checks so I could be freed up to split firewood. Getting at the woodpile in the constantly thawing and refreezing mess meant first using a beefy sledge to break up the ice locking the logs in place. It made for double the work, so by the time twilight fell and dinner came, I was beat. After eating, I was sitting in the kitchen guiltlessly relaxing with a glass of home-brewed ale and watching Arielle experiment with a new cookie recipe while Daphne and Natalia bantered back and forth as they did the dishes. Down in the basement, the ancient grandfather clock chimed off 8:00 p.m. I stood up and stretched. My arms had the pleasant warm soreness of a hard day's work and I was just a wee bit stiff. A walk out to the barn would loosen me up a bit. "I'll do the evening check," I told everyone. Arielle suggested I not stay out too long because the cookies would come out of the oven soon. I nodded politely, but I confess to being weird: I like cookies best at room temperature.

I went to the arctic entry and pulled on high winter boots and threw on a heavy-duty work coat. The days at this time of year might promise warmth, but the nights were as wintry as ever. There was no moon, so I dropped a flashlight into my pocket. My faithful Australian Shepherd, Willowisp, appeared at my side, eager to join me on any little romp. He's very good with the barn animals, so I let him come along.

We stepped out of the cottage and I felt at once the keen bite of the air. It was like that in early spring. A mild cold just below freezing can feel far sharper than the deep freeze of midwinter. I walked along the dirt path toward the barn with my hands tucked into my pockets, wishing I had thought to bring along a pair of gloves. It was pitch black and no stars shone in the sky. I went slowly, but I knew this path intimately and I picked my way by memory around small indents and outcrops of stone. Beside me Willowisp plodded, nose high in the sharp air. A dog's world is all about smells, and his perception of the night was doubtless far different from mine, for the night tells its tales in scent far better than it does with sight.

At the turnoff to the barn, we took the worn path through the small doors south and worked our way past the horses. Aval noticed me and leaned his head over the rail to nuzzle me. I held the great beast's head in my arms and stroked his cheeks. He is a kindly fellow and loves attention. His dark eyes asked the question I knew was on all the animals' minds: *When can we go outside again?* I felt so keenly for them. I wished it could be this moment. I rubbed his ears and whispered to him, "Soon, big fellow. Soon as the ice melts from the meadow and you can run safely."

I slipped past the horses under the beam that separates the goats' section. I found the yearling doe in her stall, lying upon soft bedding. Her belly was round. I felt she'd have twins, and she was so late, and both those facts had me concerned. The first birth is by far the one most likely to get complicated. But the doe, who had been sleeping, opened her eyes to regard me placidly. I leaned over the rail and stroked her neck, then stuffed a little fresh hay into her feeder, and Willowisp and I left the barn. There was simply nothing to do but wait.

Outside the barn, I noted the air felt a little warmer but heavy. That could only mean the haze of cloud blocking the stars was descending, bringing precipitation. *More snow coming*, I thought with a grimace. I sighed deeply. Nothing to do but grin and bear it. I whistled for Willowisp. "Want to go for a walk, buddy?" The Australian Shepherd wagged his bobbed tail briskly as if it was his favorite thing. Of course, everything a dog does is its favorite thing. "Heel!" I commanded and turned to walk the last little bit up the path to the dirt road. Willowisp fell into step beside me. I had been looking down to pick my way over a slippery patch, and just at the edge of the dirt road where the ice ended I lifted my eyes.

My mouth fell open and I froze. What I saw before me, just across the narrow dirt road along the western hedge of the Highland Meadow ... *it could not be!* It appeared at first to be a firefly ghosting through the air, just at the border of the hedge. Its light was bright and pure as a star, a lucent jewel-like blue. It moved slowly, about the pace a man would leisurely walk, heading north along the hedge. "Firefly," I murmured to myself, but I knew the moment I said the word it could be no firefly. Not at this time of the year. Fireflies were creatures of the early side of midsummer. They appeared only after all danger of frost was past, long after the spring peepers began to chirp down at the pond near Grandfather Apple. They had no tolerance for cold whatsoever and would die instantly in these temperatures.

And then I perceived the light was not moving quite smoothly as I had first thought. The air was utterly still and the little starlike light was making small movements back and forth as it progressed northward. It was almost … almost as if it were a tiny lantern being carried by the hand of small being. Tentatively, I took a step forward, and then another. My heart pounded, not out of fear but of elation. To be privileged to glimpse into the Otherworld, to see living enchantment right before my eyes. I took another careful pace forward, in the direction of the light, now halfway down the hedge. But I hesitated. I felt no reason to be fearful of the spirits of the Hollow. They had always been friendly to us, looked after our land and animals and even we ourselves. I just did not want to break the magic of this sacred, silent moment. Here I was seeing real magic right before me with my very flesh-and-blood eyes. Anyone who says enchantment is only a thing we imagine, or encounter upon meditative visions, doesn't know the half.

We had always been sure the barn had a bruanighe. Things had a way of working out in the barn. Oh, sure, occasionally a small predator like an ermine might enter and eat a chicken, but such creatures were like mice around here. Just part and parcel of the landscape. But no real predators ever entered the barn even though we never shut its doors. We had a barnful of goats and other vulnerable livestock, and we lived in the middle of hundreds of square miles of forest abundant with bears, coyotes, martens, and various wildcats, and none of them ever even came around the barn. Every farmer in these parts had lost livestock to the wild predators but us. And according to them, we didn't do things right. We didn't keep up impenetrable fences. We didn't shut the barn. We didn't even keep a sheep dog or llama running around the meadows. What we did … well, they'd have thought it insane. Every morning and evening when it was time to milk the goats, we just put the first few squirts into a saucer, ostensibly for the barn bruanighe. More often than not, the barn cat got to it first, but the bruanighe didn't seem to mind. It was the gesture that counted. And as I watched this magical light, I could only ask myself: *Did I stumble upon the bruanighe coming to look after the barn?*

They say such beings are shy creatures, and if you spy on them they will go away. Well, I wasn't spying, I had merely accidentally encountered it, so I didn't think it would take offense. It had always proven itself reasonable and understanding in the past.

They also say that such creatures are secretive and if you tell others where they are, they will take offense and leave, so I will only say what I have told others, a thing which it doesn't seem to mind. We have a barn bruanighe, I am sure, and he (or she) helps a great deal. I won't tell you where or when it appears, and we rarely ever see it ourselves, and we don't go looking. But be sure, the faerie world is real. I share this with you only because the faerie faith is dying in this artificially rational, industrial era, and it is important folk remember the truth of a deeper reality. I do not believe our bruanighe will find offense in such motivations.

So, I stood there like a statue, Willowisp still and attentive at my side, and we watched the beautiful, peculiar light make its way down the pitch black hedge. I strained my ears to catch the sound of snow crunching underfoot, the rustle of shrubbery being pushed aside, but there came no sound... none whatsoever. *The silently moving people.* I recalled the children with the white-blond hair we'd seen on the island of Cape Breton. The stick that threw itself in the forest when Natalia longed to see faerie magic.

The thought occurred to me to pull the small but powerful flashlight from my pocket and shine it at the lantern, but it felt very, very wrong to do so. Like a twisted voyeurism. That would be spying. So Willowisp and I stood there in the impenetrable dark of the starless night and regarded the fey light in childlike wonder.

And then, at the end of the hedge, it vanished. *Poof!* Just like that. And all was hushed and the night was ebon and impenetrable. Willowisp chuffed and I placed a hand on the soft ruff of his neck to comfort him and quietly said, "Enough." The dog made no further complaint.

And then I noticed the first of the anticipated precipitation. It fell and brushed my hands and cheek like a butterfly's kiss, the lightest of touches, leaving dampness in its wake. *A snowflake*, I thought, and automatically lifted my hand to my cheek to brush it away. But when I dragged the back of my fingers over my cheek I realized it had not been snow, nor ice in any form. I rubbed the wetness on the back of my fingers with my other hand. It was wet. Just wet. And so warm. The clouds that had rolled in after dark must have come in out of the south. Nova Scotia, all but for a tiny isthmus that connects it at midpoint to the mainland, is an island cast out into the Atlantic sea, and warm currents pass round it. The climate can change so rapidly here, depending upon fickle weather that might suddenly descend out of the arctic or rise up from southern seas. And this night, though the air was still upon Earth, enchantment stirred. A new spiraling season's enchantment. It would break the ice and set the animals free.

I realized then how anxious I had been for them. The winter snows had been so fierce and lasted so long. Our poor horses, who took being confined indoors the hardest, had been so despondent. But with the fey light's passing, the first spring storm was coming. Another little drop brushed my cheek, or was it a tear of relief? I lifted my open palm to the air and felt the rain begin.

I thought of my glimpse of the fey being. The Otherworld was experienced best at moments between. What better moment between than just now, when spring and winter collided.

The rain slowly increased. It was warm, but the air was still cold. "Inside, buddy," I told Willowisp quietly, and turned back for the cottage. It would be a wet night, it seemed. No chance for a walk in the nightwood, but I did not mind.

The storm rolled gently in and it rained for several days, working a transforming magic upon the landscape. The snow heaped in the north faces of meadows dissolved away. In windswept areas where there had been only slick ice, the bare Earth was revealed. The grasses of last year were winter-flattened and brown, but over the coming weeks green things would revive and grow. Immediately the exposed soil gave breath to a fragrance that was like new gardens and old leaves at once.

On the day after the rain departed, we went to the barn early. It had been sunny since yesterday, and the water had had a full day to flow away down the brook. It was cool that day, down to temperatures just barely above freezing. It would be a while yet until the warmth really set in, but at least we could set the animals free. The girls stood nearby as Daphne and I approached the barn doors that had sealed the horses in their communal stall. The doors were really a simple barrier; just a pair of crossbeams supporting plywood, held in place by enormous steel catches. I took one side of the upper crossbeam and she the other, and on a count of three we lifted away the upper set, then the lower set. The horses knew they were being let out and eagerly crowded the exit. The girls had to drive them back by waving orange carrot sticks (a four-foot-long rod with a rope of equal length attached to its tip) in front of them, so they didn't burst out and injure Daphne or me in their eagerness. When we had cleared the way, I called, "Let 'em go!" and the girls stepped aside. The three horses trotted out of the barn into the bright dawn's light. First thing they did was drop to the Earth, rolling and stretching. Natalia giggled upon seeing them at play like puppies, and we all smiled from giddy happiness. It was such a joy to see them out and frolicking again. The goats cried out to be let out, too, but had to wait till the horses had worked off their initial steam to be done safely. Soon as the horses had settled, we would open the goat stalls and lead them out to their meadow. Willowisp waited at the edge of the barn corral, little tail wagging furiously. A sheepdog, he had a strong herding instinct and loved to help drive the goats. In truth, the goats knew exactly where to go and what to do, and unlike sheep, they were much too spirited to allow a mere dog to boss them, but Willowisp never cared. He was happy to just prance around them, feigning lunges and nips that he thought helped them get toward their meadow.

Sidhe Bheg the quarter horse, ever the diva among our three horses, did not deign to roll over the ground, at least not while the two stout Belgians—whom she looked down upon much the way a prim older sister looks down her nose at a muddy, scrape-kneed little brother—were hogging all the bare ground. Arielle called, "Look at Sidhe Bheg's mane!"

We all glanced toward the brown and white quarter horse. Her mane had been woven into dozens of double- and triple-strand braids. Daphne walked over to Sidhe Bheg, who accepted her pets as if they were only her just due. Daphne stroked the horse's neck while she examined the braids. She gave the girls an arch side glance and said, "Did either of you do this?" Arielle shook her head. Arielle had always been crystal transparent—she couldn't tell a straight lie if her life depended on it. Daphne turned to Natalia. "Did you braid Sidhe Bheg's mane?"

Natalia replied, "How on earth would I do that?"

Well, Natalia could tell a fib. She had always had a strong dose of the Trickster in her, but one thing Natalia couldn't do was braid—she couldn't even braid her own hair properly. She'd lived most of her life in the Alaskan bush, and then this highland homestead. She was a tomboy's tomboy.

Full of perplexity, Daphne turned to me. I held up my hands and said, "Now, you know I wouldn't have the first idea how to do a braid. I'm more the rough and tumble *throw-on-a-hat-to-hide-your-hair* type." I tapped the wide-brimmed Aussie hat I nearly always wore out of doors.

Daphne regarded Sidhe Bheg's mane with increasing bewilderment. We all did. "This is really fine work," she said.

About then the two Belgians had enough stretching and rolling over the ground. They stood up and lowered their heads to the Earth to nibble at the remainder of last year's grass. Natalia pointed and said, "Look at Aval and Acorn!"

We glanced their way and, sure enough, both the Belgians' white blond manes had been finely braided, too. I stepped up to Aval and clucked my tongue, said, "Halter!" which is the command for him to bring his head to chest height. Aval took a great bite of old brown grass and lifted his head, friendly black eyes full of intelligent patience. "Good fellow," I said, stroking his neck as Daphne studied his mane.

"It's just like Sidhe Bheg," she pronounced after a moment. "The same kind of braids."

I turned to the girls. "You sure one of you two didn't do this?" I asked.

Arielle said, "Come on! Who braids horse manes? They wouldn't even stand around long enough; they're so antsy from being stuck indoors."

Good points, both, I thought.

"Faeries braid horses' manes," Natalia said. "Remember, we read about that once."

"And we saw it in that documentary about the faerie faith," added Arielle.[2]

Daphne, who is unarguably the most grounded of the four of us, walked over to the Belgian mare, Acorn, and studied her mane. "Same kind of work here, too. Why would anyone braid a horse's mane?"

Natalia, who loved to read about horse sports, said, "Some people do it for horse shows and dressage."

Daphne frowned at her and said, "Yeah, that's true. So you're sure you didn't do this?"

I said, "How could she, Princess? The horses' manes were normal yesterday and she was inside all last night. Unless she sneaked out here after we all went to bed and did it in the dark, it's impossible. And little Natalia

---

2. Walker, John, dir. *The Fairy Faith*. © 2001.

is nowhere near strong enough to control these big Belgians. Acorn is only half trained."

Daphne conceded the point.

Natalia said, "We have a bruanighe in the barn."

I nodded. "Indeed, we do." I had not yet told any of them about the faerie light I had seen several nights ago. I wanted to, but the experience also seemed very personal. The time hadn't yet felt right.

"But why braid the horses' manes?" Natalia asked. "It's a prank, isn't it?"

"Yeah, I am quite sure the old lore says it's a faerie prank. A harmless one. Just something to let you know they're around. A little jab to let you know they're on to you."

"On to us about what?" Arielle said. Ever practical, Arielle was already heading back into the barn now that the horses had settled so she could let the goats out.

I smiled and said, "Maybe just a reminder not to peek, even if the opportunity presents itself."

"We don't peek," Natalia replied firmly.

I smiled broader. "No, we don't. Not on purpose anyway. Put a double portion in the milk saucer tonight when you girls milk the goats. Our bruanighe's been busy ... and helpful, and perhaps a little miffed, though I never meant it."

Arielle was already off with the goats, and hadn't overheard, but Daphne and Natalia regarded me quizzically.

"I've got a story for you tonight," I said.

"A story of when you were a kid?" Natalia barked eagerly. She was fascinated by tales of life among the Cajuns and the mischief I'd gotten into back deep in those bayous.

But I shook my head. "No, this one's about just a few nights ago, when a certain Good Folk was going about some very good business and forgot to mind his privacy."

They had more questions, but I put them off till night when I could tell the story without interruption over dinner. For now, the animals needed tending, the barn cleaning, the goat fence had been crushed by snow and had to be mended, and we had chickens that were dying to get out and scratch at the new earth. Beyond the barn corral, the wooded mountains and their secretive valleys glowed in the rising sun. Ravens greeted the new dawn and the new season, and below the brook chuckled with vigorous melt-water. I had seen a *sith* on the night that spring broke the snow's grip, and for it, our horses sported braided manes. Enchantment likes to keep its secrets, and plays little pranks when we stumble upon it uninvited. But enchantment, like the sunbeams of a warm day, is a friendly thing, and we show our gratitude by living its mystery and remembering its story in due course.

BEALTAINE

The Earth Folk

This old mountain is ancient even by the standards of geological time. Once it was part of a range that was even grander than the Himalayas. But it was formed almost half a billion years ago in an ancient primal era, and over long ages, wind and water and time have worn this northernmost part of the great Appalachian Range down to its roots. Still, the mountain remains high enough that our climate is similar to that of more northerly Newfoundland, and the snow lingers in the high shaded places and northern exposures. But Twa Corbies Hollow enjoys a southern exposure on our side of the mountaintop valley and for us spring had arrived in earnest. It was very odd, though, to step out of the cottage and see snowbound woods all around while we had clover growing in our meadows.

But with the departure of the snow, the farming cycle had begun anew. In mid-April, I had given our little tractor a checkup to make sure everything was in good working order. The tractor works hard through the year, and preventative maintenance ensures efficiency and reliable function while it tills ground, flattens fields, drills fence posts, and hauls firewood. But it is a faithful little beast and always manages to get the job done, which is good because it would work hard this Bealtaine eve.

As soon as I'd finished breakfast, I drove the tractor over to the barn and hitched up the tiller. Then I used its bucket to haul a load of composted soil to the Old Asparagus Bed. I lowered the bucket but left the soil in it. I would have to spread it out by hand so as not to damage the perennial ferns. But before I could do that, I had to pull last autumn's final growth of weeds from the bed. The Earth was soft from a winter's worth of snowmelt, and I was able to tear the weeds entirely out of the ground. I pulled for an hour, wearing gloves to protect my hands from sharp leaves and stems, then used a hoe to gently work the soil between the asparagus, breaking up any weed roots I might have missed. Once the ground was all turned, I used a shovel to dig the compost out of the tractor's bucket and scatter it several inches deep over the soil. Then I covered the entire bed with black plastic, with foot-square holes where the asparagus stalks would emerge. This has the dual effect of killing any remaining weeds while kick-starting the growth of the asparagus by warming the soil.

While I did that, Arielle, without ever being asked, cleared the weeds that had intruded between the strawberry beds. Meanwhile, Daphne prepped the raised beds for growing her wonderful culinary and medicinal herbs.

Four huge strawberry beds and a double row of raspberries behind
them yield vast quantities of fruit. The beds have been freshly
mulched with compost and the raspberry canes recently pruned.
Almost as soon as the weather warms, they will start blossoming.

No sooner were their chores finished than Arielle and Daphne went
to inspect the thousands of feet of fences and repair any places that may
have broken under the weight of the snow. And while they did that, I set
to looking after the berry bushes and fruit trees, which needed pruning,
mulching, and feeding with manure tea.

The tasks were endless but the work was pleasant, going along at a
busy but unhurried pace. It was an especially exciting time, for with the
coming of Bealtaine Eve, we saw the land coming back to life—and we
were part of that rejuvenation. When I finished tending the fruiting trees
and shrubs, I fired up the tractor and started hauling compost from the

mounds to the main gardens that provided thousands of pounds of varied produce each harvest season, which we used, bartered, sold, and gave as gifts. Each bucketload of compost (a blend of rotted manure from the barns along with garden and kitchen scraps) averaged about two hundred pounds, but the tractor made hauling it easy. Still, it took three hours to complete the job simply due to running back and forth to the compost piles, about fifty yards away, because I had to go slow so as not to spill it when I hit small bumps. (A tractor has no suspension.) When I was done, seventy piles of rich, black compost dotted each garden. The whole family met with rakes and hoes to spread it out. While we did that, we also inspected the compost for stones and lengths of twine from hay bales which have a way of getting everywhere. The stones, which seem to migrate up out of the ground, were tossed onto a nearby wall of fieldstone. The twine can tangle up the tractor's bearings and tiller and cause enormous strain on the otherwise efficient machine. Daphne gathered it for later cleaning and recycling.

Only when the compost was stone and twine free and evenly spread did I begin the tilling. Again, the tractor made easy work of it and it took only twenty minutes per garden. Over the coming month, I would till the soil twice more as part of our organic-growing strategy. Each tilling broke up and weakened the weeds. By the third tilling, the weeds are so weak that they cannot compete with our domestic plants for months, and by the time they have regained their strength our plants are so well established they actually choke out the weeds. But it is the first tilling that is best. It is then that the soil transforms from just another bit of meadow to sweet, fluffy black loam—a beautiful sight to any gardener.

Several ducks appear to be discussing their plans for a fine spring day. "Hey! Want to go down to the pond and swim?" The ducks form an integral part of our strategy for living in balance with the land. They eat the grubs in the freshly tilled earth come spring, protecting future crops, and they weed out the Firefly Pond.

Such intimate work with the land at this time has given us a profound appreciation of Bealtaine. To us it is far more than dancing 'round Maypoles and toasting the rebirth of the Green Man. It feels like our own lives are reborn with the waking Earth. Not only is it becoming warm and pleasant, but our food and activities will be intimately shaped by the play of the spring elements. So, in a very real sense, all this Bealtaine Eve work is our ritual. We worship the rebirth of the land by nurturing its resurrection. We honor the Green Man by getting our hands dirty.

It was not until a couple hours before sunset that the day's long work was done, and we retired to the cottage for a huge, well-earned dinner made from the best of last year's harvest. Fennel sausages of ground venison. Mashed potatoes rich with garlic. Grilled onions and the last of the big round cheeses—an overlooked round, actually, that I had noticed hanging half-concealed between shelves in the root cellar. And all around, there was cider wine, made from juice pressed from the previous year's apple harvest. Yet as good as it all was, this was only a practice feast, as it were, one we gave ourselves as a family as a reward for all the hard work of this special day. The real feast would happen tomorrow when friends would arrive for a proper Bealtaine celebration. There would be croquet for the children, and horse rides if the fickle weather permitted. At night, the fire would blaze high in the chimenea and we would sit nearby and drink hot, spiced peach melomel and tell stories of legend and lore. If a friend who is inclined to ritual happened to attend, then we would hold a ritual and perhaps even have a Maypole.

But for now I needed to do something else, a private tradition of honoring the season I have done every year since I resided in a cabin deep in the Alaskan bush—where I first took up the way of Earth in earnest. The cabin was remote, nearly two hundred miles from Alaska's only real city: Anchorage. The nearest village was fifty miles away, and getting there was difficult. It required crossing a vast lake by boat in summer, or snowmobile in winter, or if the lake was impassible (as during freeze-up) it meant hiking several miles along a roundabout trail through a vast forest of white spruce and enormous birches and cottonwoods. Needless to say, we didn't get much company. So in those days, when Bealtaine rolled around, I would grab a musical instrument—back then a Celtic harp (clarsach)—and head off to an abandoned cabin a few miles away with a little bread and drink as well as a meal for myself. There I would build a fire and spend the frosty subarctic day playing for the spirits, my way of welcoming their return to the living land. I would leave bread and drink out for them and then spend some time meditating, then have a quiet meal near evening as I watched the sun slide into the interior lake before heading back.

Twa Corbies Hollow is accessible enough that we occasionally have guests, but I had kept up my tradition of time alone with the spirits on Bealtaine Eve. I no longer played the clarsach, though. One needs slightly long fingernails to play it, only two or three millimeters, but I couldn't maintain them with all the heavy work required of the homestead. So I had given up the clarsach and focused on my fiddle.

Before it was quite dark, I snagged a bit of bread and a bottle of ale, and grabbed my fiddle on the way out. I slipped quietly through the library and meandered around the south yard, past the smokehouse and the fruit grove, then turned north, going along the archery range, passing the various gardens. The Berry Garden held four huge beds of strawberries and a long double row of raspberries, two extremely hardy perennials that were both already turning green. Soon, the strawberries would be producing fruit. A little farther on I passed the Old Asparagus Bed that I had been working on earlier. The dark tarps I had laid over it to kill the weeds were now weighted down with hefty rocks taken from the fieldstone wall just beside the gardens. Just beyond the Asparagus Bed were the experimental arctic kiwis, planted just last year, still small but dogged on their little support posts. If those worked out, they'd grow up to forty feet long and shade all that part of the ground, providing us a couple hundred pounds of the sweet arctic kiwis every year for wines and preserves.

Past there was the Old Garden, the first vegetable garden we had established. Here we grew various greens, turnips, and hundreds of pounds of tomatoes every year, most of which were canned and stored in the root cellar. The freshly turned black earth smelled like ... well, from a farmer's perspective I can't describe it adequately. To me, it smelled like warm sunbeams and balmy breezes, summer stars, and nights of peepers and the cries of great horned owls.

Then I passed the Raised Gardens, much of which were Daphne's demesne except for a section I used as an additional asparagus bed. There she raised rhubarb and her many herbs. She had been out here the previous two days, weeding and turning the Earth by hand ever so lovingly with hoe and trowel.

Finally, I passed between the enormous New Garden and the even larger Potato Patch. The Elfwood abuts the gardens, full of wild apple trees, spruces, and birches that offer ample perches and nest-building sites in the nooks of branches, and spring songbirds sang lively melodies as the sun neared the horizon. I always loved the evening chorus.

From there I trekked just a bit further north to Hedge Witch Hill, a small hillock of open meadow that sticks like a thumb into the Elfwood. I walked to the backmost corner of the hillock and set down my instrument case. I was also carrying a large fannypack that I normally use when hiking with a bow. It's big enough to carry several meals and a water bottle without getting in the way of the back quiver. But tonight it served another purpose. I unzipped the pack. From it I withdrew a saucer and the bread, cheese, and dark, rich home-brewed ale, and I withdrew a small cup, too. I set the bread and cheese on the saucer and put it at the very edge of the wood. Then I poured some of the ale into the cup and set it down beside the saucer. The faerie plate was set. I stood and enjoyed the rest of the ale, drinking it slowly as I watched the sun hovering just over the western ridge. It was practically twilight now. In less than an hour it would be full dark. But time enough . . .

Dropping the empty bottle into the pack, I lovingly opened the fiddle's case. It was an exquisite fiddle, a relic of a folk music store Daphne and I once owned. I enjoyed scraping out tunes with it and was decent at it, though I sometimes yearned for the crystal-under-water voice and haunting sustain of my old wire-strung clarsach. But the fiddle's voice was sweet and in this instant, perfectly acceptable for the task. I breathed deep, inhaling the fragrance of the wakening land, and stood with the instrument to my shoulder, plucking the strings to ensure it was in tune. Then I began . . .

First I played a series of glissandos to loosen up, then I scraped out a few random tunes, barely moving the bow to keep the volume down. I practiced till I felt full flexibility enter my fingers, then I slipped into a few jigs and hornpipes from old Celtic repertoire. I bowed faster, and the fiddle's voice carried into the forest, sweet and blended in measure, a songbird of spruce wood and flame maple.

Then I let the melody fall away. The still, spring air carried the first nip of evening. It felt pregnant with anticipation, or was it just me? Did it matter? Is enchantment a force in the heart or a force of Nature? I knew the answer was not rational. The answer to both was: Yes!

So I switched to my favorite kind of music—the old airs and tunes not quite meant to be airs but which I found translated well into them. I played "The Great Selkie," a haunting ballad of the aquatic faerie folk. Though the Hollow is well inland and high above sea level, it is a right tune for this place, as the entire province is a long, narrow strip of land and the sea is never more than a few miles distant. I let the air die away and slipped back into pensive bits of melody and let those melt into a song for the trees: "Bonny Portmore." It is a sad air mourning the fall of a lovely forest to greed. After it, a song for the fey spirits of this high country, "Tam Lin": the tale of a poet who stumbles into Faerie and falls in love with the elf queen. And when that song had played out, I concluded with the haunting sea chantey: "Nova Scotia." I didn't know why. Maybe to honor everything here. I was just following my heart.

When I finished the last song, the light was fading to the point I could barely see the strings, and in the darkness the contrasting silence felt palpable. But it was a good silence. It felt calm and approving. I had offered my modest musical skills to the land's spirits, and I was sure they had accepted.

And so I cased the fiddle and set it against the base of a maple and meandered over to a fire pit where we sometimes built bonfires in autumn. I did not build a fire but instead reclined on the ground, folding my hands under my head for a makeshift pillow, and there I lay in the declining light, watching the stars one by one find their way into the darkening sky. It was Bealtaine Eve, and tomorrow when our guests came, we'd hold a proper feast and a more formal celebration, but for now I was part of the Earth and welcoming the dawn of summer in my own way. A private moment with the Green Man and the land's spirits. It was a perfect end, and a perfect start.

Traditional Living

*Faerie Plates: An Old Way
to Honor the Good Folk*

In the Maritime provinces of Canada, the tradition of the faerie faith was strong until only a generation or so ago, yet even today it lingers and reports still trickle in of odd pranks happening to rural dwellers: hikers turned around by fey lights in the woods; picnickers fleeing the forest after encountering strange, diminutive beings; and snatches of pipe music in the remote hills. And not far away, on the great neighboring island of Newfoundland, there are even more dramatic tales related by its folk, most notably of persons going out upon the wild meads to pick berries and vanishing for a few days only to turn up later in some village miles away with no inkling of how they got there or how much time has passed.

I have always perceived the oddities of Otherworld encounters as, at worst, friendly pranks, or otherwise something akin to cultural misunderstandings—the results of realities that operate under different rules coming together. Indeed, the work of witches, shamans, and the nearly forgotten Celtic faerie mage, known as the tabhaisder (CHAH*vawsh*der) had a lot to do with easing and mediating encounters with this other reality. Nevertheless, people tend to fear what they do not understand, and so it was that in many places, from Scandinavia and the Germanic countries all the way west to Ireland, there has long been a tradition of leaving small offerings of food and drink to appease the little spirits that shared the land.

This faerie plate, left in the shadows of the Elfwood at dusk, offers soft, fresh-baked bread, a portion of Daphne's herbed-vinegar cheese, and bubbly hard cider. The next morning we always find the plates empty and no sign of whatever took them.

The tradition goes back millennia and the offerings usually consisted of a bit of porridge with butter, or bread and honey, and a drop of ale or milk. Shepherds and other folk of the fields were inclined to leave the offerings in natural hollows of boulders, but more domestic folk left them in small plates or bowls for beings such as the house bruanighe, or in the meadows for the helpful faeries that looked after the livestock and gardens, such as the glaistig. For the more wild spirits that lived in the shadows beyond the hedge, the offerings were left at the edge of the woods. These faerie plates were considered an act of essential courtesy, and the faeries rewarded those who kept the tradition with good luck, fine harvests, and the safekeeping of their lands and folk.

Ideally, the faerie plate should be left out each night, especially if one believes the home has a helpful resident faerie such as a hobgoblin (which are not evil, as they are misrepresented in the modern fantasy genre, but are domestic sprites of the hearth) or the land has a warding spirit, such as a Brown Man. But the tradition becomes especially important as one approaches the seasons of growth and harvest. A few apples are to be left on the tree for the Apple Man. A little produce should be left in the garden for the Earth spirits. And with the richness of the harvest coming in, the faeries become persnickety if they aren't allowed a drop of ale or even a bit of cake from time to time. Look, I'm a rational person, but I have noticed that when the ale and cake are set out, our gardens yield best and the animals thrive. And if passing creatures like raccoons or stray cats should get the faerie offering first, it is no matter. I am sure the faerie folk don't mind letting the animals have it. The point is the generosity. The old lore mentions over and over that the spirits have a universal respect for sharing persons.

At Twa Corbies Hollow, about the time of Bealtaine the goats have freshened and are yielding their best milk on new spring clover and tender shoots of young grass. At the sunup and sundown milking we always put the first few squirts from the udder into a tiny bowl which we tuck in a corner near the milking stand. And when Bealtaine arrives, I am especially careful to set out a proper faerie plate at the edge of the Elfwood not too far from the cottage. It's nothing fancy, just good, honest food. A slice of Arielle's homemade bread with a bit of Daphne's pumpkin preserves, a sliver of cheese made from the goat milk, and a drop of one of my home brews is typical. In the morning, it's always gone.

Does it help to leave out the faerie plates? We always seem to enjoy good luck in the Hollow, and happiness and richness always seem to reside over our little homestead. I remember one time when it seemed the chicken eggs had vanished only to turn up the next day in a huge clutch right where we had looked the day before. Just a little harmless mischief by our fey neighbors, and when the eggs reappeared, it was with a bonus—more than could be accounted for by two days' laying. So, yes, the faerie plates help. The spirits of the land understand through them that we remember them, and they, in turn, look after us.

So, honor the spirits and set out the plates. They just need a bit of simple fare, a little bread, a sliver of cheese, perhaps a dollop of butter and jam. Say a few words that let the spirits know you have put it out for them, but never thank. The old lore is pretty consistent that the spirits find being thanked offensive. (Don't ask me to explain it. Their logic is different from ours.) And see if in taking up this courteous tradition, luck does not turn in your favor, as well.

MAY

The Stag and the Doe

Deep in the enchanted forest, the gloaming was near, the air just cool and sweet enough to make it impossible to go inside. And Aval, my great horse of eighteen hands, standing eight feet tall at the ears, was as eager as I to wander into the wood. And so I set aside my work of planting young raspberry canes in a new bed a bit early and walked him down from the Highland Meadow, where he passes the spring among new grass and a seasonal pond. I led him to the grounds beside the woodshop, currently doubling as a tack shop, and got his saddle and bridle.

The late day was calm, the air fragrant and soothing. Though darkness was not far, the atmosphere called for calm and patience. I took my time scraping Aval's great hooves and combed him with massage brush and fine brush. The big brute is still shedding his winter coat and burgundy fur ghosted away upon the slight breeze emerging from the spruce and birch woods that surround the cottage. I threw his saddle blanket over him and then his saddle, patiently tightening the girth while tempting him with some homemade molasses cookies that Daphne baked for him. I fitted his bitless bridle. (Who needs a bit to control a horse? If you love it, it will willingly do what you ask. There is no need to stick a harsh metal bar in its mouth.) And when all was said and done and the sun would fall in less than an hour, I climbed up into his high saddle and waved goodbye to Daphne, still shaping beds out in the new berry garden.

Aval started off into the sweet early evening air, and in a few minutes we were off the main section of Twa Corbies Hollow, beyond the cottage and the barn, the chicken coop and the goats' meadow, green and rich due to its southern exposure and fortuitous spring. Pigeons were coming to the barn to roost and nighthawks were setting out. In the far woods, an owl hooted, accompanied by a dove too silly to quiet herself in the presence of the predator. Aval's ears were perked and forward, horse body language for *happy*, and we rode up a dirt path to where it split and turned east onto a rarely used way.

Calmly we traveled on and soon the last meadow of the Hollow gave way to woods—young forest of spruce on the left and old forest of maples and birch on the right. Shadows grew long and cool, promising mystery, and more than once I have seen strange lights dance among them, but not this evening.

The Old Wood lies a mile or two east of Twa Corbies Hollow,
at the very top of this lonely old mountain. It is graced
with trails and hidden ways of haunting beauty.

But there was a sound from the old wood, a crack of a branch, a muffled scudding upon the duff of the forest floor. I halted Aval and looked
right. I wasn't afraid. The woods are my home, and I have passed nearly all
of my life in such wild places. And I rode a horse that weighed nearly three
quarters of a ton. Not even a bear or a pack of coyotes could threaten us.

Then she ghosted into sight, not fifty paces away, flowing liquidly as
she leapt over a great windfallen branch. A doe: silent as a whisper, gentle
as a breeze, delicate as beauty. And a moment later, a great stag leapt the
same branch and landed beside her, graceful also, but in a strong, very
masculine way. They paused in the twilit wood and watched me in utter
stillness, just as I contemplated them. A long time passed, or a moment. I
am not sure. I only know the moment was sacred.

A slight touch of my boots to Aval's flanks and he walked on, calmly. I watched the path but kept my eyes in the forest as well. And to my amazement, the doe and stag kept pace with us, staying off the path, in the settling shadow of the woods. I rode Aval up the mountain and the doe and stag followed us all the way.

At last my way led north, through a break to the old cabin where I sometimes like to go and camp or contemplate. I halted Aval again and inclined my head to the pair of deer, and they watched from the silence of the great trees. Unless they wanted to follow me into the open lands, here we must part ways. Another push to the flanks and Aval passed an old rusted gate and we rode down a long trail out to the cabin.

The cabin sat in a grove of truly ancient maples near the summit of the mountain. The woods were quiet and surreal, except for the song-birds of evening that sang of elder mysteries and enchantment that must have been here since the first twilight of the world. I sat upon Aval, facing west, and together we watched the ruby sun go below the horizon, Aval occasionally stealing a tuft of tender spring grass.

Then we turned back toward the Hollow, and I urged Aval into an easy trot. Over meadows of wild blueberry, past rabbits feasting upon sweet spring green. Then again to the foot of the old growth wood beside the path, but the doe and the stag were now not there.

Who were they, this pair? And why would such shy creatures follow beside me, a large man riding an enormous horse whose ancestors were bred for war. I have no illusions and know Aval and I together make an imposing sight, even though we would harm nothing in this sacred wood. But most of all I wondered why I felt such kindred with these two deer, two among many that grace this forest.

It was a living oracle, a shaman's vision, a wood witch's dream. Some-times this forest gives me such, and they are precious moments. And it is for this reason, these summits in life, for which I have lived my days in the wild places and follow the Way of the Green Man and keep to the

Old Ways. He Who Walks Among the Trees, such gifts as these come from him and the Lady Brighid, deities both of life, beauty, and wild wisdom. And such gifts, they are more valuable than gold.

JUNE

Firefly Nights

The very day June arrived, winter once again declared war on summer. The cold descended out of the far north and days and days of a drizzling, chill rain commenced. The wind blustered continuously, never hard enough to be really called a gale, but never gently enough to be thought of as a mere breeze. In fact, the best way to describe the season was "confused," summer ceaselessly trying to reassert its proper place while winter held out listlessly.

The milk goats, which had been delighted to be let out of the barn for the season, had to be returned to their warm, dry, but otherwise boring stalls. The horses are bigger and hardier and we leave them out unless an icy rain should fall. But that didn't happen so they got to graze, and when they weren't eating they took shelter beneath the trees at the hedge around the Highland Meadow. But days on end of ceaseless wet are no fun and even the horses were becoming sullen. Of all the domestic animals that live in the Hollow, only the chickens, geese, and ducks enjoyed the weather. The wet soil brought countless grubs and worms to the surface and the poultry feasted upon them, and, as a result, our fridge filled with shelves and shelves of free-range, organic eggs. You can always tell a real free-ranged egg. When you crack one open, the white tries to hold its shape in the pan. And the yolk of a healthy egg is not bright yellow, as most people think these days. That's actually the sign of an anemic, poorly fed and exercised bird—typical of what one finds in grocery stores that get their eggs from modern industrial farms. The color of a healthy yolk is more a reddish gold, or a deep orange, like the sun just as it rises over the horizon on a clear day. We enjoy good eggs, which was a good thing because our two dozen birds were yielding them by the flat thanks to the feast the rain made for them. We made every kind of egg dish we could think of: quiche, custards, tapas, omelets, and what we could not use we traded at the farmers' market in the village forty-five minutes away.

But June is normally the time when the homestead really comes back to life. We mend fences and outbuildings, do maintenance on the cottage, work the horses, and tend the land. The weather becomes balmy but the biting insects haven't yet gotten their numbers up, and evenings are marked by bonfires around the chimenea, barbecues, and sometimes horse-drawn carriage rides about the trails and paths that wind through the mountains and forests. But we'd been able to do all too little of that since the first of June. We did what outdoors work could not be avoided, and had to simply skip some essential tasks, such as mending the fences that had collapsed in the Blueberry Meadow under the immense snow of the previous winter. Otherwise, we were stuck inside where we passed our time playing board games and reading. Daphne began experimenting with new vinegar cheese recipes. Arielle and Natalia taught themselves how to play gin rummy. And I took advantage of the lull to brew several batches of wine and ale, and fully restocked the cottage's substantial wine cellar. But we're outdoorsy folk, and though we have always been good at keeping ourselves busy, we'd all have rather been out and about.

One morning near dawn, our younger daughter called from up the stairs on the main level. "The weather is nice!" she cried. "We're making pancakes!" It was unusual for Natalia and her sister to be up before us, but they had awakened, seen bluing dawn skies, and couldn't keep themselves abed. After so many days of rain, everyone wanted to get up and do things! Daphne and I took quick showers and went to the expansive kitchen which takes up a full third of the main level and poured ourselves cups of strong black tea and enjoyed juice and whole wheat yeast-risen pancakes with pumpkin syrup that Daphne had made last autumn. After a fine, big breakfast and a brief break to let it settle, we went outside and got onto the day's chores. The long wet period had set us back and we spent a lot of time in the gardens, but we also had goats to put out, plus I had to rewire the electric fence's energizer and make some modifications to the corral to deter our two mighty Belgian horses from casually pushing through the fence between training. They are just so strong they can walk right through all but the strongest fences and hardly notice, so I beefed it up by driving some posts in deeper and adding reinforcing wire between them.

There's as much play as work. A game of horseshoes
between the cottage and the Elfwood is good for morale
and the spirit. Later, we'll barbecue in the chimenea.

By lunchtime we were all sweaty and ravenous, but having a great time
with the outdoor work. The girls knocked off and played fetch with Willowisp, and Daphne made a huge shepherd's pie using some of the new
goat cheese and the last of last year's beef. I took pride knowing the only
thing in that meal that we hadn't grown was the wheat, and that only because I simply have not yet had time to get around to establishing a wheat
field and purchasing a small mill to grind the grain into flour. We ate lunch
on the picnic bench in the little yard near the cottage and afterward, while
the food settled, I cut grass while the girls went exploring. They came back
an hour later glowing with excitement to tell us they had found faerie rings,
which are naturally occurring circular growths of mushrooms. I followed
them back out to the Hedge Witch Meadow, surrounded on three sides by

the Elfwood, and sure enough, there were several faerie rings growing at the top of the hillock. Arielle noted that she had read that the mushrooms of faerie rings were edible. I confirmed that these were probably Scotch bonnets (a common edible faerie ring mushroom), but explained that in my opinion they resembled the death angel (common in these parts) and other amanitas too much to chance harvesting them. If you ingest a toxic amanita, it's three miserable days of pain, then death, and there is no antidote. We harvest wild mushrooms, but I wanted the girls to understand clearly we never chance eating anything that even remotely resembles amanitas, even if we're 100 percent certain it's safe. Mycophiles (mushroom lovers) say: There are old mushroomers, and there are bold mushroomers, but there are few old, bold mushroomers. Besides, there were plenty of other mushrooms in the forest we could harvest with no danger, such as the friendly chanterelle, dryad's saddle, and penny bun. "And also," I told the girls, "would you really want to break a faerie ring? I hear it's very bad luck." Natalia and Arielle shook their heads briskly, manes of blond-brown hair flying. "Good! We can always get other mushrooms later in the year. We'll leave these to the faeries."

There were more chores for the afternoon, mostly related to the gardens, and early in the evening the girls and Daphne brought the goats back to the barn to milk and put to bed. I decided to surprise the girls by getting a fire going in the chimenea. There was still plenty of leftover firewood in the pile from last winter. I took a hefty maul out to the pile and chose a couple logs and split them down to the size of baguettes. These I carried back to the fire circle in the yard ensconced in the Elfwood and deposited next to the chimenea. Then I went into the trees for a bit of kindling. I gathered windfallen twigs and passed a wild apple tree, noting there were still a few desiccated apples among its branches. Squirrels would probably discover them soon. I brought the twigs back and piled them at the center of the chimenea's fire pan and lit them using a handful of dried leaves as starter. The air was still and they took easily.

As the twigs smoldered, I added larger and larger twigs until the fire was a healthy, flaming glow. Then I left it and went inside and collected marshmallows, graham crackers and chocolate—the essentials for s'mores.

At twilight, when the light still had a few minutes of strength left, the girls came back from the barn carrying stainless steel pails laden with warm goat milk. Natalia noticed the fixings waiting on the picnic table and yelled, "S'mores!" Daphne passed by and said she would grab a jar of mint water she had set out that morning on the deck, and maybe we'd lay out some sleeping bags, too. For all of us, a bonfire meant much more than treats; it was high-quality family time. We'd lie out beneath the dark country sky regarding a scatter of stars like dust of diamonds, tell stories and yak late into the night. Sometimes we didn't even bother to go back inside and just fell asleep around the fire. The moment Daphne opened the door, Willowisp bounded out over to me, and I tossed him a graham cracker and a marshmallow, which he caught out of the air and gobbled down. Willowisp will happily eat anything except bananas, as far as I can tell. After he inhaled the treats he found a stick and begged me to play fetch with him. I tossed it a couple times then told him no more—I was just too tired from the day's labors—and he settled down at the foot of the picnic table. Daphne paused in the kitchen to put dinner (leftover shepherd's pie) in the oven and came out with the girls, carrying the mint water jar and cups.

For a while we just roasted marshmallows and munched s'mores, talking easily between nibbles. Natalia had never quite gotten the knack of roasting marshmallows, though, and more often than not hers flamed like a torch at the end of her roasting stick, but it was all fun and we were just glad to be out of doors doing stuff together. Overhead, the welkin transformed into true night, which is not to say it became black. A vast panoply of stars came into being, first with luminous Venus, then the next-brightest heavenly object: Jupiter. Soon we could make out constellations, as owls began to call secrets to one another in the distant reaches of the great forest. The Milky Way came into view—a haze of light like the backbone of the night. The country night was so clear that one could make out the Milky Way's details: the black places where distant stardust blocked the path of interstellar light; where it broadened in the direction of the galactic core. When we'd had enough s'mores, we all kept our heads turned away from the fire to sharpen our night vision and oohed and aahed at the glorious celestial revelation.

Just then we heard a rooster crow, and it wasn't the muffled sound it might have been had the bird been calling from within its coop. The chickens know instinctively they must spend the nights in the coop otherwise they might fall prey to any of the small predators common to the forest. By night the chickens will gather in their coop and the girls will shut them in on their way back from the barn. Natalia pressed an open palm to her forehead and cried, "Oh! I forgot to shut the chicken coop."

Daphne said, "Well, the rooster is letting us know he's not happy about it. Why don't you go shut it?"

Natalia nodded and left the table. Despite the complete dark, she didn't carry a flashlight. She's lived in the woods all her life and she is quite comfortable going about on dark nights. She strode off in the direction of the chicken coop, which was all the way out on the other side of the goats' meadow. We expected her to be gone ten minutes or so because she'd probably have to use a little grain to lure the silly rooster and any stray hens back inside, but just a moment after she left I heard her call, "Dad! Come see!" She sounded urgent but not alarmed. I had just lain down on a bench and was just on the edge of dozing off, but I forced myself back to wakefulness. I rose promptly and marched off in her direction, stretching as I went.

I came upon Natalia standing at the edge of the path just past some young fruit trees we planted three years ago. She was yet two dozen yards off and staring down the southern slope in the direction of the pond at the edge of the goats' meadow. I couldn't yet see what had caught her interest because a hedge extending from the Elfwood obscured my view, but as I approached her the pond came into sight, and what had halted her trek to the chicken coop was breathtaking.

In our first year in the Hollow we had dubbed the goats' paddock the Firefly Meadow because any early summer night you might see a couple hundred of the insects down there, attracted to the lush grass and warm microclimate near the pond. I am no entomologist and can't tell you the specifics of fireflies, but I grew up with them in Louisiana where they are abundant, and I've seen them aplenty in Maine, too, when camping during visits. There is something different about the Nova Scotia variety. Especially the ones atop this mountain. Their light is of a remarkable clarity; azure, like the midday sky. But the brightness of the Nova Scotia fireflies is what is truly remarkable. They are so bright that a firefly flying at the height of a man's head can light up the ground beneath it. I've seen them in the deep woods glow so bright you could count the leaves of nearby trees. I suspect a dozen in a jar could make do for a lantern. The firefly is one of the most efficient light sources in Nature, and scientists long ago realized Edison's light bulb was crude and ineffective by comparison. Even today, in the era of florescent bulbs and LED flashlights, the humble firefly still outperforms anything Man has dreamed up by far. And for some reason, tonight, down there by the pond, thousands upon thousands had gathered, covering an acre of ground between the hedge and the brook.

"Look at them all!" I gasped. The naturalist part of my mind started trying to make sense of it. I know so little about entomology, but I knew the fireflies of these parts favored water. They could be seen anywhere upon a June night, but concentrations would always be found gathered around a pond or brook. But what drew them here in such numbers? Maybe they had just multiplied in the unseasonable rain? I just didn't know. In the moment, it didn't matter.

A pair of fireflies ghosted by. They don't fly fast, seeming more to drift like dust motes upon a breeze. They glowed as they went, illuminating Natalia's face. Her eyes were round with wonder.

"Watch this," I told her and reached into my pocket, withdrawing a tiny but potent flashlight half as long as my palm. I clicked it on and the intense beam shone powerfully enough to illuminate the hedge of woods beyond the pond, sixty yards away. I swept the beam over the ground from the goat fence to the ancient fieldstone wall on the west side of the pond then clicked the flashlight off. Several seconds passed and then the meadow and pond banks lit in a gorgeous display of bioluminescence. It was like a troop of summer stars had gathered in the tall grasses.

"They're answering the flashlight," Natalia observed. "Why are they doing that?"

"Birds use pretty plumage to attract mates. Deer display huge racks of antlers. Some animals, like cicadas, make loud calls. But fireflies are the most elegant of all. They call their beloveds with starlight."

After about half a minute the response began to recede and I passed the light beam over them again. Seconds later the fireflies responded with another brilliant display, all glowing at once.

Daphne and Arielle had grown curious and appeared beside us. "Look at them all!" Arielle gasped, as awestruck as Natalia and I.

Daphne stepped up beside me and said, "They're back again. So many! I hadn't seen them much this June."

I said, "No, it's been raining so much. They like it when it's damp, but I don't think they like coming out in the rain. Can you imagine what a raindrop must be like for an insect?"

"It would be like a falling boulder," Natalia declared. I nodded. Natalia seems to have the heart of a naturalist. She has a good sense of how things work in the wild world and how animals perceive that world.

Once more I shone the flashlight over the field for the benefit of Daphne and Arielle, and again the fireflies replied, all going aglow at once, the flying ones and the ones settled upon blades of grass, turning the banks of the pond into a little Milky Way.

When I was a boy, I would spend long summer nights in the meadow behind my grandfather's farm. Long before my time, it had been a cow pasture, but the owner was old and hadn't used it for cows or even haying since before I'd been born. The knee-high grass harbored countless fireflies by night and I used to run through the fields with a jar and try to scoop up a few to make firefly lanterns. The fireflies of the Deep South were elusive, though, and I rarely managed to catch more than five or six. But these fireflies were almost tame and you didn't even need a jar to catch them. I studied the grass near our feet and in moments espied several blades where fireflies were winking. Gently, so as not to startle the friendly insects, I plucked a grass blade and handed it to Natalia. "Your very own faerie torch," I told her. She held up the blade and a few moments later the firefly at its tip lit up, illuminating the little girl's enormous smile. Arielle bent and picked her own blade. The firefly on it promptly flew off. "You have to move gently or they will just fly away," I told her. Arielle smoothly plucked another grass blade and held aloft her own faerie torch.

I started moving down to the pond and Natalia came along beside me. We went carefully, walking a few paces then waiting and watching for the fireflies around us to light up so we could pick our way between them without harming any. Daphne and Arielle, a little less intrepid, stayed at the top of the slope where they could command a high view. The gods have gifted me with keen hearing, and I could make out their whispered chatter: how marvelous the firefly meadow was and then the need to make cheese faster as we were getting surplus milk with a new doe in production this year. That was so typical of my lady and my oldest daughter: two kindred souls—part magical and part practical. And as Arielle was on the verge of becoming a young woman herself, she and Daphne had grown very close—as much like two old friends as mother and daughter. Natalia, a primitive archer and an outdoorswoman, was naturally more like me and we moved in sacred silence through the grasses, carefully picking our way among the fireflies, traversing ever deeper into the heart of their territory. Around us they sparkled and floated and perched, and we were illumined by their cool azure light.

"They're like flying jewels," Natalia murmured, and, uncannily, I had been thinking a similar thought at just that moment.

"Like living aquamarines," I replied.

We made our way to the edge of the pond and sat in the knee-high grass. In silence we watched the creatures and I shone the flashlight over the banks. Moments later, the fireflies lit again, thousands upon thousands of them, perched at the top of grass blades or floating all around us.

Natalia was always hungry for stories of when I was a kid, so I told her one of my most precious and personal memories...

I was ten years old and my mother and father had only recently divorced. It was an ugly divorce, occurring in a day when it was still rare, and both my parents parted ways in deepest bitterness. I couldn't say I blamed my mother, though. My father had gambled away everything and left us struggling to get by on only a hope and a prayer. But I hardly understood that in those days. I only knew that we had left our home in New Orleans to live full time at my mother's father's farm. I had always loved the country, so the prospect didn't bother me, and I understood nothing of what a divorce meant, except that my parents wouldn't be living together anymore. Mom had told me we were poor now, but I didn't really get that notion either. At least not back then. It was too abstract for a ten-year-old to comprehend. Later on, when we found ourselves struggling to live on a few dollars per week and unable to so much as buy decent clothes or even food now and then, I would know poverty. Thank the gods for the rich soil of grandfather's farm—often it fed us.

But even as a child, I was in love with the green world and glad to be staying in the country. I had always found life in New Orleans stifling.

Here, there were endless meadows and forests and bayous, and I would get to help my grandfather grow corn and plums and watermelon and whatever other crops took his fancy. That was, when I wasn't off wandering. Almost as soon as we settled in, I was out every day. Equipped with a pocketknife and a canteen, I explored the wild country around the farm from dawn till dusk and sometimes risked Mom's wrath by staying out a bit into the night. Frequently, I would come home bruised and scratched up, with skinned elbows and knees, and happy as a lark from endless rambling through the woods, leaping over brooks, fishing for catfish and crawfish with sticks carved into spears, swinging over little stream gulches from ropey vines, climbing barbwire fences, and exploring old barns and ancient, abandoned houses. There was no end of mystery and wonder to be encountered in that wild green world around grandfather's farm deep in the heart of Louisiana.

One day early in that first summer, I had left home near sunrise. I had discovered a great forest of hardwoods northwest of the farm and I wanted to ramble through it. A stream ran through it with wonderful vines for swinging. There were really big oaks for climbing and I suspected I'd find wild pecans and persimmons there, too. Who knew what other marvels the woods held. My grandmother had warned me to be careful of the *pere malfait* (Cajun French for the "evil father," some kind of malign spirit that haunted the woods) and the *feux follets* (will-o'-the-wisp–like spirits that, in Cajun folklore, pursue farmers in their fields and wanderers in the forest, but to what end, no one knows). She warned me not to let them touch me and to flee across a stream if they came after me, and I had nodded solemnly. Cajuns believed solidly in various wild spirits, ghosts and entities that roamed the dark bayous and woodlands, and the lore she shared with me was not just empty trickery to keep a young boy close to home.

I set out and meandered all that day through the grove. It was several miles long and about a half mile wide, dividing the fields of several small farms and forming a shelter for various wildlife. I found belladonna and wild onions. Using a hatchet, I started to build a lean-to that I envisioned might evolve into a cabin and become my secret clubhouse. I found a fishing pond and went skinny-dipping when the day grew very hot. I had so much fun that I completely forgot the passing of the hours—before I knew it, the sun was upon the horizon. By that time I was back at the far side of the forest, miles from home. But I had a good sense of direction and left the woods, cutting across open meadows so that I could cover ground faster. It was a fortuitous route because along the way I discovered some lovely wild persimmon trees that I took note of for later harvesting, and I found some wild passionflowers growing among thickets of scrub. Not only were the flowers extraordinarily beautiful but they eventually transformed into fruits that were full of seeds. The seeds were fleshy like those of a pomegranate. Much of the time they were bitter, but sometimes the vines yielded fruits of surpassing flavor and sweetness, and I knew no comparison for them. I got lost in taking note of all these marvels and when I was yet a mile from home I realized it was the very last edge of the gloaming.

I cut across a final great stand of oaks that divided two cattle pastures and swung over an intervening stream using a heavy vine. It was getting so dark that I could barely see as I left the trees, but knew I still had two more meadows and a narrow hedge between me and home. I was halfway across the second to last meadow when I noticed an odd glow up ahead. I had always been prone to giving into curiosity and ignored my grandmother's many warnings about avoiding strange lights in the forest and made my way toward the phenomenon.

The darkness was so thick now the land's features appeared only as shadows against deeper shadows, and in that profound twilight I came upon something extraordinary. There was a great tree ahead and it seemed like every firefly in the parish had gathered upon it for a grand summer fair. They were up and down its trunk, upon every branch and twig. I don't think there was an inch of that tree without a firefly on it, and more hovered thick in the air.

In the far distance, I could now hear my mother's voice carrying across the meadow from the house, her tongue lilted with the drawl of Cajun French. "It's past dinner time! Get home now, *cuyon!*" She was always a chronic worrier. She would be furious with me for getting back so late, but the sight held me entranced. The entire tree sparkled with cool blue fireflies. It was as if it were a faerie city. *Were my eyes tricking me?* I wondered. I rubbed my eyes and shook my head, but the surreal vision remained.

I trailed off then and glanced at Natalia. She was so much like me. The kind to wander the woods around here, carrying her woods knife and a heart full of wonder, exploring every nook and cranny of the countryside. She had a dreamy look, illumined by azure firefly light and softened by the darkness. In the pond, the peepers—tiny frogs unique to the region which chirrup like little birds as soon as spring thaws things—had started singing to the night. I thought for a moment Natalia's mind had drifted and she was no longer listening. Couldn't blame her, not in this moment surrounded by so much natural beauty. But then she surprised me and said, "When you got home, did you get in trouble?"

I chuckled, but quietly, to myself. It was just the sort of question a mischievous tomboy would ask. "You know, I hardly remember," I told her honestly. "I know Mom—your grandmother—would have been miffed, but the only memory that really stands out in my mind was staggering dirty and tired and banged up from a day of hard woods-wandering into that meadow and encountering the firefly tree." I paused, thought about it, and added, "I was stunned by the sight, you see. I mean like really dazzled—like my mind just locked up. I don't think I was exactly thinking clearly after I found the tree. Remember in Alaska how the aurora would glow like a curtain of flame in the sky right over the cabin? It was like that in a way. Unearthly, beautiful beyond what words can tell. It stole all my thoughts for weeks after and I used to go back there at nights to see if the fireflies would come back, but they never did."

She brightened. "Could it have been faeries?" she asked. Her voice held that yearning quality.

I thought hard about it, trying to recall every last detail of that long-ago twilight. The memories of finding the tree were so keen, but they blurred from the moment I walked away and only now did I realize why. I had never expected to see such a wonder again, and walking away had hurt, like saying a final goodbye to loved one. And so the long years had passed and I never again saw such a thing, not until this summer night thirty years later. But I realized something else, something Natalia had to know.

I shook my head. "No, it wasn't faeries, Natalia. But look around you. It's like we're sitting among the stars. Magic comes in many ways, and there is enchantment in so many things. All you have to do is really open your eyes. It's everywhere."

She pondered my words there in the June's dark beside the bank of the pond, with the peepers singing spring tunes and the fireflies shimmering. I looked to my right, saw one glowing upon a blade of wild mint and pulled the herb from the earth. I held it before my face. The firefly winked out and I held out a finger to the insect and nudged it gently. It stepped onto the pad of my finger and I reached over to her. A moment later it lit up again. I closed my fingers loosely around it, and for an instant it appeared as if I held the pure radiance of a star. Then I opened my fingers and encouraged the firefly to climb upon another blade of grass, and then I crushed the sprig of mint, filling the air with a fresh, cool scent. And all around the fireflies sparkled. She looked around and I could see in her eyes that she got it. She was experiencing magic, honest-to-goodness magic, just here and now, as much a part of the green world as she. The lines between Nature and the otherworldly are thin, and often real magic is right in front of us. We just have to know how to look.

At the end of the day, this is what it's all about. Loving our
animal brothers and sisters. Living well with Mother Earth
and Father Sky. Being good to one another.

Traditional Living

The Kitchen Witch's Secrets:
Imbolg—In Milk and "In Cheese"

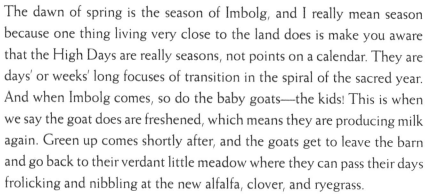

The dawn of spring is the season of Imbolg, and I really mean season because one thing living very close to the land does is make you aware that the High Days are really seasons, not points on a calendar. They are days' or weeks' long focuses of transition in the spiral of the sacred year. And when Imbolg comes, so do the baby goats—the kids! This is when we say the goat does are freshened, which means they are producing milk again. Green up comes shortly after, and the goats get to leave the barn and go back to their verdant little meadow where they can pass their days frolicking and nibbling at the new alfalfa, clover, and ryegrass.

The new foliage is tender and especially nutritious, the best grazing of the entire year. Consequently, the goats will produce their best milk, far more than their kids will need. So, not long after Imbolg we're getting daily fresh milk again. And while Imbolg has come to mean so many good things to us—for the activities of our lives will pivot upon that turn of the Wheel—one of things it means most is *cheese!* That might sound silly, but cheese in the ancient world was such an amazingly important food, especially if you lived in country that did not readily lend itself to agriculture, like post-glacial Europe (not unlike these rocky, cold highlands). It was an important source of protein and fat. It was a way to make the goodness of milk keep through the year. It came to be perceived as especially sacred to the spirits, and a bit was often left out for the helper sprites around the farm or flock. Best of all, it tastes wonderful. We cannot think of spring's dawn without thinking of cheese.

Our cheese begins with the milking of the goats, but anyone can make cheese with good quality whole milk. Here, Natalia milks Dew Drop while Rhys the barn cat waits for a saucerful.

Cheese is a fermented milk product, and the making of it is none too hard, though like brewing, organic gardening, animal husbandry, and so many other arts of earthy living, it has been lost on the average person. Daphne is a mistress of the art, and she is perfectly happy to share what she knows.

There are essentially two kinds of cheese: soft and hard. Both are made by causing the proteins and fats in milk to coagulate into curds by adding acid. The more complicated cheeses, such as Havarti and cheddar, are made by adding rennet and various kinds of lactic bacteria. The rennet forms a large curd and the bacteria ferment the curd, giving the cheese varieties their distinctive flavors. Working with rennet and bacterial fermenters is tricky and takes some experience and specialized equipment. Measurements and timing must be precise and the equipment sterile. But some household acids will cause milk to make curds, too, and make the process easier, so Daphne is going to get you started with a relatively simple Twa Corbies favorite: vinegar cheese. Anyone can make vinegar cheese with only a modest outlay for equipment. And few foods say spring better than it. Of course, at the Hollow we are using goat milk, but the preparation is essentially the same for cow milk.

You will need:

A stainless steel pot of at least 3 quarts
　　(a double boiler is preferable)

A stainless steel or glass measuring cup

A stainless steel stirring spoon

A 3-quart colander

Cheesecloth

A large, handheld tea strainer with a very
   fine mesh sufficient to hold at least
   four tablespoons

(Optional) A floating thermometer

¼ cup vinegar of any kind (you may substitute
   vinegar with lemon or lime juice)

Finely ground sea salt and herbs

2 quarts milk (it doesn't matter if it's
   pasteurized, but whole is best)

Note: It is important to use stainless steel because the acids involved will eventually corrode ordinary metal. Glass is acceptable for the measuring cup. Plastic may not do well as it may become soft due to the heat.

Pour two quarts milk into the pot and heat slowly over medium heat. If you are not using a double boiler, you must gently stir constantly so the milk doesn't burn. Add the thermometer and try to keep the heat around 185 F, or turn down the heat when the milk is near boiling.

This simple double boiler was made by putting a stainless
steel bowl inside a stainless steel pot. A small baking
thermometer is sufficient for monitoring the milk's temperature.

When the milk is hot, slowly dribble in the vinegar, stirring gently as
you do. Continue stirring through the entire process of forming the curds.
They will be very small, sometimes no bigger than grains of sand. You will
shortly be able to see the clear whey. After three to five minutes turn off
the heat and begin the next step. But note that curd-making may require

more time. It depends on the age of the milk. It may also be influenced by the quality of the milk. For example, ordinary cow milk will have less nutrient value than organic, pasture-fed milk, and spring milk will be richer than autumn milk. These factors can cause it to take up to several minutes longer for the milk to fully curd. You have to get a feel for when the process is finished, and it is based on observation. When you don't believe you're seeing any more curds form, it's time for the next step.

There are two ways to go about the next step. You can either spread a cheesecloth into a colander and pour the curds and whey through it, or you can skim the curds (which mostly float) out of the whey and set them into a cheesecloth sack. The former produces a creamier, spreadable cheese. The latter produces a denser cheese with a texture like tofu. You can increase the density of the skimmed curds by tying off the sack, placing it on a plate and stacking several more plates over it, and leaving it in the fridge for several hours. The moisture will be pressed out of the cheese.

Within moments of stirring in the vinegar, the curds have formed.

Daphne uses special strainer cups (at bottom), bought from a cheese-making supplier, to form the vinegar cheese. A jar of beans set on top is sufficient to press out the excess liquid over a few hours.

Save your whey and use it in place of water for baking, or soup and stew stocks. It adds flavor and protein. Daphne sometimes makes lemonade out of the whey, too, which is like drinking protein-enriched lemonade. Either way, you won't be able to taste the vinegar because its acids bind with the milk proteins and fats to make the curds. If you substituted lemon or lime juice, there will be a distinctive citrus flavor in both the curds and whey.

Whether you pour or skim the curds, now is the time to flavor the cheese. If you leave it plain, it is almost flavorless and in texture and taste is much like tofu. If you don't want a tofu substitute, Daphne suggests adding crushed herbs to taste and two teaspoons of fine sea salt and mixing thoroughly. Over the years she has made chili cheese, chive cheese, basil cheese, blended-herb cheese, bacon cheese, and garlic cheese—only your imagination is the limit. But if you are going to make a very dense, pressed vinegar cheese, be sure to add your spices and salt before you put it in the press. Daphne also says you can just salt the plain cheese then marinade it in an herbal oil overnight. Next day, fry it for an unrivaled taste treat. Vinegar cheeses don't melt and can be fried till crisp directly on a skillet.

Vinegar cheese doesn't keep any better than milk. It will last about a week and is best used fresh. It goes great on sandwiches, in salads, and most anyplace else you would use cheese or tofu. But since it won't melt, if you want to use it on pasta or pizza, it's best to crush it and sprinkle over your dish after it's nearly cooked. Then heat just enough more to warm the cheese. We've even made sweet varieties that are like extra-smooth custards.

You can make vinegar cheese sweet or salty,
spicy or mild. The only limit is your imagination.

When the High Days come, or when we just want to do something for the spirits, a bit of vinegar cheese often finds its way onto the faerie plates that I leave out in the Elfwood. Sometimes, if I'm out hiking and I've stopped for a repast, I'll leave a bit in the nook of a boulder or flat of a fallen log. In the doing, I keep a tradition that probably dates back to not long after Man first began keeping dairy animals, and, unsurprisingly, the vinegar cheese is always gone the next day. Whether taken by the spirits or by the local wildlife, Earth seems to approve.

A fine vinegar cheese is a work of art as well as an ancient
tradition that draws upon the bounty of the sacred Earth.

JULY

Green Man's Weave

After the night of the fireflies, the rain resumed, and June proved to be as wet a month as we had ever seen. We didn't count sunny days in the Hollow—we counted sunny hours. It was cold, too, sometimes nearly freezing here atop the mountain. It was so unsummerlike that the young peach tree near the cottage gave up and lost her spring shawl of foliage; the poor goats didn't even want to come out of the barn; the horses meandered forlornly in their meadow where they nibbled at sodden grass and wondered if the heady days of riding and games would ever commence. The rain was the worst kind, too, a heavy mist that worked its way into everything, leaving behind a cloying damp. It kept everything dripping without ever really falling. It made you feel wet through and through the moment you set foot outdoors. But despite the unpleasant weather, we found ourselves often out inspecting the gardens. They were high up on our list of concerns because May had been unseasonably sunny and pleasant, and we had taken advantage of the early warmth to till and plant a couple weeks early.

We had planted a large variety of vegetables, including the usual basics such as tomatoes, corn, and Swiss chard. We had also decided to experiment with a few new things, such as rutabaga and Chinese cabbage. And because potatoes have long been a hardy, reliable staple in the Maritimes, we had enlarged the Potato Patch. It had been the work of days, getting all that seed in the ground. But the cold, misty rain went on and on, and those days it wasn't raining, it was usually dark with heavy gray clouds. The Hollow is high enough up the mountain that rain-heavy clouds don't pass over us, they slide around us, so even the clouds left us chilled and wet.

Some plants reveled in the cool, wet weather. The strawberries loved it and soon gave the heaviest yields we had ever seen. In the space of a few weeks, blossoms unfolded and became ripe fruit, and every day we wandered the beds collecting them. It wasn't long before a quarter of a deep freezer was filled with frozen strawberries. The young asparagus beds didn't seem to mind, either, and we were soon harvesting stalks that were a foot long and as thick as my middle finger. And the Irish Cobbler potato vines, ever durable and tolerant, were springing out of the ground. And, thankfully, this year we had planted Nova Scotia tomatoes, an especially hardy variety bred for this climate, and it was holding on, even if not showing much sign of growth.

We had expected the cold-loving plants such as the broccoli to germinate and at least start showing some growth, but the incessant wet was too much and it never even sprouted. Pole beans, traditionally a heavy yielder atop the mountain, made a heroic effort, but the tender new shoots were promptly mowed down by piranha-schools of slugs born of the damp soil. We turned our chickens loose in the garden and they ate slugs by the pound, and at any dry moment I sprinkled the beds with diatomaceous earth—which is anathema to slugs though inert, organic, and harmless to any life form higher than an insect—yet it was barely enough to contain their slimy hordes. They reproduced so fast in the perfectly moist conditions that they even mowed down the corn and squash, normally little bothered by the voracious little beasts.

By mid-June more than half the gardens had either succumbed to the wet cold or the slugs it bred. For homesteaders largely dependent on the produce of our land, it was a real blow. We had made a firm commitment to eating locally grown, preferably our own foods, as part of our effort at creating a greener world. Many people are not aware how much energy is wasted shipping food. Walk into your local grocery and take a good look at what is available. Mutton from Australia. Beef from Argentina. Tomatoes from California. Lettuce from Arizona. Rice from China. Beets from Europe. On and on it goes. Chances are that your local grocery offers very little in the way of foods from less than one hundred miles away. A vast amount of energy, usually in the form of fossil fuel, is expended moving this food around. For example, if you live in Toronto and your lettuce comes from Arizona, some 30,000 calories of energy have been spent to ship that head of lettuce worth thirty calories to your body. The local food movement was established out of recognition that this is a wasteful and unnecessary practice. It propounds the idea that wherever you live, local foods are a better option for your body and the ecology. Local farmers will grow better foods if they know it will be eaten by people in their communities, and local foods are fresher, offer a variety of taste sensations, and consume much less energy through shipping. The local food movement lives the adage: "Think globally; act locally." But as we looked over our gardens and saw little more than the chard, strawberries, and the Irish Cobbler potatoes flourishing, we thought it would be a long regime of monotonous meals this year.

Then mid-June came along and the weather finally gave us a break. We woke up one Friday morning to discover clear skies and warm air. By day two it was more of the same, and the ground was already drying. We decided to replant everything not flourishing. Daphne and I sat down over breakfast on Saturday to revise our growing plans. Rutabaga are big and tasty but slow growers that need some hundred days to mature. We didn't think they could reach maturity with half of June now lost, so we decided to replace them with fast-growing turnips. Broccoli loves cool weather, but it also requires a fairly long growing season, so we replaced it with kohlrabi. We had planted Sunnyvee corn, a short, stout variety that is resistant to the winds we get toward the end of summer when Nova Scotia often catches the tail ends of hurricanes and tropical storms as they head north to peter out, but it had proven vulnerable to the cool dampness. But with the weather warm and sunny at last, we decided to risk replanting the Sunnyvee. It grows fast and we figured it should still have time to mature. Besides, the year before we had lost 20 percent of a more cold-tolerant but less stout corn variety called Seneca to the end-season winds, and all that waste was still fresh in our minds.

Our gardens are immense, nearly a quarter acre of intensely managed grounds, not counting the fruit groves, and it took all four of us the better part of two days to replant everything that had failed, which was almost everything. And all the while the weather was beautiful. Warm but not too hot. A mild breeze. The sky clear and azure. There were not even insects just yet, the rains having set them back, too. We finished the replanting late Sunday, feeling very proud of our hard work. On Monday I dusted the beds with more diatomaceous earth, which did away with the new crop of slugs, and then I set about pulling the rain-fed weeds that were taking over thousands of square feet of soil. Normally, weeds never troubled our gardens because of our practice of triple tilling the ground over several weeks in spring to weaken them and planting deep, dense beds that allowed the desired plants to choke out the hangers-on. But the rain had set our plants back this year and given the weeds an edge. It was a lot of work hand pulling all those weeds, but I got it done, and now there was nothing to do but let the land work. Within a couple days, we saw the first new sprouts of germination.

But before the following weekend, the cool rains returned. Voracious mobs of slugs emerged again and attacked all the plants that did not have a natural resistance. I hammered them with diatomaceous earth anytime the weather broke, but it washed away as soon as the rain started up again, so I was not able to do away with them entirely. We had to remove the chickens from the beds because they were turning up so much soil in their pursuit of slugs and worms. Dejected and helpless to change the circumstances, we watched from the cottage as our hard work was once again undone by treacherous weather.

A couple days before June's end, the rain let up, though heavy clouds still brooded over the mountain. The sun was down and it was full dark, but I had been stuck inside so much I felt like I had to take advantage of the break and get out. I slipped on a pair of high waterproof boots and went out to ramble the south side of our land where a path runs alongside a babbling brook. The darkness was like pitch, but I hadn't bothered to take a flashlight. I couldn't see much more than the path before my feet, and that was mostly only as a lighter strip among the darker, surrounding woodlands. All around me, the accumulated wetness of weeks dripped and plashed. The brook, normally only a few feet wide and placid, was swollen and gurgled and foamed like an angry little river. Typically, I like the rain and I enjoy evenings in the woods, but tonight I was brooding far too darkly to appreciate any of it. We had worked so hard to do the right thing for Earth. We had plowed and tilled and nursed the soil. We had dug in literally tons of compost that we had gathered from the leavings of our kitchen and the droppings of our animals. We had poured ourselves into the land and all our work was being washed away by fickle weather. I could imagine what it must be like to be a farmer of old and see one's crops desiccated by drought or ravaged by pests. There was a profound sense of anger and betrayal. At least, unlike the plight of many farmers, we wouldn't starve or go broke if we could not bring in our crops, but we would keep our vow to eat local, so our meals would become quite monotonous. Chard, even supplemented by wild greens and mushrooms, only goes so far, and even strawberries become bland if they are dessert every night. And there was an immense sense of helplessness. Despite all our hard work, ultimately the productivity of the land was beyond our control. We could, in a sense, only set the stage. In the end, it was Nature that must perform the play.

Often, when I go for a walk in the woods, I find myself becoming calmer, more grounded, and seeing things more clearly. Frequently, I will even think a way out of whatever problem vexes me. But not this night. We could not force the gardens to yield so much as a mouthful if the cold and rain continued to burn up all the growing season. And in Nova Scotia, especially atop this mountain where the climate is like that of an even more northerly province, the growing season was very short. Already, we had lost a full third of it to the unstable climate that didn't seem to want to give up the ghost of winter. I kicked angrily at a stone that tumbled away into the darkness. Somewhere down the path, I decided to head back. I turned back for the Hollow, in no better frame of mind than when I had left. Every step I took, my boots splashed in puddles and mucked through mud. It was like lemon juice on the wound.

When I reached the two-hundred-yard-long driveway, I began the long walk toward the cottage. I passed the compost piles where, every year after removing what we need to feed the gardens, we plant squash to break up the new organic matter. The young zucchini plants were stunted, half eaten by armies of slugs thriving in the rain. I had promised my youngest daughter, Natalia, that I would grow her some giant pumpkins this year, and now we were a third of the way into the growing season and the delicate plants were no bigger than seedlings, dilapidated and sulking in the unrelenting wet even though I had planted them where the compost was well rotted and perfect for growth.

I continued up the long driveway, flapping through the odd puddles. The new serviceberry, Saskatchewan berry, and Honeycrisp apple trees were holding their own against the weather but not showing any real signs of growth as a result of the incessant cold. I closed my eyes and clenched my fists. A whole year's growing, wasted!

Near the head of the driveway, I turned right and followed my feet out into the tract where the gardens are. There are currently eleven sections: the raised beds where Daphne grows herbs, asparagus, and rhubarb; a larger asparagus bed that I tend; a region for the new arctic kiwis; various berry beds and plantings; and the three major plots for vegetables and potatoes. I walked slowly among the gardens and regarded the beds—mere shadows in the ebon night. By and large, they were just bare soil, saturated and lifeless. I had worked this earth so lovingly and so long that I knew it intimately; I could feel its emptiness in my soul. I could sense the languishing tomatoes, tough as they were, at last succumbing to sodden roots; the young corn sprouts, their life force drained by the incessant strain of the damp chill; the summer squash, staggering beneath an onslaught of slugs. But then I passed the snow pea bed, and even in the dark I could sense something different. I couldn't see any detail, but I had the sense that something didn't fit the pattern. *It felt better here.* I walked into the garden and carefully knelt, feeling over the soil like a blind man, for I could barely see in the near total, cloudy blackness. Beneath my hand were a tangle of foot-high sprouts of determined growth. The valiant snow peas were defeating the cold and the rain, even the incessant slugs. They were fighting for life and winning. I don't know why, but I took such encouragement from that. It filled my heart with hope and suddenly the despair lifted. I stood up, turned my head in every direction, toward the Potato Patch, the New Garden, the Old Garden, the Raised Beds, the Berry Patch. I felt energy filling me. Green energy. Green life! Resilient Life! Somehow, this place in the garden was determined to find its spring. Determined to overcome adversity! Life was coming! I had only to hold on and believe. In what, I wasn't sure. In me? In the promise of spring? In Nature? In magic? Life seemed more important than the specifics of the answer, and I found myself raising my hands and turning my face to the bordering forest we call the Elfwood.

"Green Man!" I cried. "He Who Walks Among the Trees! We are just four people trying to make a better world. What we can do is small, but we can teach, we can share. But it is nothing without life. You are the lord of Nature, the keeper of life. Life! Let it grow! Life! Let it flourish! Life! Make the gardens hale!"

I felt it, then. The flux, though *flux* is a poor word to describe it. It is like the shaping of a thing not yet born but sure to come. It is like the making of the thing that yet exists only in the craftsman's mind. It is like the moment between when art goes from dream to canvas. It is that magical point where things find a turning point and a new path emerges. The Green Man had heard. He Who Walks Among the Trees was coming. He was emerging out of the forest and pushing up out of the soil. Somehow, just then, I knew this. I closed my eyes and felt the wondrous green energy of this hinterland pass through me, like a shock, like a deliriously pleasant healing thing.

But calling upon a god and feeling the awakening of enchantment is no excuse for sitting on one's laurels. I took a deep breath and cleared my mind, grounded myself. Insight poured into me. I wouldn't say I channeled it because I definitely wasn't meaning to open myself to anything, and I certainly don't think of myself as psychic. But without a doubt, the knowledge of what I had to do was just suddenly there. Life was coming, and it needed me. It needed all of us to help it along.

When I returned to the cottage, I found Daphne sitting at the kitchen table, sipping tea and reading while between steps in making cheese. I sat opposite her and snagged the seed catalogs. "We're going to replant," I told her. She looked weary. We had already planted twice and it was so far just a lot of wasted hard work. "I know," I told her. "It seems pointless just now. But we're organic gardeners, and we've been forgetting something. We're organic gardeners! That means we cultivate to fit Earth's needs. We find what she wants to grow and we figure out how she wants to grow it. So the wind-resistant corn doesn't want to take off in this cool air. We'll find an alternative. So the kohlrabi drowned? We'll move it to a more sheltered place. We'll go beyond planting a garden—we'll weave a garden into the land."

Daphne began to take heart, too, and we sat at the table a long time, looking through seed catalogs, selecting varieties that seemed most suitable for our mountain's near boreal and unseasonably wet climate. Three hours later we had a list of plant varieties we had never attempted before, some of which we had never even eaten. The next day we went back to the village and purchased the new seed: an even hardier version of kohlrabi, purple bush beans that would even grow in Alaska, yet more corn seeds, this time the cold-forgiving Seneca, and much more. And this time we wouldn't just plant hardier varieties, we would plant in a way that played to the dictates of the land. Humans have been in charge of Earth so long they tend to overlook their own place in Nature's pattern. We forget how essential and utterly real the weave of life is. Even at the Hollow we were forgetting, thinking that organic gardening meant simply not using pesticides. But what we needed to do was blend our garden into the local ecology. So we dropped every plan and set aside our experience from years before and determined to revise the gardens according to the new dictates of Earth and Sky.

The next day was another damp one, but at least it wasn't saturated, and the four of us returned to the gardens. We pulled up all the struggling corn shoots. They had been weakened by weeks of trying to grow in the difficult weather. We replanted them with the Seneca corn (which are hardier in the cold, but their thin stalks can all too easily be knocked down by the mountaintop wind), but this time we sowed pole beans between and around the corn seeds. Pole beans grow impressively tough little vines that climb up and cling to everything. The pole bean plants would weave themselves up with the Seneca corn and essentially form tie-downs, anchoring the stalks against the wind. As an added bonus, they would enrich the soil with nitrogen, which corn loves, and that would speed up its growth, allowing the corn to take advantage of what would now clearly be a shorter growing season.

We pulled up all the kohlrabi starts and replanted them near the back of the garden, against the Elfwood and behind the broad beans, which are super hardy and were flourishing despite the weather. Now the kohlrabi would be fed by the broad beans and shielded from the wind by the woods. Also, being at the edge of the garden, they could be well drained. We went to the Potato Patch and added pole beans, bush beans, snow peas, corn, and squash, each plant intended to reinforce and feed the other, and the lot of them together intended to hold the soil in place against the rain that was trying to dissolve the beds. Plus, the wide variety in the Potato Patch would draw in a varied ecology of insects, birds, and other animals, which would manage any problem insects and slugs for us. On and on it went, this weaving of a garden ecology. We planted mixed crops so that each plant could support its neighbor: some by strengthening the soil, some by feeding it, some by reinforcing fragile plants, some by summoning protective creatures such as ladybugs and predator wasps. And as we planted, I felt that this time we had really gotten it right. We had been here for several years and our gardens had always done well, but this time we were not just growing an organic garden, we were joining the weave of life.

July came, and almost with the turning of the calendar, so turned the weather. The rains departed and it warmed. It was not going to be a hot summer, but it was warm with intermittent showers. By the end of the first week of July, many of our new plantings had already germinated, and within another week everything else was growing vigorously. Daphne, the girls, and I watched in wonder as the plants thrust from the soil into the light with a vigor we had never before seen. Every day we would walk out and look at the beds. Fingerlike vines of Yukon Gold potatoes, which were less enthusiastic than the Irish variety we had also planted but kept longer, suddenly pushed high from the soil. Between them, peas, beans, corn, and squash grew and formed a protective, soil-retaining, weed-inhibiting network. In the New Garden, the beds of corn grew by inches every day and vines of hardy pole beans wove among the stalks, anchoring them solidly against the wind. The nitrogen-enriched soil fed the corn and soon silky pollinating threads emerged from the tops of the stalks. The zucchini, pumpkins, and summer and winter squash which had struggled so long rebounded with unbelievable vigor. Sometimes the pumpkin vines grew as much as a foot in a day. It wasn't long after July that we were harvesting our first zucchini and summer squash, with dozens of sugar pie pumpkins and a couple giant pumpkins ripening on their vines. The chard that had always been hardy, but only a fair yielder, exploded from the Earth and I could find no logical reason for it—we had made no changes to its beds. But we had to harvest it every other day for weeks, bringing it in by sacks for blanching and freezing and canning. We finally had so much of it that we cut it all down to the soil line, which should have vastly weakened the roots, but it regrew faster than before. We did it again and it just grew back again, even faster! By the end of July, it took the four of us hours every weekend to bring the harvest in, using every reusable grocery sack and milk crate we could scrounge up. By August we gave up on sacks and crates and started transporting the harvest with the wheelbarrow. Eventually, we had to resort to hauling it with the tractor. Everyone had their job. Natalia is the smallest, so it was her task to patrol the berry beds and harvest the chard, both of which are tedious, but not heavy, labor. Daphne likes repetitive tasks, so she took to harvesting the snow peas, which were yielding the heaviest harvests we'd ever gotten, filling grocery bags every week. Arielle is strong but likes variety; she took to harvesting the miscellany: green, windfallen tomatoes, yellow beets which give fine tubers along with glossy green tops, turnips that needed thinning, and so on. I am the strongest but also arguably the most cautious, so I took the strenuous work of harvesting the potatoes, which must be dug out of the ground, and the delicate work of picking broad beans, which grow on huge bushes that are surprisingly fragile.

One of our goals for the Hollow is for it to serve as a model and a teaching place, to show people that one can truly live green while living well, and to impart the skills for doing so. To that end, we have always kept a running blog (just look up cliffseruntine.wordpress.com) of daily activities and among other things have reported the amazing growth and immense harvests we experienced after the challenging month of June. During this period, many people wrote back to us from around the Maritime Provinces about how their gardens were struggling. Often their plantings had never even germinated or had withered soon after. It didn't matter if they were using organic or nonorganic methods. Some of those persons were dubious of our reports, so I often posted photographs on the blog of the latest harvests. And we had a few guests up to see and learn for themselves—and honestly, we needed their help getting everything in. I shared what I knew of gardening with those guests and posted more on the blog. In the end, I attributed our success to just four things:

(1) We didn't despair. Though the weather wiped out most of our planting twice, we kept at it. (2) We didn't try to force Earth to give us what we wanted. We adapted to the changing weather and cultivated what Earth indicated she was willing to grow. (3) We had always gardened smart by positioning the beds where they could make optimum use of sun, shelter, and drainage, but this year we planted and intermingled crops so that they could nourish, support, and protect one another. We even encouraged the growth of local foliage around the beds to help the gardens blend with the local flora and fauna. We didn't just plant a garden, we wove it into the ecology.

And all that is very important, but it was the fourth thing that I consider most essential: that one dark night in a moment of despair I called upon the Green Man. It was in that moment that things turned around. It is said that Nature is indifferent, and in my years I have seen Nature be both surprisingly abrupt in dealing death and unbelievably warm in nurturing life. But I no longer feel Nature is indifferent. Nature is very much attuned. All things live; all things die. But live in harmony with life's weave and Nature keeps you.

All around Canada and the USA that summer, strange weather affected the land. Farmers in one place lost crops to floods while in another they lost them to drought. Many eastern Canadian and Ontarian gardeners could not coax a harvest from their soil. I read of all their plights, even heard from many of them, and I felt for them as I offered what counsel I could, yet our deep freezers and cupboards and root cellar filled to overflowing with produce. That rebounding life started the night I called to the Green Man and the knowledge of what to do came to me.

The gardens exploded from the Earth after that fateful June. Here,
Daphne is harvesting yet another bucketful of snow peas.

So, did our gardens turn around because the Green Man heard my call and worked some marvelous enchantment in our gardens? I would say, absolutely yes! Or did enchantment have nothing to do with it and our gardens turned around because we began cultivating better than we ever had before? Again, I would say, absolutely yes! That's the thing with natural magic: what we perceive of it depends entirely on our perspective. What is ultimately important is a simple lesson: respect Earth and she will care for you. However you look at it, she is aware. Ultimately, Earth responds to how we live with her.

LUGHNASADH

Harvest Fire

A hot period had come to the Hollow. Most of the year, Nova Scotia's temperatures are moderated by the sea, but just as winter usually brings a week or two of arctic cold, so during the summers we usually see a couple weeks of ghastly hot weather, made all the more unbearable by accompanying extremes of humidity. When that happens, nothing is happy save the insects. Even the trout inhabiting the babbling brook that runs along the south border of the land hide in rock shadows from the heat.

So we rose before dawn and completed our outside work before the sun had climbed even halfway up the sky. Then we retired to the cottage for a long midday break in the library down on the first level. It was once a basement but had been partially dug out and converted into another full story of the house. The master bedroom was down there, along with the library, the root cellar, and a few other odd rooms. But being fully in the earth on three sides, the lowest level was naturally cool. It was the best place to dodge the midsummer heat. Arielle and I were reading on the couch by the French doors while Willowisp contentedly dozed at our feet, and Eldritch, our old black cat, dozed at the dog's head, the cat's nose barely touching the wet tip of the canine's nose. Willowisp was affronted that a cat would so deign to touch him, and he glowered at Eldritch beneath lidded brown eyes. Eldritch considered the dog's sentiments entirely inconsequential, however, and blissfully ignored him.

I was enjoying a novel when I thought to check an arrow I had started repairing the day before. It was mounted on a special jig used to repair broken fletching. I got up, unclipped the jig, and noted that the replacement feather was solidly glued to the shaft now. I tucked the arrow into my practice quiver with its seventeen brethren and was just walking back to the couch to continue my book when I noticed it suddenly grew several shades darker outside, and just at that moment the old grandfather clock past the tapestry at the end of the hall struck eleven chimes. It felt portentous.

I walked to the French doors and stepped out. The cloud shadow had brought coolness with it. I glanced up and saw the sky filling with billowing cumulonimbus clouds piling over one another. In the far distance, shadowed streaks traced from cloud belly to earth, marking where rain fell. I was relieved. The gardens could use a bit of rain and the storms would bring the temperature down. The tomatoes had been sulking in the heat and this would pep them up. The wind was mild but coming out of the east, a sure sign in these parts that the weather would become more serious shortly.

The door was still open and I turned and told Arielle, "Hey, it's cool outside. You up to helping me finish mending Sidhe Bheg's stable?" Sidhe Bheg was our quarter horse, and she had damaged her stable a bit during the winter by leaning against the wall while sleeping. It had slowly loosened the joists that held the planking in place. Last time I was in the village forty-five minutes away, I had purchased steel braces to reset the joists. Then I would fashion and bolt wooden blocks around them, setting the joists far stronger than they had ever been before.

Arielle, almost always willing to help with any task, nodded and set her book aside. We stopped briefly in the woodshop where I gathered a few essential tools. I took note that the large wind chime that hangs just to the side of the shop's door was being stirred by an increasingly eager breeze. At the kitchen window just a little beyond, hummingbirds were visiting the feeder, their wings beating the air in noisy fashion. Yellow finches were suddenly active in the cool air, too, visiting the seed feeder, and in the surrounding Elfwood, songbirds had struck up various tunes. I smiled and Arielle and I set out to the barn.

Over the Hollow, Father Sky is fickle. In minutes, a day can transform from lucent cerulean to the wildest storms and back again.

❖

An hour later we had gotten two of the joists in place, but there were several more to do. The job was taking longer than I had anticipated because I had to cut shims to custom refit each joist to the baseboard. Meanwhile, Sidhe Bheg was regarding us suspiciously from the barn's entrance, as if to say, *Excuse me, but why exactly are you renovating my bower?* We paid her no mind, and Arielle held a steel brace in place while I tapped hefty nails into it.

Suddenly, an enormous explosion broke over the sky. It was so loud and deep that the barn shook—literally shook—and we could feel the powerful sound deep in our guts. But I shortly put it out of mind. "Just a thunderstorm," I said, dismissively. Arielle nodded and went over to the opposite side of the barn and unplugged the energizer that charged the electric fences. We don't get many thunderstorms up here, and they are rarely very impressive, but electric fences are a natural lightning rod, especially if they are powered when a storm hits, and a lightning strike could easily fry the expensive energizer that put a safe, but powerful, charge on the fences. As she walked over there, the first drops of rain began to spit on the barn's steel roof, forty feet overhead. She had just started to walk back when another bright flash shone outside the barn, followed by another mighty explosion.

"That was close!" she exclaimed. The flash and thunder had occurred less than a second apart. The strike could not have been more than a mile away.

But no sooner did she finish the sentence than there was another powerful strike. Again, the thunder followed it in only a second, but before the thunder even arrived there was another bright flash of lightning. Even as the thunderburst echoed among the hills and ridges, more lightning strikes flashed across the sky, one after another in such rapid succession that there was a constant percussive sensation of pulsing air, and it felt like our bones were rattling.

"It's a full-scale bloody electrical storm!" I bellowed. I had to cry out at the top of my voice to be heard among the continuous crashes of thunder even though Arielle was mere yards from me.

She nodded, remembered the horse and looked to see the mare was no longer standing at the barn entrance. "Where's Sidhe Bheg?" she shouted over the din.

We dashed over to huge main entry and I leaned against the timbers as I peered out. Beyond the corral we could see the Highland Meadow. The Belgians were galloping off for the east side where they knew instinctively to take shelter in the hedge of woods at the lowest ground. But Sidhe Bheg for some reason had gone into the middle of the corral by the barn, and she stood frozen with her head held low, tail drooped, ears sagging, her back slightly arched. It was equine body language for sheer terror. We squinted our eyes and looked away as several more blindingly bright flashes bolted across the sky, and I saw one blast like artillery into the hillside south, not an eighth of a mile away. Thunder ripped through the Hollow, so powerful I could feel it trembling in the foot-thick maple timber my hand was pressed against. "She's frozen in panic!" I shouted over the thunder at Arielle.

Arielle shouted back, "She's like a lightning rod out there between the electric fence."

I nodded. I stepped to the middle of the entry and tried to present a calm figure, for horses match their mood to their people. I whistled her call. Each horse has a name and a unique whistle-call, but she wouldn't respond. She didn't even glance my way. The horse was petrified.

The lightning flashes became even more intense, striking so frequently they were like a barrage of cannon fire. I bellowed as loud as I could so Arielle could hear. "Rope!" She nodded and dashed over to the coops where we keep some horse tack. She came back with a thick length of rope and a halter.

I took the rope but not the halter. It's a lot easier to handle a horse in a halter, but there was no way to use it. A terrified horse is a dangerous horse. She might bolt or kick or rear just as I was putting it on. And in the time it took to put it on, I would be just one more lightning rod out upon this high ground in that wild storm. To save Sidhe Bheg and avoid getting killed in the process, I would have to move fast.

A few quick turns of the rope put a locked bowline knot in it, a trick I'd learned sailing long ago. I slipped a loop through the open portion of the knot and made an improvised lasso. I took a deep breath and bolted out into the open. The moment I did I realized the storm was weird. The winds were substantial but not fierce. There was rain, too, but it wasn't pounding. It was as if the sky was ablaze, though. The storm cloud overhead was so thick, little light seeped through. It was like the hypnopompic brightening in the hour before the sun wakes over the eastern horizon. Lightning spilled out of the cloud in ceaseless flashes all around. Thunder growled a wild cacophony, and it seemed lightning even struck within the cloud so that it blazed from within. *What the hell was going on?* I thought. It was like the end of the world. Like the gods were at war.

No time to worry about that. I slid on the wet grass to a stop beside Sidhe Bheg and cautiously approached the last couple feet. The horse didn't even glance at me. She had gone deep into some mindless, dangerous panic. I widened the loop and slipped it over her neck without problem. A quick pull tightened it and I shouted, "Walk on!" at her, the command to walk whether in the saddle or on a lead. She wouldn't budge. I urged her more and more firmly, but she wouldn't move. Carefully, ready to leap out the way should she bolt, I got in front of her and heaved on the line, trying to pull her forward. I might as well have tried pulling an oak from the ground with my bare hands.

There was no time for this. We'd be struck by the crazed lightning if we stayed out here much longer. So I did something then I never do. I slipped the line off her neck, lengthened the whole thing to make a triple strand six feet long and spun it hard overhead, then lashed it into her flank. The thick wet rope was heavy and struck hard, cracking across her rump like a bullwhip. I knew it had stung her smartly, but it was enough to break through the blind terror. She whinnied and charged toward the barn.

My valiant little Arielle was just venturing out into the storm to come help me, and she dodged out of the horse's way as Sidhe Bheg ran through the great entry. I ran for the safety of the barn, too, yelling over the thunder: "For the gods' sake, girl, get back inside!" I don't think Arielle could hear me, but when she saw me dashing in, she ran back for the shelter of the stout old barn, too.

Sidhe Bheg had come to a stop in the middle of the great midsection and turned around to watch the storm. In the safety of the barn, the wild fear had left her eyes. I stopped ten feet in front of her and Arielle was about that distance to my right. Over the thunder, I yelled, "She looks calmer now, but we should get her in her stable in case she wants to panic. The less she can move, the less she can hurt herself." I stepped slowly toward the mare, holding out the backside of my hand in what is sometimes called the horseman's handshake. Sidhe Bheg seemed to understand the lashing I'd just given her—the only lashing I'd ever given her—had been a desperate ploy to save her life. She accepted the "handshake" and stretched her muzzle forward to brush my hand, but when I was about a yard from her, it was like a tiny bolt of lightning lanced between us. The shock was powerful, like grabbing a hundred electric fences all at once. Experience told me there'd been a lot of voltage in that charge, but thankfully little in the way of amps. Volts just hurt. Amps killed. Sidhe Bheg winced and looked around, as if wondering what had just stung her.

Arielle had seen it and even felt some of the discharge. She blurted, "What was that!"

"I don't know," I shouted back. "The ground must be so ionized by the storm that it's making super static electricity."

She started to step toward me and a charge, this time invisible, lanced between her and me. She jolted and stepped away, and we stared at each other alarmed. Horse, she, and I all realized we had to keep our distance from one another or the charge would try to leap through us.

Another bolt of lightning ripped the sky, and in that moment there appeared in the barn on of the most bizarre and rarest phenomena in Nature. A brilliant blue sphere of light, bright like the sun and the size of a cabbage, appeared over the rail that divided the horses' section of the barn from the goats. Ball lightning. A fireball. It lasted several seconds and then winked out, and Arielle and I regarded one another. As if to affirm the obvious, she said, "Did you see that?"

But no sooner had it vanished than another appeared, directly overhead at the central apex of the roof, about thirty feet high. This one was much bigger and magenta in color. It hovered there several seconds, then vanished. The moment it did, another glowing sphere appeared over one of the doe's stalls, right over the metal feeder, also about the size of a cabbage. This time it was a darker blue, like the sky at the end of the day, but still dazzlingly bright, and over it appeared numerous golden spheres the size of tennis balls. The little spheres were arranged in an arc over the large blue fireball like a crown.

"It's ball lightning!" I gasped. Then I realized Arielle could not possibly have heard me over the incessant thunder and yelled it again, louder.

All around us the barn lit up with the electrical spheres, in ones and twos, sometimes seven or eight at a time. They came each time the lightning flashed and lasted only a few seconds. An electrical sensation built up in the air, making the hair on my arms and neck rise. An unbelievable charge was building in the barn. I realized that with the deep grounding rods around the barn, the dozens of steel panels that formed its roof, and the attached electric fence—thousands of yards of it—the barn may have become some kind of unintentional capacitor. I had built such a thing when I was child: an experiment I had come across in a book of science projects. One enclosed an empty space with conductive material, placed an unattached metal rod down the middle, and from the top you could evoke a static spark. The barn was now a giant imitation of that science project.

I had been fascinated by ball lightning as a child. It so resembled the *feux follets* of Cajun and French myth, what the British Isles folk called will-o'-the-wisps, though experts in the phenomena will point out that ball lightning (an intense electromagnetic phenomenon) is not the same as a will-o'-wisp (a ghostly entity which in turn should not be confused with the glowing swamp gas phenomenon sometimes called foxfire). It was extraordinarily rare and I never expected to see it, but now it was happening all around us, over and over and sometimes many at a time, singularly and in formations and all kinds of colors. I also recalled that I had read that the surface of ball lightning could be a million degrees and they carried a massive charge, like any bolt of lightning. What I was seeing was perilous beauty, Nature at its most marvelous and primal, and mortally dangerous.

"Get down!" I shouted at Arielle. But the storm had built up to a peak of frenzy. She could not have heard me over the roaring thunder and she had not even seen me shout. Her eyes were glued to the incredible display appearing at the ceiling, over stalls and everywhere around us. Instinctively, I thought to press her to the ground, but as I took a step toward her I felt the charge building up between us, threatening to hit us again. The electrical force in the barn was so great now, I was sure if I got too close to her there would be a truly dangerous discharge between us. I stepped back and shouted for her to get down again, but she simply could not hear me over the incessantly blasting thunder. I thought of waving my arms to try to get her attention but feared the movement might make us a bigger, more attractive target for an electrical discharge.

Then an amazing sphere of deepest blue, extraordinarily bright, appeared over the buck's stall, only a dozen feet away. It swelled instantly to the size of a huge pumpkin, and then it shrank and fizzled out. It took only a moment, but it felt like several long seconds had elapsed. And just like that, the lightning outside stopped and the ball lightning in the barn ceased. There remained of the freakish storm only a wet wind and the humming of rain on the steel roof that picked up in moments to a torrent. Arielle and I stepped over to the great entry, looked out. In the back of our minds we expected to see smoke rising from a lightning blasted hillside and craters as if they'd been hit by artillery shells. But there was only the rain, the immutable mountain, and a couple downed trees.

"What just happened?" Arielle said. I could hear the tension blended with wonder in her voice.

I grew up in Louisiana where I saw the wildest hurricanes and witnessed up close and personal wicked tornadoes. I have sailed a goodly portion of the North Pacific and seen mighty storms called Chinooks rip down out of seaside mountains over waters that had been dead calm only a moment before, tearing foam off the waves with 70-knot winds though there was not a cloud in the sky. Once, in the far north, I saw the entire sky lit up with the aurora in the peculiar form of a vast cloud of flame, the whole sky flashing beneath it in an eerie, pulsing rhythm. But never in all my days and in all my wandering had I seen anything like this. In answer, I could only shake my head, as baffled as she.

So Lughnasadh came to the Hollow with fire, and after the fire came a warm summer rain that lasted three days. It drove away the stifling heat. It lifted our spirits. By night, Daphne and I slept on the covered deck at the edge of the Elfwood to listen to the music of the rainfall and the play of the breeze across the wind chimes. By day, the gardens drank the pure sky waters and the brook south of the cottage chuckled merrily, full to the banks. The geese played in the puddles that gathered in their paddock and the goats chewed cud contentedly in their run-in beside the turkey coop in the Firefly Meadow. And on the third night, the showers simply faded away, leaving in their wake a dazzling dawn and a world that smelled of the clean, wet forest. It was said that a gentle rain upon Lughnasadh was a portent of abundant late-season crops, and if that were so, then autumn would bring a rich harvest indeed, for already the gardens were exceeding our expectations, especially given their late start due to an unseasonably cool June. But the fireballs at the eve of the High Day—they stumped me. They were so rare and marvelous. Did they have meaning? I could not help but think so.

If nothing else, Lughnasadh had come with omens and wonders, and I wanted to be sure to celebrate the season properly. I had never been a great one for ritual, so I tended to find more direct ways to honor the spirits. This year I had planned to honor the grain goddess (the Goddess in her Mother aspect) by making a traditional grain sheaf doll and staking it out at the edge of the Elfwood where it could overlook the gardens. However, the cool June had set all the growth back, so there were no grain stalks available.

Well, from the Gallic Taranis to the Nordic Thor, lightning was a masculine device. Maybe it was appropriate that this season I honor a masculine god: the little spirit who becomes the life of the grain. Out in the Potato Patch, I had planted a considerable amount of an early variety of corn to help stabilize the soil. Much of it was about ready for picking, so one early August morning, I set out beneath a clear sky to gather corn and keep an old tradition . . . in a new, and hopefully better, way.

According to old myth, as the grain is harvested, the corn spirit must retreat to the remaining stalks. It wasn't bad to take the grain: it was part of the natural spiral of life. But eventually the harvesters would come down to the last remaining stalks. No one wanted to be the one to cut that last refuge of the corn spirit—it was bad luck. So, traditionally, the harvesters would gather around the last sheaf and throw their sickles at it till someone succeeded at toppling it—the idea being that it would be hard to tell who made the felling blow. Well, there was only me working the patch, so it would be obvious who did the harvesting no matter what. And one doesn't cut down corn to harvest it anyway; you just rip the ear off the stalk. So I went around the patch taking the good ears, but when I reached the central stalks I just left them. Why not let the spirit have a few ears to himself this Lughnasadh? And as I harvested all but the last of the corn, an ancient poem that has been made into many a folk song came to mind:

There were three kings into the east,
Three kings both great and high,
And they hae sworn a solemn oath
John Barleycorn should die.

They took a plough and plough'd him down,
Put clods upon his head,
And they hae sworn a solemn oath
John Barleycorn was dead.

But the cheerful Spring came kindly on,
And show'rs began to fall;
John Barleycorn got up again,
And sore surpris'd them all.

The sultry suns of Summer came,
And he grew thick and strong;
His head weel arm'd wi' pointed spears,
That no one should him wrong.

The sober Autumn enter'd mild,
When he grew wan and pale;
His bending joints and drooping head
Show'd he began to fail.

His colour sicken'd more and more,
He faded into age;
And then his enemies began
To show their deadly rage.

They've taen a weapon, long and sharp,
And cut him by the knee;
Then tied him fast upon a cart,
Like a rogue for forgerie.

They laid him down upon his back,
And cudgell'd him full sore;
They hung him up before the storm,
And turn'd him o'er and o'er.

They laid him out upon the floor,
To work him further woe;
And still, as signs of life appear'd,
They toss'd him to and fro.

They wasted o'er a scorching flame,
The marrow of his bones;
But a miller us'd him worst of all,
For he crush'd him between two stones.

And they hae taen his very heart's blood,
And drank it round and round;
And still the more and more they drank,
Their joy did more abound.

John Barleycorn was a hero bold,
Of noble enterprise;
For if you do but taste his blood,
'Twill make your courage rise.

'Twill make a man forget his woe;
'Twill heighten all his joy;
'Twill make the widow's heart to sing,
Tho' the tear were in her eye.

Then let us toast John Barleycorn,
Each man a glass in hand;
And may his great posterity
Ne'er fail in old Scotland!

* John Barleycorn
  Robert Burns (1759–1796)

When I finished harvesting the corn, I stood beside the Potato Patch, wiping sweat from my brow and smiling. The little spirit still had some corn to himself, and I felt sure he'd be pleased. I loaded the ears into the tractor's great bucket, then gathered some more of this and that from the other garden beds till the bucket was full. Then I drove the tractor back to the cottage. The produce had to be stored, and there was far more to do this day.

According to old tradition, Lughnasadh is a time to celebrate when Nature is most generous and life is at its sweetest. In elder times there would be an early harvest fair with singing and dancing, fine fresh foods, rituals for a good late harvest, and games of skill and athleticism. But we live in an industrialized era when some 90 percent of the world's population live in urban areas, and with it has come a global food system. Want a peach in midwinter? Chances are your grocery store has them, flown in from Australia. Want grapes in May? You can find them because a greenhouse a thousand miles away is forcing them to fruit out of season. Such a lifeway makes it hard to fully appreciate summer's generosity. But we lived immersed in the spiral of the year and know full well the impact of its turning.

So, while Daphne and the girls husked the corn for storage (organic corn in these parts must be promptly husked to deal with a little caterpillar that likes to feed on the kernels), I began setting up for our own little festival, and that afternoon our guests came. We offered a dinner of the early fruits of our abundant garden: buttered corn on the cob, steamed Swiss chard, green and potato salads, and quiche of summer eggs. Our guests also contributed with their own hors d'oeuvres and dessert. After eating, it was near twilight and the children visited the horses and played chase and Frisbee and other games while the adults talked and laughed over home-brewed wines and ales at the picnic table. When it grew dark, we built a bonfire in the chimenea at the edge of the Elfwood and the good cheer continued under the light of evening stars with roasted marshmallows and sparklers handed out for the children to run and scream with.

The fun lasted till nearly midnight when our guests, themselves also early risers, bade their farewells. We saw them off, and then Daphne and I wandered back out to the chimenea where the fire still crackled. We were so tired from all the pleasant work and play of the day that we didn't have the energy to clean up or even go inside. Daphne laid down on a blanket by the fire and was soon sound asleep. I climbed up on the nearby picnic table and lay on my back, regarding the myriad stars in a vast, lucent darkness. I thought just then they looked like little fireballs. And I realized, with my heart still full with the echoes of mirth, that a star and a fireball were so much alike. A star is ultimate destructive power contained in balance, and so it becomes a thing that provides life to worlds.

Our own sun is a star, and its steady strength is the very lifeblood of this green Earth. And the fireballs we saw in the barn: they were power, too. Not the unleashed power of lightning, which is the weapon of gods like Taranis and Thor. We had been so close to the fireballs, yet we had not been harmed and nothing in the barn had been damaged. The fireballs were power contained. Power in balance—the root of creation.

I smiled at the thought as my eyes drifted shut, there on the picnic tabletop, by the fire near my beloved wife. I had no scholarship to prove it, for ball lightning is the rarest thing, little touched in the annals of occult lore, but the insight felt right. The gods had touched the Hollow, showing us the full power of land and sky. It had been followed by the good omen of a gentle Lughnasadh rain. Power in balance was working to make something good here in the Hollow. We gave to the land and its spirits, and they gave back to us. And, oh, how they would give. I didn't know it just then but autumn would, as if in response to the magical touch of the fireballs that day, yield a legendary harvest. But in that moment, what I knew mattered is the spirits were happy, we were happy, our children and our friends were happy. Life was in balance and the spiral of the year reigned over the Hollow. And with that pleasant thought sleep came on quiet cat's paws, and as I drifted off overhead the stars kept silent watch.

Arielle prepares to set off into the Elfwood to find
adventure with her friends. Somewhere back there,
they have a secret hideout. I just haven't found it yet.

Traditional Living

*A Concert of Owls:
Immersing in Nature by Night*

In the beautiful documentary, *The Cave of Forgotten Dreams* (2011), we are taken to the Chauvet Cave in the mountains of France, where Homo sapiens who dwelt in the world primeval left their mark with astounding paintings on cave walls 32,000 years ago. This enormous cave is special because the artwork was partially covered by lime crystals and has thus been well preserved, and it is not the simple creations of our Neanderthal kin. The work of our early ancestors possesses depth and range, shading and dimension. The cave was visited over a period of five thousand years, each succeeding generation leaving a tableau of creatures, some still with us, some, sadly, extinct, such as the mammoth, cave lion, and cave bear. The cave was, doubtless, the sacred domain of early shamans who sought to record the soul of their world. And that soul is redolent of Nature. Not abstract designs or occult symbols. Just Nature. The creatures they shared the world with. Some, like horses, painted with such detail, shading, and loving attention that it is obvious early folk saw the creatures as beautiful and spiritual. And for tens of thousands of years, Nature remained at the heart of spirituality. It was the abode of spirits and material beings alike.

But the spirituality of Nature got lost around the time of the birth of civilization. Civilization was a force bent on reshaping the world to suit Man's desire for wealth and comfort, and with it, comforting gods were sought. Anthropomorphized gods. Old men upon mountains and in the sky. Even leaders became gods, seen in the Egyptian and Roman proclivity for viewing their rulers as divine, or at the very least, of divine origin. And in the present, when technology and vast urban centers make it possible to spend entire lifetimes within artifices of concrete and steel, that separation is more dire than ever.

As our ancestors knew, Nature is full of spirits. And sometimes, if one looks very carefully, you might espy them. Can you see the two fey folk hidden among these spruce boughs?

It is essential that persons keep in touch with Nature. It is healthy and healing for the soul and body and helps us stay in balance, so several times a year we offer outdoor hikes in which we show guests how to do such things as identify useful wild herbs and observe wildlife. But my favorite hikes are those we do after dark. Many animals that used to be diurnal have taken on nocturnal habits to avoid Man. And many other creatures simply prefer the dark, such as porcupines and flying squirrels. And some marvelous things you will only encounter after dark, like a meadow full of fireflies.

Anytime you go hiking you should be prepared, but a few additional steps should taken to make a nighttime hike go well. Ideally, have a guide—someone who knows the area well and is competent in the back-country. But that is not always easy to find. Alternatively, hike the area by day and get to know it. You'll want to know where any dangers are that could be concealed by darkness, such as drops and thorny thickets. If you are not absolutely confident you can find your way, mark the trail in advance with reflective, biodegradable tape about every twenty to hundred yards, depending on how thick the country is. Trust me, unless you are following a good trail, this is essential. I can assure you it is unbelievably easy to get turned around in a thick wood at night. Even a flashlight will do little to help you find your way after dark. A light beam has a way of turning a lovely forest into a directionless tangle of unfriendly logs, look-alike trees, and tripping stones. Mark your way in advance.

Bring two flashlights. Both should be small and very powerful. That is easy enough. New LED bulb flashlights can boast thousands of candle power and run for hours off a single, tiny battery. Having two flashlights gives you a backup, and when you're in wild places, it never hurts to have backups. Plus, you should put transparent red tape over one of the flashlights, or get a flashlight that has a built-in mount for a red gel cover. Many animals don't see or respond to red light, so they will act normally and you will get to watch them in their usual activities. Plus, red light will interfere little with your night vision.

Bring a pack of matches in a waterproof container because you never know when you might need a fire. Trust me on this. If the weather turns or you get lost, the best thing is usually to hunker down, and a warm fire makes that not only bearable but can turn it into an enjoyable adventure.

Bring a bit of extra food. A few granola bars or some high-calorie trail mix are good. A bottle of water should be brought along, too. Few things make an excursion unpleasant like hunger and thirst. You'll burn up calories and your body's liquid quickly when moving in backcountry, and if you don't have food or water you'll come to regret the trip.

Bring a roll of toilet paper and a plastic bag to remove waste, or a trowel to bury it, depending on the country's conditions. In the far north where the ground is acidic, don't bury used toilet paper. The ground acid will keep it from degrading for years. But in other regions, I favor just burying all such waste. As long as it is biodegradable it'll just be compost in a matter of weeks.

Some persons advise bringing a radio or cellphone in case you need to call for help. I suppose this is a good idea, though I hate to feel linked to the human world when on such outings. But it's a good safety precaution, especially if you aren't competent in backcountry.

Very importantly, dress in layers and carry a large fannypack or small daypack so that you can strip, add, and stow things as needs require. Remember, it might feel chilly when you start a hike, especially at night, but when the body gets working hard, you'll get hot. If you just wear a coat and heat up, you'll have your choice of wearing it and being hot and miserable, or taking it off and being cold and miserable. Experienced outdoorsmen get in the habit of wearing layers of shirts, pants, sweaters, and weatherproof shells so they can always have just the right garments for the conditions. Those few times I have neglected this rule, I have always regretted it.

Likewise, get appropriate footwear. Good hiking boots at least ankle-high are a MUST. Nothing will ruin a trip or present a danger faster than a turned ankle, and without good footwear, it is very likely to happen. I once had a pair of women drive over two hours to attend a Nature by Night hike at the Hollow. Though I had emailed them a list of required equipment, nevertheless one arrived in semi-high-heeled dress boots, and the other had only light sandals. I would have made exceptions for any other equipment they might have lacked, but not proper footwear. I refused to allow them to come along even though they had driven all that way because there was little doubt in my mind one or both of them would be limping out of the woods with a sprained or broken ankle by the end of the hike. It's that serious. Invest in a good pair of hikers. It's worth every penny.

One of my favorite nighttime Nature experiences occurred just last summer when Natalia and I planned a daddy-daughter camping trip up the mountain, a mile or so from the Old Wood. The area had been logged a couple decades ago and was half grown back, so the blend of cover and open area was perfect for browsers like deer and various birds of prey. It wasn't rare to even find wildcat tracks and sight bear, and a pack of coyotes often sang there by dawn. Natalia and I had arrived around noon and pitched our tent in a little glade. We were going it easy, so we had some comforts, namely a pump gas stove and a folding picnic table and a couple folding chairs. The tent's floor was soft and comfortable with sleeping pads and several extra blankets to accommodate the rocky ground. We had hiked about in the early afternoon with our bows, stump shooting and observing the abundant rabbits and songbirds. I taught her how to tell the difference between predator and herbivore spoor, and if a predator, how to identify what it had last eaten. But it was a very hot day and we returned to camp in the early afternoon to take our ease in the shade of the trees.

Late in the afternoon, we gathered firewood and made a ring of stones. When twilight fell, we started the fire and let it burn down to coals, then set up spits to slow roast some steaks. At the edge of the fire we set some potatoes to bake on hot rocks. It grew darker as the food slowly cooked. I put a pair of candles in two small lanterns and lit them, and we reclined and talked until, suddenly, we noticed a breathtaking spray of silver light illuminating the trail ten yards from our campsite. We rose and walked over to it. The trail divided the trees and ran directly east to west, and through the break in the forest canopy we could see a magnificent, huge full moon at the edge of the horizon, positioned so perfectly up the trail that it looked like it was coming over to visit. We continued to watch, awestruck, and slowly it rose and painted the woodland an otherworldly hue like hoarfrost. The moonlight was so strong it cast long shadows behind us, and we could have taken our bows and hunted in the dark.

Natalia and I stood on the trail and admired the rising moon a long time, then we recalled the roasting steaks. They would need a dousing so they didn't dry out, and the spits would have to be turned, so we started back to the campsite. We had just reached the fireside when two huge black shadows rose like phantoms from a great old tree, taller by far than the rest. Their winged forms flew ghost-silent up and up, toward our encampment, and then they began a bizarre dance, flying around one another. They were positioned just perfectly so that it seemed they were circling that brilliant full moon, now just over the treetops.

Round and round they went, silhouettes waltzing to an unheard music. Then they broke apart, one great owl to a high tree on the southeastern edge of our clearing, the other to the southwestern point. As soon as they alighted upon the branches, they began their eerie calls—the thrilling "Hoo! Hoo!" that people have associated with dark and spooky nights since time immemorial. Their calls echoed throughout the mountain forest as if they were serenading one another, or perhaps us. It was so beautiful, and we watched in silent reverie as the duo performed their nocturnal concerto.

And then, as if the lunar conductor had tapped her baton, the performance was ended and the two owls spread their wings and fell out of the trees, catching the air in the complete silence of the species. They sailed high over the wood and swerved north, in moments out of sight.

In that moment was magic. Pure, true, earthy enchantment like our distant ancestors at the Cave of Forgotten Dreams must have known. In such a moment are ancient spirits, shaman secrets, and eldritch beauty of such depth it is a wonder humankind ever looked away from the perfection of the green world. Only when you touch such magic can you know how essential it is to our own well-being.

AUGUST

The Coyote's Tale

Nightfall had come over the Hollow and the great forest slept, only the occasional sigh of a breeze or the haunting cry of an owl breaking the deep silence. In the cottage, the ancient pendulum clock on the living room wall that we call Grandmother struck midnight and I wandered out to the back deck to watch the moon slowly sink toward the mountain's west ridge. The vast maple wood was silvered by its light.

There was a slight bite in the air, and even though it was only the first week of August, Earth was hinting that in the none-too-distant future, autumn would come. It was not close, but in this land of dramatically varied seasons, the next turn of the Wheel of the Year is never far, so we lived each day with an eye upon the seasons: the time to break soil and set out the bruanighe's first spring milk, the time to sow seed and invoke the Green Man, the time to nurture crops and stake the corn doll, the time to harvest crops and set out the faerie plates. Living in harmony with Earth kept us attentive of the Wheel.

And now thoughts of the Wheel kept me up late, for it was in motion and its turning was not entirely clear. Today it had brought us to the beginning of serious harvest time, and with that came elation. It had been a perfectly beautiful day, with mild temperatures and a cyan sky where scattered puffy clouds drifted lazy and high, and Daphne, our daughters, and I had spent the better part of the afternoon gathering in the gardens. In truth, the gardens had been yielding since June when the asparagus emerged and the strawberries began to come, but today was the first really big harvest of the annuals. We spent the better part of the afternoon uprooting the fattest turnips, breaking magnificent leaves of Swiss chard from their roots, and harvesting snow peas and early potatoes (a highland favorite). And the gardens yielded far more than that. Plump red currants slated to become jams, huge yellow beets with their lush, glossy green tops, and even some early broad beans joined the sacks and crates accumulating at the foot of the beds. All told, it was an enormous harvest, and when it was all brought into the cottage, we worked late into the night preparing the produce for freezing, canning, and storage in sawdust in the root cellar.

But despite all that, the majority of our crops were still maturing in the soil, and some would not be ready for months. The success of those crops depended upon the weather, and we knew only too well how fickle it could be atop this mountain, in this land half cast out into the sea. But a gentle rain had fallen over the Hollow upon Lughnasadh and that was an ancient omen of good fortune for the farmer. Having witnessed the incredible fireballs, and then the perfect rain, I could not help but feel that our gardens would fare well late into the year.

So what ate at me, I wondered as I leaned against the rail near the large wind chime that played in the ever-so-slightly-cool evening breeze. There was a lot more work to do tomorrow—strawberries and asparagus were still coming in, and fruit trees needed to be pruned and the horses worked. The innumerable tasks of the farm had made us a family that rose and slept with sun, and I knew I should get to bed. But sleep eluded me despite a powerful physical fatigue after a day of hard work.

This was the month of Lughnasadh, and thoughts of the meaning of the High Day came to mind. The holiday comes out of old Irish mythology, and it has to do with the goddess Tailtiu (CHUL*ch'yoo). According to legend, she cleared the plains that would become the heart of agriculture in Ireland; however, she succumbed to the strain of the work and died. It is said that Lughnasadh is when we honor Tailtiu's heroic deed, but profound myths are rarely so simple. Tailtiu's act is said to represent a mystery of transformation: the heroine who gives all of herself to the land and so is reborn as the land's vitality. But I was never sure if I quite bought that scholarly interpretation. It always felt too obvious to me. They don't call them mysteries because the truths they sequester are easily discerned.

Oh, why am I up after midnight pondering things I am too tired to wrap my mind around? I asked myself for the tenth time. *Go to bed!* But still sleep eluded me. Fireballs and balmy rains. Good omens and the honest hard work of the harvest. The simple pleasure of watching jars and cans and crates of good food being stowed in the root cellar. So much was coming together in August, a heady blend of effort and Earth and enchantment. Suddenly, I knew this feeling. I had experienced it before, that cloud-black night back in June when I had stood in our rain-wrecked gardens at the edge of despair and called upon the Green Man. This was the flux—that pregnant moment when vision meets reality. And that realization brought me back to another memorable event of the day: the first ride of Natalia's young Belgian mare, Acorn.

Acorn is sixteen hands, meaning she is sixty-four inches tall at the withers (shoulders). I have raised her since she was six weeks old, and she is a little over three years now. Since last year, I've been prepping her for riding by teaching her how to work in partnership with humans, starting with simple games that horses find fun but also teach attentiveness, patience, and confidence. In the last few weeks, I had begun saddling her and riding her around the corral. But riding a novice horse can be tricky. Even a mild-mannered horse like Acorn can be dangerous without meaning to just because she is so large and strong. Just the previous week I had put Natalia in the saddle, and after fifteen minutes of riding around the corral, Acorn decided it would be fun to roll on her back and stretch. Fortunately, I had taught Natalia to bail if a horse pulls a stunt like that and she bolted out of the saddle before Acorn had even lowered herself to her knees. No one was hurt and I promptly forced the horse upright again and made her back up a few paces (horses hate backing) so she would feel scolded for that moment of inattention. The horse hadn't meant any harm, but she's as heavy as a small car. It could have gone really bad had we not acted so quickly. So for the past week, I had been working closely with Acorn, teaching her that when she is in proximity to people she must mind her manners—no exceptions! And Acorn was coming along fine, so today was her big test. I'd try her on a long ride outside the corral, and if she performed up to standards, she'd be ready to become Natalia's.

Horses of the Belgian breed are closely related to the medieval heavy
war horse. They are the largest, most powerful breed in the world,
but they're never too tough to just stop and look sexy.

Near twilight, I had Natalia lead Acorn to the woodshop. The horse
had to learn to see herself as Natalia's, so I had Natalia groom her and
check her hooves. Then Natalia helped me throw on her saddle blanket, set and fasten the saddle, and put on the bridle. Then I mounted
Acorn, tapped her flanks with the heels of my boots. She started walking, and I guided her up the two-hundred-yard driveway. Out on the
dirt road, I steered her south toward ever remoter paths, following the
back ways to the old Acadian forest in the deepest regions of the mountaintop valley where I have tracked black bears and take deer. The sun
was very low in the west. On the road, there was still plenty of day-
light, but Acorn was very aware of the deepening dark beneath the

looming tangle of boughs. I had known she would be and it was what I had intended. To ensure she'd be a safe horse, I needed to help the young mare develop the confidence to set aside her fears.

But this is not so easy, even for a big, powerful Belgian steed. Horses are an ancient species and have long ancestral memories. Long before they began their alliance with Man, they were herbivorous prey animals found throughout Africa and Europe, and those lands were ruled by mighty predators. The days when they were low on the food chain are still keen in a horse's instinctive memory, and every horse learning to be a trail horse must learn to face the darkness, especially around woods and ponds and places of high brush from which predators ambush prey. I guided Acorn into this place so that she might experience that fear and learn to trust in her rider to look after her. This, as much as obedience and attentiveness and manners, is necessary to creating a worthy trail horse.

Soon we were deep in the woodland. As I had expected, Acorn was skittish and a little rough on the reins. Often she directed her ears into the shadows, perhaps overhearing the movements of a porcupine or the activity of a squirrel up late. She stopped at such times and wanted to turn back, but I held the reins firm and did not allow her to retreat. I made her hold her ground, occasionally patting her neck and whispering an encouraging word. In this way she confronted her fears, and as she did she learned confidence. She began to ride ever steadier. When at last I turned her back for home, I had also gained this harvest season a transformed horse. The fledgling filly was gone. For Acorn, the Wheel had turned.

Back in the present, upon the deck at the edge of the woods, I stared into the dark and pondered this, another mystery for the pot. There was a pattern here, something elusive and significant. The mystery of Tailtiu was in all of this, wanting to be known, I felt, if I could only tease it out. A stiffening breeze began to rustle my hair and brought me back to the moment. The wind chimes sang for that breeze, an unearthly tune of air elementals. It was beautiful and fey, a thing one never wants to forget yet cannot hold in memory. The bright half-moon had slid even lower into the west. It was well past midnight now and soon it would sink below the mountain ridge. Then a true country night, so black you can barely see your hand before your face, would fall over the land. As if to signal the coming dark, off in the distance a coyote howled. I smiled. It was always good to hear my canine brothers, so long as they kept to the forests and stayed clear of my livestock. But I do not fear them. I have always respected their territory and they, in turn, have respected mine. It called again, a loner trekking through the nightwood, and the cry felt like a summoning.

I entered the cottage. Moving quietly so as not to wake Daphne and the girls, I slipped down to the library, past the great old grandfather clock, which chimed a quarter past one. From a shelf, I grabbed my puukko. I always carry it on my backcountry rambles. I love the forest, but I am not naïve to its dangers. I've lived too long in wild places for that. Several times I've been challenged by wild predators, bears mostly. They've always backed down, and the creatures and I were able to avoid injury because I stood my ground and made it clear that I was as much a predator as they. Wild predators do not attack other predators—they understand full well that even a minor injury can mean starvation and death. I belted the puukko and slipped a small flashlight into my pocket and walked over to the French doors that exit directly out the library in the direction of the brook. Faithful Willowisp had been sleeping near the shelves, and he lifted his head and regarded me with concern. I knew he wanted to accompany me, but tonight I felt the need to be alone. "Next time, buddy," I told the eager shepherd as I set out.

I picked my way down the tangled foliage of the hillside, past the spring-fed pond, and along an ancient rock wall that was built by Scots settlers more than a century ago. At the foot of the hill, the brook babbled among a hedge of high trees, a mix of silver birch, sugar maples, and white spruce. Long ago I had made a path of steppingstones through the brook, and I used the flashlight to illuminate them. I dashed across the stones, through the remainder of the hedge, and a minute later, emerged at a dirt path. I swung west and walked down deeper into the valley, in the direction I had heard the coyote howl. Down there it is very wild, an old-growth forest predominated by massive maples—the region we call the Rusalka Wood. It was the only place in these parts that I ever felt like there was something of dark spirit—the rusalka: the spiteful ghost of a murdered woman, drowned more than a half century ago. The horses always seemed to sense it, too. They hated being ridden over that part of the brook, shying as they approached and bolting away after they passed. Yet it was in that primal place that illumination awaited, I was sure.

Ten minutes' walking took me to the western boundary of the Hollow, but the wildwood began long before, for we have always left the west flank for the feral spirits and as a sanctuary for the forest's creatures. Only a couple weeks ago I had ridden Aval out this way and come across some of the largest black bear tracks I had ever seen. I like the bears, but I have learned to respect them. They are not really dangerous, so long as you don't stumble upon one and startle it, so I kept my ears open, but all I heard were the echoing calls of horned owls and occasionally the cry of some eastern night bird I did not recognize. I considered putting a red gel lens onto the flashlight in hopes of spotting raccoons or a rare flying squirrel but decided against it. This was a night for focus.

I drew the flashlight from my pocket and flicked on the beam. It was extremely bright and instantly ruined my ability to see in the dark. I should have put on the red gel lens—red doesn't wipe out night vision. But I needed the light in the near-total dark of the trees' shadows, so I swept the beam over the path as I continued ever deeper into the valley. It was not long till I came across fresh coyote spoor: canine prints crossing the path. They were sharp-edged and the detail was crisp. It had not been long since it passed this way. Perhaps, with the Green Man's luck, I would see the coyote myself. I flicked the light off and stood still for several minutes, letting my eyes readjust to the dark. There was just enough remaining moonlight to find my way so long as I stayed to the path and went carefully.

When I could see again, I started walking, doing my best to be quiet. I've been living in the woods a long time, and I can do a fair job of it, though occasionally my foot skidded along a stone I failed to see, sending it rolling and clattering away. In the silent wood, such small faux pas sounded like thunder to my ears.

I made it all the way to the Rusalka Brook, but I had not come across what I had hoped for. I still had not met coyote. Alas, it was a long shot. They are elusive, clever creatures, and in general one comes across them only when one isn't expecting it. I stood there several minutes in silence, listening to the song of the brook. But the night drew on and I could not linger. I had to be up early the next day; a farm's work never waited. I drew the flashlight again, intending to use it all the way home to speed the journey.

I no sooner turned, though, than the beam fell over coyote. I didn't think it was aware of me. It had emerged on the path not thirty yards away while I stood silent and still upon the bridge, my noise and scent muffled by the rushing water. As is often the case with animals when artificial light falls over them, it didn't react. It didn't understand the flashlight made it visible despite the dark. But it must have been hunting because it froze, cocked its head, and perked its ears in the direction of the forest on the opposite side of the path. I suspected it was listening for rodents or rabbits—coyote favorites.

It was alone, and it was huge, as big as any canine I had ever seen. It stood broadside to me, all feet upon the ground, its body in rigid attention. It had to be the size of a German shepherd, but with longer, gangly-looking legs. It looked every ounce of a hundred pounds. I had seen coyotes out west in their native Mohave Desert, and they were nothing like this beast.

The real coyote is a relatively small canine. They always hunted in packs and were noisy on the move, using their calls to set prey in terrified flight and then howling and yelping to coordinate the chase and run it down in unison. But this creature—it was nothing like those. This was an eastern coyote, once referred to as the *new wolf*, a creature whose origins had been till only a few years ago mysterious, and whose behavior remains poorly understood. The eastern coyote can be as small as the western variety or as big as the mightiest wolf. They might hunt in tightly coordinated packs or they might wander alone. They are unbelievably intelligent and often elude the best manmade traps. Attempts to remove them from agricultural areas where they love to prey on sheep often prove futile. In fact, while many creatures have been on the decline with the advent of voracious Man, the eastern coyote has been on a steady rise, occupying forest lands and suburban areas where other predators have virtually vanished.

"A great one," I whispered at the sight of the huge beast. I felt no fear. Coyotes almost never attacked humans. They were much too smart for that. You'd have to run and really act like food to get a coyote to abandon its natural leeriness of humans. And besides, I was here to see coyote. So I held my ground, and I watched. If the coyote even knew I was there upon the bridge, it paid me no mind.

Suddenly, without a sound, it bounded into the forest on the opposite side of the road. Perhaps it had scented quarry. And just like that it was gone, just as the moon fell behind the mountain and the night became, at last, truly black.

I stood upon the bridge and pondered the beast I had felt compelled to see, and had been fortunate enough to encounter. I couldn't tell if it was the same one I had heard earlier, but no matter, I felt certain I had encountered the one I was meant to. It had truly been a great one. Before coming to Nova Scotia, I had wandered the far distant wilds of the Alaskan bush over many years and seen more than a few wolves, but I don't believe I had ever seen one so impressive as this mere "coyote."

In this day and age, how does a predator such as that manage to survive? Humans have overpopulated, spread everywhere, and wherever they go they declare war on large predators even as they rob the landscape of its wildlife and natural resources. Coyote's cousins, the red and gray wolves, have been virtually eradicated from all but the remotest areas and the far north, and yet coyote is more numerous than ever. Somehow I sensed the riddle of coyote was also part of the mystery of Tailtiu that seemed to compel me this sleepless night, and I recalled the saga of the coming of coyote to the east.

Only a couple centuries ago, coyote had been entirely a creature of the west. But as humans settled the land, they inadvertently created a "predator trail." Following human roads and taking advantage of the food that always accompanies human habitation, whether in the form of luckless livestock or garbage, the coyotes made their way into New England and ultimately up the Atlantic coast into the Maritime Provinces of Canada.

At the same time, the wolves of the East Coast of North America were being systematically eradicated by the European settlers who hated them for reasons based partially on superstition, partially on the fact that wolves occasionally preyed upon their livestock, and partially because they thought American wolves might behave like European wolves, which were much more aggressive toward humans. By a century ago, the gray wolves were gone from the East Coast, like the great flocks of wild turkeys and the caribou herds of Nova Scotia. Of the great predators, only shy, elusive black bears and a few red wolves remained. But whereas the black bears were learning to adapt to encroaching humanity, the red wolves, too, were on their way out. They were strong and capable, and a bit more elusive than gray wolves, but they could not learn to adapt to the new pressures humanity was forcing upon the natural world.

But coyote was always clever, the Loki-like trickster of aboriginal American myth, and as coyotes came east they became ever more adept at coping with humans. Used to evading bigger predators due to their small size, they quickly learned to hide from humans, too. They became so good at it that they could even live right under the noses of human settlements. Always opportunists, they made do with many food sources. They targeted anything handy: a stray cat, a lame deer, a wandering chicken. They'd even survive on rodents happily enough. They hunted in packs when they could and alone when they had to. Those original coyotes out of the Mohave were Nature's survivalists, even though they were small and basically unimposing.

It was inevitable that coyotes would eventually encounter the last of the red wolves as they expanded into the eastern woodlands. Once, when the wolves' numbers had been greater, they would have attacked the interloping coyotes on sight, but humans had so reduced their numbers that it seems the red wolves simply allowed them the territory. Then something extraordinary happened. When Man had virtually broken the wolves' packs and ancient, almost tribal ways, it seems the coyotes took pity on them and adopted them into their own packs. Interbreeding occurred. The two species were close enough genetically that some of the offspring were fertile and from their union a new creature emerged: the *new wolf*. This is a remarkable creature that has all the adaptability and intelligence of coyote, and all the speed and brawn of the wolf. Some biologists who study these creatures estimate their intelligence to be on a par with ours, though very different.

The sacrifice of Tailtiu. The yield of our gardens. Acorn becoming a trail horse at last. And now the coyote-*cum*-wolf. All of these pointed at some mystery yearning to be known, and I suddenly realized what it was. Lughnasadh ... this was the time of the apex of the flux, that point where a thing comes into fullness and must be remade. Tailtiu died in making Ireland fertile, and from that self-sacrifice she was remade into the life-giving power of the land. The crops of our gardens were reaching fruition and being remade into our life. Acorn had been a carefree and unpredictable fille but was remade this very twilight into a reliable saddle horse. And, most dramatically, both coyote and the red wolf of the east found their apex moment together and were remade as the *new wolf*. The ancient druids believed that such transformative moments were full of enchantment. In such moments, possibilities and the numinous become entwined, and who knows what might come thereof. The insight was powerful and made me shudder. I had to wonder, there on the little bridge over the Rusalka Brook, is the Hollow, our work of living in harmony with Nature and its spirits, our apex? And if so, what will the thing that comes of it be? Our dream is to teach others that they can love Earth and live better in doing so. Our hope is to see a greener, kinder world.

The mystery revealed, my mind relaxed and fatigue quickly overtook my exhausted body. It had been a very long day filled with lots of hard work, and there was much again to do tomorrow. So I began the long walk back to Twa Corbies Hollow. In time, I came upon the hidden path that led through the hedge to the brook and stepped across the stepping stones, climbed the little hill to the cottage. Quietly, I entered the library and set my flashlight and puukko upon the shelves. I wanted nothing more than to climb in bed beside Daphne.

I undressed and slipped under the covers, careful not to disturb her. Somehow she always knows when I've gotten to bed, though, and sidled up beside me in her sleep. I closed my eyes. A peace settled over me and, as I tossed an arm over her waist and drifted off, I knew that no matter where we were in relation to the apex, we were on the right path. Whatever the future, we were becoming what we were supposed to be. It is part of the magic of every enchanted forest.

SEPTEMBER

The Way

Natalia and I were deep in the forest up near a ridge overlooking the Old Wood and a vast valley beyond. She stood not twenty feet away, still as a statue. Between us was a tall spruce and in its lower branches were a pair of fat grouse. I had nocked an arrow to the string of my longbow and was trying to find a clear shot, but from every angle a tangle of branches threatened to interrupt the arrow's flight. Even the smallest twig could send it off course. I would not fire unless I could be sure of a clean kill. This shows respect for the beast.

Very slowly I slipped around the trunk, creeping at a snail's pace, careful to watch the grouse only out of the corner of my eye. Animals are sensitive to movement. Bear, deer, even birds will hardly notice you if you go very slowly. I once walked right out in the open to within thirty yards of a black bear by taking my steps no faster than the big hand of clock moves. Likewise, animals also know good and well when they are being watched, so we kept our gaze off them. I crept around the tree as if wading through a viscous fluid. The pair of grouse cooed and preened in the lower branches of the spruce, and then, without warning, one flew into a tall neighboring pine, the loud flapping of its wings disturbing the autumnal quietude of the wood. I noted where it landed halfway up the tree, then returned to stalking the largest, fattest one, still perched in the spruce about seven yards away.

When I found a position where all the intervening twigs and needles were out of the line of sight, I lifted the longbow, slowly pulling back the string. It's a powerful bow so I only drew a third of the way, pulling about twenty-five pounds. I could feel the arrow shaft slide between my index finger and the narrow shelf upon which it rested against the stave, and in my mind's eye the grouse, my arrow, and all the space between became as one when the shot was true—a phenomenon traditional archers in Britain refer to as "mushing." Opening my string fingers smoothly, I released the arrow and it flew quietly and took the bird out of the tree. Because the bow had only been at partial draw, there hadn't even been a snap of the string against the heavy leather bracer armoring my left arm.

I turned almost on my heel, still moving in that same viscously slow way, drawing another arrow from the leather quiver at my back and setting it to the string. Two paces to clear the line of fire at the grouse in the next tree, pull to one-third draw, and let the arrow fly. It took the second grouse with a *thwack*, and it fell from the mid-high branch and was instantly still.

I don't like to use guns. If you miss with a gun, the bullet can travel miles and maybe hit a person or some other creature far away. But there is more to my disdain of guns than safety concerns. For me, hunting is a shamanic experience—a process of profound immersion in the natural world that draws every sense, every movement, every skill deeply into the ancient cycle of predator and prey. A bow requires daily practice—not just to develop the skill of barebow archery, but also to learn to track, to stalk, to become one with the forest shadows and terrain. To hunt with a bow one must enter the very zeitgeist of land and quarry. Even the act of aiming is a Zen kind of experience. There are no sights on a longbow. One must envision a joining of target and self, and in the mind's eye become the arrow at all points of flight. It is a deeply meditative experience that can only be developed through countless hours on the range and in the forest, tracking, stump shooting, and ultimately truly stalking the quarry.

But bows don't kill like guns. If what you know of how bows work you learned from watching movies like *Robin Hood* and *The Lord of the Rings*, you've been misinformed. A gun may kill game instantly through the mere shock of the impact of the bullet, but an arrow kills by bleeding the game. Think of it as drawing out the life force. An instantaneous kill can only be attained by a perfect shot into a vital organ. I could see that the second shot had killed the grouse instantly, but no sooner did I see it hit the ground than Natalia pointed toward the first grouse, behind me on the ground under the spruce and called, "The first one is flopping about!"

There was no more need for silence or stillness now. I set my bow down quickly, drew my puukko, and darted across the duff to the bird. Without a moment's hesitation, I grasped the grouse, pressed it up against the trunk of the spruce and decapitated it, using the beefy puukko like a hatchet. A single sweep, a moment's shudder, and it was over. The grouse was still.

Natalia, barely a teen and in the forest with me to learn the skill of the ancient longbow, winced. "That was so fast," she said. "Why were you angry?"

I shook my head. "That wasn't anger. That was the Way." She look puzzled and I found my mind drifting back across the years to the days I resided deep in the Alaskan wilderness...

It was late August, and in the far north of the Alaskan interior it was already autumn. The wild blueberry scattered over the tundra was becoming a distinctive red and the odd willow, alder, and birch took on hues of butter and rust, standing out against the evergreen spruce like bright harbingers of winter. I walked up a trail, hundreds of miles from the nearest city, far away from any signs of civilization. As I went, I studied the ground. There were fresh caribou tracks through here. I was fairly sure a great herd was passing through, broken up among innumerable scattered groups. I needed only find a spot in the shadows and wait. I spied a thicket and walked over to it, stepped into the foliage, and vanished. Just before I had, though, I saw movement about a half mile down the trail on another hill's ridge. Someone else was out there, also hunting. I wanted to let him know we were here, so I waved my arms and whistled, but he didn't seem very attentive. I didn't believe he'd noticed me.

I glanced north to check the other ridge for my friend who had come out to assist me on this hunt. My family lived deep in the wilderness and, as such, were accorded the privilege of subsistence hunting. We were dependent upon the caribou to get by through winter, and an extra hand would increase our chances of success. I spotted Skye at the top of the rise and waved a sign that he should stay put. Between the two of us, we commanded a wide view of the surrounding lands.

Several quiet hours passed and the day moved on. In Alaska, the sun doesn't move across the sky so much as around it. Night and day are somewhat abstract concepts until winter, and I wasn't paying much attention to the passing of time. I was focused on watching the bush. Even though I had a good vantage, it was thick scrub in which I could easily miss a small, passing herd if I wasn't careful.

Suddenly, the caribou arrived! A vast herd. There were so many, moving like a forest of antlers across the clearing. They had come through the thickest part of the taiga, and so had been nearly invisible till they were almost on top of our position. Skye and I made three easy shots in quick succession, but over the racket of fire I thought I heard a fourth shot. But it could have just been an echo. The hills played odd tricks with sound.

I set my rifle down and waved a signal to my friend. He waved back. Between us we had bagged three caribou. The rest of the day would be full of hard work, cleaning and hauling them by hand out of the bush. But it would be good work. Our families would eat well this winter and tonight we would have a small feast in celebration. But as my friend started walking toward my position, I glanced toward the opposite ridge and saw the other fellow had slung his rifle and was trotting up the trail in our direction ... fast, like he was retreating. *Was he afraid?* I wondered. Maybe he'd seen a grizzly on the approach. Grizzlies are huge and fierce, and everyone in Alaska worries about encountering them. I loved them. They were a symbol of the most primal wild, but one had to be respectful of them and cautious. They were huge, powerful predators with little fear of Man. Some grizzlies had put two and two together and realized that gunfire often meant fresh killed game, and they would come from afar to claim it.

The fellow came past my position just as Skye reached me. He looked around sixty, thin, with the softness you see among people who don't spend much time out of doors. "You okay?" I called. "Do you need help?" He ignored me and kept going, straight and fast in the direction of the trailhead.

Skye called, "Did you see a bear?"

But the old fellow didn't so much as give us a sidelong glance. He hastened past, head down, shoulders leaning forward as if he were forging into a cold wind, though there wasn't so much as a breeze. Skye and I exchanged meaningful looks, but what could we do? He'd clearly wanted nothing to do with us. We glanced at our three caribou, sizing up the task before us. The deer are made for cold weather and the meat is delicate. If left untended, it will begin spoiling immediately. But I couldn't shake the feeling that something was very wrong. I turned to Skye. "Start gutting those, will you? I'm going over to that ridge and see what that fellow was up to."

He nodded. "Signal if you need me, brother," he said.

I shouldered my rifle and started down the hill then up the next. I watched the landscape carefully as I went. I kept thinking the old fellow must have seen a grizzly and panicked, but it just didn't feel right. Why would he not have accepted our help? I thought back to the moment the herd came through. I was sure I'd heard a fourth shot timed almost exactly with our own. I froze on the trail as a cold fear gripped me. Had the man hit someone? Was he running away from a tragic accident? I started jogging up the trail.

I reached the top of the next ridge and called, "Hello!" but no answer came back. I pulled my binoculars from their case and glassed out the surrounding area, but I couldn't see anyone. Suddenly, I heard a small crashing sound in a copse of birch and spruce about twenty yards away. I dropped the binoculars in a jacket pocket and approached the forest. "Hello?" I called again, but there was no reply. I entered the copse and in moments came to a tiny glade ensconced by the trees.

A young caribou lay among the grassy brush. It wasn't half the size of a full-grown animal. Probably late born and only a few months old. Its foreleg was broken where a bullet had grazed it. Suddenly, I understood what had happened all too clearly. The old fool hadn't had idea one what he was doing out here. I recalled seeing at the trailhead a huge, expensive new truck with a trailer carrying an ATV. The entire rig was worth as much as some people's homes. No one from the bush who needed to live off the land could afford something like that. First guess, he was some lawyer or dentist from Anchorage, one of those fools who thinks killing a wild animal makes him a man, and he'd been after a trophy. He had gotten overexcited and shot the first thing to come out of the trees. It's illegal to shoot a juvenile caribou and, seeing his error, he was taking off. As I put the pieces together, a cold fury began to burn inside me.

I shook my head. No time for that. I had to do something for the little caribou. For a moment I entertained impossible fantasies of nursing it back to health. I envisioned bringing it back to the cabin and setting its leg with a splint, tending it over winter and turning it free next spring when the bone had mended. I took a single, tentative step toward the young buck, thinking to somehow restrain it so I could carry it back. But it didn't, couldn't, understand my intent. It rose and tried to flee but fell promptly on its useless leg, making a pained cry that is impossible to describe. I winced in empathy, and the moment brought me back to reality. Caribou were creatures of movement—they lived active and hard in some of the toughest country on Earth. No splint I could possibly set would last more than a day. The bone would never mend, the creature would endure weeks of pain, and ultimately infection would set in and it would die a lingering death. I had to face the truth that there was nothing I could do for it.

I took a shaky breath as I realized there was only one mercy I could give it. I could make its end quick. I had no ethical problem taking game out of necessity, and always strove to make the kill swift and clean. But this ... the old man shooting wildly, without thought of the irrevocable consequences of that action; the prospect of taking the life of this little one; the lingering pain and fear it was even now in. Everything about the situation was wrong—and there was no right way out of it. Only a path of the least of evils.

I leveled my rifle at the young caribou. "I'm sorry, little brother," I whispered. I aimed, gritted my teeth and tried to squeeze the trigger. But I couldn't. I just couldn't do it. I kept thinking, *Put it down. End its suffering.* But I just couldn't make my finger move.

Skye appeared beside me. "Brother, I was worried about you," he said, then he saw the young one before me. He frowned. "That son of a bitch!" he hissed.

Without pause, he unshouldered his rifle and pulled the trigger. In a moment the young caribou lay still in the grass. I wanted to curse Skye. No, I wanted to throw a punch and break his nose, but I knew he'd only done what had to be done, but I could not. But the anger wouldn't subside. It was damned wrong! I turned on my heel and punched a birch several times, hard, hurting my hand a lot more than the solid trunk of the tree.

He looked at me sympathetically. "Had to be done, brother," he said.

"I know," I replied flatly. "I'm glad you made it quick." But a deep sadness crept into me. What had to be done was done, but it should never have had to be.

Skye and I returned that evening to my family's little cabin tucked into the cove of a vast inland lake surrounded by roadless wilderness. We dressed out the meat, and I gave a third of it to him. The rest we put in a storage shed because the days were already icy and outside the meat would shortly freeze. With two caribou for my family, and a stock of rice and potatoes and whatever greens we could acquire during our infrequent trips into the tiny village fifty miles away, we were set to ride out the winter. I knew I should have been happy, but the shadow of the day pervaded my thoughts and I became sullen. To keep from taking my mood out on Daphne and the girls, I excused myself after dinner and went for a walk along the lake's edge. What that old man had done ate at me. An ethical hunter never shoots without being certain of the target. Just as much, an ethical hunter never leaves a wounded animal to suffer. My grandfather, an ornery Cajun who spent his entire life on his farm deep in the bayous of Louisiana, had taught me to spend all day tracking down injured quarry, if need be. I had no illusions about the way of the wild. Caribou are prey animals, and eventually something always takes them down. But that little one should have had some good years before it to run free with its kith and kin. The whole affair had left me feeling dark inside.

A year later we moved to Anchorage so I could attend grad school. During that brief stint in the city, hunting was no longer a necessity so I gave it up. Several years after I graduated we went east, to Maritime Canada, wanting to live in a place that was still in the north but warm enough to farm. It was a relief to find Twa Corbies Hollow and resume our rural lives. Soon we had gardens, groves, livestock, and pets, and because I felt it was the right thing to do for the land, I resumed hunting—taking up the longbow to do so in a manner much closer to Earth and its creatures. And as we re-entered Nature's spiral, I told myself if I was ever confronted with a suffering creature again—something beyond hope—I would do what Skye had done and put a quick end to it. But Nature has her own Way, and it is never simple. She had more to teach me about what it means to walk her Way.

It was early spring in the Hollow and all the goats had given birth to their new kids except Fey, a year-old doe born to our flock the previous year. This had us worried. It would be her first birthing, and if anything was going to go wrong, that's when it usually happened. Already there were problems—she was more than three weeks late and so huge she could barely walk. A goat's gestation period is about half that of a human, so it was like she was a month and a half late. I was considering inducing labor, and we had all been making frequent trips day and night to the barn so that, if labor did start on its own, we could be ready to assist her.

Despite all our efforts, she managed to go into labor right after her Friday noon check. When we came back an hour later, we found her in the stall with twins. One was small and stillborn. The other was large and alive, but Fey had been too weak after labor to remove the amniotic sac. It was wrapped around the kid's head, drowning it. I cut it off and dried the kid, then tried leaving it to Fey's ministrations, but she was too weak to nurse or even tend it. The little one would have to go to the house, so Daphne stayed at the barn to look after Fey while I brought the kid to a kennel we keep as an animal infirmary in the arctic entry. But the kid was too weak even to be settled into the kennel, so I had to pack her in a basket lined with dry towels and covered her with old blankets. I tried several times over the course of the day to feed the kid, but it didn't even have the strength to swallow.

If you live on a farm, you see animals die from time to time, sometimes by illness, sometimes due to predation, sometimes even because they've been picked on by their own kind (poultry are notorious for that). But it was hard to watch a day-old kid fading away without ever even a chance at life. It was so unfair. And if time and chance had just worked out a little differently, if I had just checked on Fey a few minutes earlier, I might have been able to give crucial assistance.

By 6:00 p.m. Daphne and the girls had come in and reported that Fey was eating and drinking again and it looked like she would be all right, but I had been fighting a hopeless battle to save the kid, and I was emotionally exhausted, my nerves on edge. I snapped at Daphne, something stupid about it being just wonderful for Fey. Then I caught myself and promptly apologized. Daphne understood and forgave me, and put a hand on my shoulder as I knelt beside the basket and racked my brain yet again for some way to help the kid. But it refused the bottle, and when I tried to force-feed it, it choked on the vital colostrum, of which I had only a limited supply. All I could do was stay there beside the basket, making soothing sounds and keeping it from wriggling out of the blankets.

It was getting well on into night when Daphne returned to check up on both the kid and me. I glanced up at her and knew what she was thinking, and I didn't like it. But the kid was suffering badly. It was time I give up and let it rest. She told the girls it was time to look in on Fey and they all went out to bring hay and molasses-sweetened grain to the animals.

I stared down at the tiny creature, feeling utterly helpless, for I didn't know what else to do. The juvenile caribou Skye had put down years before kept flashing into my thoughts, clear as the present moment, and I kept thinking, *No! I'm not letting another little creature die!* But the little doe was suffering and sometimes there is nothing to do but give what mercy one can. I drew my puukko and put the point against its ribs. A quick thrust and its suffering would be over.

But I was conflicted on so many levels. So many times I had taken game without guilt, and on many occasions killed domestic livestock. But there is something profoundly different about taking a mature beast in a fair hunt, or killing an adult chicken. Those animals had lived outdoors, digging and eating, playing and sleeping under the sun and stars—like an animal should. And when I had taken them, I had done it swiftly, without warning in an instant. Most times the animals were gone before they knew it was coming. But this little doe, she would never have her days to romp in the meadow. All she'd known was pain. It was so unfair. So damned unfair!

But in the end I couldn't get myself to thrust the puukko, and that surprised me for I had told myself that, like Skye, I would not hesitate if the need came again. But this wasn't a wild caribou. Nor was it the deep Alaskan bush. And then it came to me: *You walk the Way you're on.* And here and now there was another path. I knelt to one knee, stroked the down-soft fur of her delicate neck. Then I drew the blanket up to her shoulders and tucked her in and left the basket in the warmest corner of the entry. I decided I wouldn't try to force-feed her anymore. I wouldn't keep waking her when she started to sleep. Death would come, and there was nothing I could do about it, but I could at least give her warmth and be with her as she passed. In minutes the little doe quit squirming and settled into the blankets and became still. Sleep came over her, a sleep from which I knew she would never awaken.

When Daphne returned from the barn she found me leaning against the doorframe that led to the entry, looking over the basket where the kid slept. I could see in her eyes she was surprised I hadn't put it down. My voice broke as I told her, "She's just a little thing. She can't last the night. But we can at least let her pass away warm and cared for. We can give her that."

Daphne nodded solemnly.

Long ago we discovered a glade in the eastward forest that
became a regular site for a base camp, and as Nature is a wise
teacher, it has often served as a learning place for all of us.

Back in the present, Natalia and I began the two-mile hike back to camp. About halfway, we came to a spring-fed brook and stopped. The brook was tiny but at least it was clear and pure. We washed our hands in the icy water, then cleaned the birds properly so we could spit them for dinner. I showed Natalia how to remove the skin and clean a carcass inside and out so the meat stayed fresh, then she cleaned the second herself. When it was done we walked on, picking our way among the tall grass of a half grown-over trail that would probably vanish in a couple years as the forest continued to reclaim this ground. We went in companionable silence for a long time, watching for useful herbs and mushrooms. When we reached a fork in the trail and turned west, the woods opened out. Sunlight spilled through the loose canopy of boughs and we began chatting idly. It wasn't long before we were talking about the hunt.

Natalia had lived on the farm long enough to understand that animals live and die, but she remained perplexed by how swiftly I had dispatched the injured grouse. I hadn't hesitated an instant, and she asked me about it again.

"It was an act of mercy," I explained to her. "The right mercy for this branch of the Way." And then I told her about the little caribou Skye had put down in Alaska, a memory I had never shared with anyone before. I explained to her that I didn't know what I would have done had Skye not shown up, though it would have been a great wrong to let it suffer. I had determined at that time not to let my feelings get in the way of doing the right thing again. But then years later the little goat had been born and sure enough my feelings got in the way, but then it had been a good thing because I realized there was a better way to end its suffering.

"So why kill the grouse so fast?" she asked again.

"Because the grouse was going to be dinner. From the moment we decided that, the right choice was to make the kill quick and clean." The lyrics of a song came to mind. Natalia knew it, but I quoted it for her anyway:

"Let the death be clean as life's released
So we show our honor to the beast
For your own death you will understand,
When you hold life's blood within your hand.

Though we draw a bow and we wield a blade
We respect the code that nature made
For we know not when the shadows fall
And the huntsman comes to take us all."[3]

Our little camp was coming into view. The bright-yellow fly of the tent almost glowed against the dark-green backdrop of the forest. We were tired, thirsty, and hungry from a long morning of hiking and gathering, and when we reached camp, we each drank our canteens empty and fell into chairs beside the ring of stones we had gathered for tonight's fire.

Natalia looked very thoughtful, and after a bit she said, "So mercy doesn't hesitate."

I went to the ice chest and dug out a couple water bottles filled with Daphne's cold herbal tea and tossed her one, then fell back into my chair. "Not quite. We do good where we can. We are hard where we must be. We are merciful when and how it is right. We act with forethought so as to be wise, but we also act without undue delay. It is not simple to balance all these things, but they are essential. The aboriginal shamans would have called this delicate balance the Way of a true human being."

---

3. Heather Alexander, *The Hunt Is On*. Sea Fire Productions, 1997. Compact disk.

Natalia nodded, but remained pensive, and that was fair. Nature's deepest truths are often right there before our eyes, yet subtle enough to occupy the thoughts of the wisest shamans for a lifetime. In time she would understand. Nature is the teacher, and this is also the Way.

Traditional Living

Harvest Cider:
A Taste of the Land

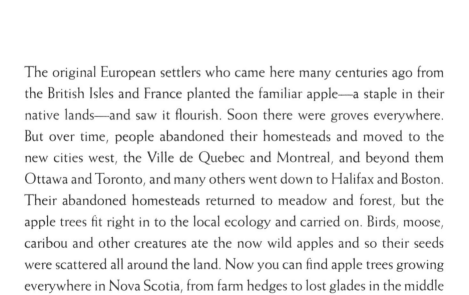

The original European settlers who came here many centuries ago from the British Isles and France planted the familiar apple—a staple in their native lands—and saw it flourish. Soon there were groves everywhere. But over time, people abandoned their homesteads and moved to the new cities west, the Ville de Quebec and Montreal, and beyond them Ottawa and Toronto, and many others went down to Halifax and Boston. Their abandoned homesteads returned to meadow and forest, but the apple trees fit right in to the local ecology and carried on. Birds, moose, caribou and other creatures ate the now wild apples and so their seeds were scattered all around the land. Now you can find apple trees growing everywhere in Nova Scotia, from farm hedges to lost glades in the middle of the grandest forest.

As I noted earlier, there are many wild apple trees in the Hollow, but the one that produces the largest, sweetest apples grows just above a spring down by the Firefly Pond, not one hundred feet from the cottage. Grandfather Apple is very old and likely to fall to wind or snow-load one day, so I have planted several Honeycrisps in our groves to replace it when it happens, but for now it is our best loved fruit tree.

In spring, it is covered in delicate, fragrant blossoms like little roses (the apple tree is, in fact, closely related to the rose). In summer, we spend several hours each week pruning excess blossoms off its prolific branches so that those selected for maturation can become plump, sweet fruit. And when autumn comes we cannot think of changing leaves and Samhain celebrations without thinking of apples.

I am sure it was the same for our ancestors. The apple was a sacred fruit and staple crop, and a good part of their livelihoods over winter relied upon its yield. It was so important to them they conceived of faerie spirits that oversaw the trees, such as the Apple Man. The apple became part of their magical and spiritual rites. And when the fruit came in, they were baked into pies and puddings, used in stews and garnishes, and often enough eaten raw, savored for their crisp, tangy sweetness. But one tradition of the season would have been especially dear—the making of cider.

At the Hollow, cider-making starts the Old Way—harvesting the apples from the tree. Then a couple hundred pounds are halved and quartered and cut up still more, a joint effort of the whole family working at the enormous picnic table ensconced in the Elfwood, upon a clear, cool day. The apple bits are then placed in a hefty tub and partly crushed with a clean maul. Then we spill the pulpy mass into an apple press, about thirty pounds at a time, and start the long process of crushing the juice out. We use some fresh and barter some, but the best has a special purpose—a purpose as old as Samhain, as vaunted as harvest. It will be turned into hard cider. In elder days, hard cider was important to the peoples of northerly lands. Hard cider naturally keeps for years if made and stored right. It would have been a way to set aside the goodness and nutrition of the harvest until the next year. And, best of all, it is delicious beyond comparison.

To make hard cider, you need only a few things, which can be acquired for a very modest expense at any brewing shop. If you're skilled, you can substitute most of this equipment, but I would suggest a novice at brewing stick closely to my instructions until you get the knack of it. By the way, if you're worried that brewing things is very complicated, trust me, it isn't. That's only a myth, one that I'm sure has been helped along by the brewing industry. Brewing is an ancient, essentially simple practice, and any liquid with sugar in it naturally wants to become a brew. The art of doing it right is just understanding proportions, and ABOVE ALL, cleanliness. Everything needs to be meticulously sterilized, from the first moment the raw cider (also called must) is poured into a primary fermenter bucket to the moment it is bottled. But don't worry, it's not terribly difficult. I'll explain it all.

To begin, you'll need the following things, all of which can be easily acquired at a brewing story for under $100. (If the initial expense of the equipment bothers you, remember that your first batch will yield thirty standard wine bottles or sixty-six standard beer bottles of cider, a minimum value of $360, though good cider often sells for much more. And you can use this same equipment to make wines, meads, and ales forever after.)

The primary fermenter, shown left, is just an eight-gallon bucket, usually made of food-grade plastic. It is overlarge to allow brews in the vigorous early stage of fermentation space to foam up. It also makes it easy to blend in fruit and spices for beverages such as melomels. It has an airtight, snap-on lid to keep insects and oxygen out. The carboy, right, is usually a glass bottle of six gallons capacity where a brew finishes fermentation in airtight conditions over weeks or months. The carboy shown has an airlock inserted into the opening to stop all inward airflow. Some carboys have wider mouths.

A six-gallon glass carboy

An eight-gallon food-grade primary
fermenter bucket with cover

An airlock and bung

A rigid racking rod with six feet of tube

A bottling rig: This uses a bottle filler, six feet
of flexible tube, and a rigid plastic rod the
length of a carboy plus a few inches. Attach
the rod and bottle filler to each end of the
tube. It will make bottling much easier with
a lot less spillage.

A brewer's spoon (a large spoon with a two-foot
long handle, made of food-grade plastic)

One packet of brewer's yeast. Montrachet yeast is
a personal favorite, but any brewer's yeast will
do. You can find a variety of brewing yeasts
at your brew shop. You can also use ordinary
baking yeast from a grocery, but the results
will be weaker and won't store as long.

3 lbs white sugar

3 lbs brown sugar

Acid blend

Pectic enzyme

Yeast energizer (or a quarter cup of
currants, washed in cool water and
crushed but not pulverized)

Grape tannin

Diversol or its equivalent. (This is basically
powdered bleach. An experienced brewer
can use pure bleach, but I would advise
you stick with Diversol for now.)

A small packet of Campden tablets

If making hard cider wine, you will need 30
standard 750 ml wine bottles (often
available free at a recycling facility,
or they can be gotten from friends or
bought from a brewing shop).
You will also need corks.

If making bubbly hard cider, you will need
66 standard 335 ml beer bottles. (Short,
stubby bottles without screw-on tops are
best as they handle a capper easier.)
You must use beer bottles or the bubbly
cider will burst the bottles due to the
pressure it creates as it primes.
You will also need caps.

6 gallons of apple cider. Unpasteurized,
unfiltered (you can tell because it's cloudy
from fruit protein), and organic is best
but not necessary. But it must be free of
preservatives and sulfites as these will inhibit
the fermentation process.

Acid blend (a mixture of citric, ascorbic, and other comestible acids), pectic enzyme, grape tannin, and yeast energizer are inexpensive and usually sold by brew shops in small portions (enough for two or three six-gallon batches) as well larger portions.

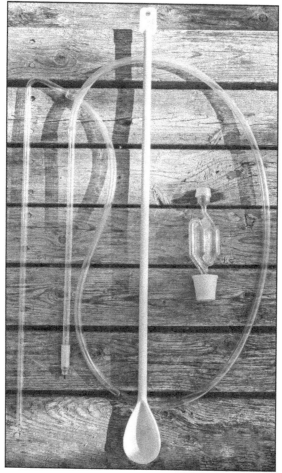

Pictured above are a brewer's spoon, airlock, and bottling rig. See how long the spoon is. This is so it can reach all the way to the bottom of carboys and primary fermenters without the need of touching the liquid. This helps prevent contamination. Note the rubber stopper attached to the airlock—that is the bung. Be sure to get the proper size bung for your carboy's mouth. The bottling rig is a simple siphoning device—a length of flexible tube with two rigid rods (one to insert into a carboy or primary fermenter, and one to insert into a bottle). The rod that goes into the bottle has a pressure-activated stop at the tip (see the lower part of the inner rod) that allows liquid to flow only when the tube is pressed down. This reduces spillage during bottling. A racking rig is not shown because it is very similar, the only difference being that it has only one rigid rod. Sometimes racking rigs are of larger diameter to allow faster flow, too.

Since you only need a few grams of each ingredient for a batch, don't get too much so they're not sitting around too long. As far as I know, they don't spoil, and I've used them years old, but it's best to avoid risking ruining a batch. They usually come in powdered form and are easily stored in empty, clean, small mason jars in a cool, dry place out of direct sunlight. Refrigeration is not necessary.

Yeast is the exception in that it will not keep once a packet is opened. It comes in small, airtight foil packets intended for immediate use, one packet per batch. Even sealed, it only keeps a year or so, so don't get more packets than you intend to use in a year. Toss out dated stuff as it loses vigor and will not ferment properly.

Lastly, for cider wine you will also need a corker. Don't stint and get a cheap one, either. You will very, very shortly regret it if you do. The good ones are $60 or so and make corking a pleasure. The cheap ones will have you struggling to cork your bottles, cursing your foolishness for attempting to brew, and possibly injuring yourself on broken bottle necks. Many brewing shops rent good corkers for just a few dollars a day, and you can cork thirty bottles of wine with a good one in five minutes. But if you try brewing and enjoy it, you'll want to buy one. It's worth the small investment.

If you are making bubbly cider, you'll be putting the cider in beer bottles which can handle the gas pressure that the priming builds up, and you'll need a capper instead of a corker. Cappers are only about half the price of corkers, so brew shops rarely ever rent them. Get the best you can afford. It should be a stationary model that sits on the floor or bolts to a table. With a good capper, you can cap sixty-six bottles in less than ten minutes. If you go cheap and get one of the flimsy, handheld designs, you're likely to curse brewing and never do it again. That's nearly thirty years of experience talking, so trust me. Above all, don't skimp on good cappers and corkers. It's a one-time expense that's worth every penny.

Always start with clean hands and arms up to the elbow. Once you start the work of brewing, be careful not to touch things unrelated to the process. If you do, dip your hands in the bleach-water solution and rinse thoroughly to resterilize them.

Step One: Sterilize your primary fermenter. To do this, put two gallons of hot water, as hot as you can stand to touch, in the primary fermenter bucket, and dissolve in 4 tablespoons of Diversol. Let the solution stand in the bucket for 30 minutes, sloshing the solution around every couple minutes to be sure it gets everywhere. Also, be sure to get the solution on the bucket's cover. To do this, just put the cover on the bucket. It should seal on quite tightly. Then turn the bucket over now and then when you are sloshing the solution around. Be sure to toss the brewer's spoon into the bucket, too, so that it also gets sterilized.

After 30 minutes, empty the bucket and rinse everything thoroughly in three douses of hot water, then three douses of cold water to get every last bit of the bleach solution out. Any hint of bleach odor will wreck the flavor, so be thorough.

Some would say this is oversterilization, but "some" occasionally lose a batch to spoilage. In nearly thirty years of brewing I have never lost a batch. Cleanliness and proper sterilization is the most important step to success in brewing. Always be attentive to it.

Step Two: Pour the must (apple juice) into the primary fermentation bucket. Crush one dozen Campden tablets (these are just sulfur) with a mortar and pestle and pour the powder into the must. Using the spoon, stir the powder for 5 minutes to thoroughly dissolve it. Put the cover on firmly and let stand one day. The sulfur will sterilize the must of wild yeasts and other unwanted microbes and vanish into the air as gas.

Step Three: Mark your start date on a calendar.

Making sure your hands are sterile (I keep a mild solution of iodine and water in a spray bottle for this purpose), open the cover of the primary fermenter, and add all the sugar. Also add:

One tablespoon pectic enzyme (this is a natural vegetable hormone that will break down fruit proteins so the must can clarify as it ages)

Two tablespoons acid blend (fruit acids like citrus are essential since things become bitter as they ferment)

1.5 teaspoons grape tannin, which helps give body and character to the finished product

2 tablespoons yeast nutrient, or the quarter cup of lightly crushed currant berries (these provide nutrients for the yeast)

DO NOT STIR ANYTHING.

Lastly, add your yeast. Do not stir it in. Just let it float on top. It will sink in and start working shortly.

(Note: If you have read winemaking books before, you know that most will tell you to make a yeast starter with a weak sugar solution a day before so as not to shock your yeast when you add it to the must, but the writers of these books also tell you to stir up everything you just put in your primary fermenter. This makes the must super rich which is what overloads fresh yeast. If you simply don't stir anything the yeast will be fine, and you can skip a tedious step. Don't worry—a day or two after the yeast is added the entire batch will be roiling to a furious fermentation that will blend everything in the must to the molecular level. Nature is remarkably efficient, if left to her own devices.)

Set the primary fermentation bucket on a table at least waist high, snap on the cover, and do not move it again. The room where it is left should be just on the cool side of room temperature (about 68 F or 20 C), but a few degrees variation is no big deal. Too cool and the fermentation will go very slowly and the timelines I'm giving you will not work. Too warm could lead to spoilage. After you've made a few batches, you'll start to get a feel for how to manage this in your location. Also, the bucket should not be in a place where it will be subjected to strong sunlight.

Leave for ten to fourteen days until it looks like the action of the yeast is done (you can't see bubbles in it anymore). The yeast is still working but too slowly to be observed. A great deal of sediment will accumulate during this time, so don't move the bucket. You do not want to stir it up.

Step Four: At this point you will need to rack the must, which involves using the rigid racking rod and flexible tubing to siphon the must from the primary fermenter to a carboy. Start by sterilizing the carboy and an airlock and bung in the same way you sterilized the primary fermenter and spoon. You will likewise need to sterilize your racking rig. Just draw the bleach solution into the tube by sucking on one end. (Be careful, of course, not to swallow the solution.) Rinse the carboy in hot water three times and cold water three times.

To rinse the racking rig, set up a small sterilized container holding about a gallon of hot water and siphon off the hot water. Then repeat using cold water. Also, remember to sterilize and thoroughly rinse your hands.

Be absolutely sure to get every trace of bleach odor off your equipment during rinsing.

Now comes the racking, which is best done with two people. It is the process of separating the must from the sediment. You merely siphon off the must into a carboy, being careful not to disturb the solution as you work. To do this, set the carboy on the floor beneath the primary fermenter and a few feet away to give the tube length to be straightened. One person will hold the rod and start the siphon action. That person will then pass the flexible tube end to the other person, who will hold it in the mouth of the carboy, making sure the tube is running in a consistent, straight downward slope for an efficient siphon. Daphne and I do this together, and I always hold the rod because I've had a lot of practice at it. It takes some dexterity, as you must learn to be very steady so as not to stir up the sediment, but with practice you will get the hang of it.

By the way, racking rods come with a small detachable rounded piece at the bottom. Be sure it is attached to the rod now. It will raise the lip of the tip of the rod and slow the siphoning procedure down a little, both of which help keep the sediment out. If this doesn't make sense now, it quickly will once you start the procedure.

Racking takes several minutes. It cannot be hurried because too much suction will draw up the sediment. With brewing, you can never go too slow, but you can easily go too fast.

The sediment at the bottom is called the dregs. If you have a steady hand and the sediment has not gotten stirred up, you can press the base of the rod down into the edge of the carboy and very slowly, carefully tip the carboy so that you can catch a bit more of the clear must, but the moment you see the dregs going up the rod, immediately stop the siphon by simply lifting it out of the must. Don't worry if you get a little of the dregs in the carboy in the transfer. It is harmless and won't affect the flavor of the finished product. Besides, there will be another racking in due time.

Cap the carboy with the airlock and bung. Most airlocks need to be partly filled with water, so don't forget that step. Place the carboy where the primary fermenter was and dump the dregs from the primary fermenter. They are harmless and can go into a compost pile or right onto the soil, or even down the drain.

If you're making bubbly cider, the next step will occur in three weeks. If you're making cider wine, the next step will occur in ten weeks. Mark the time you should get back to it on your calendar.

Step Five for Bubbly Cider: Three weeks have gone by and it is bottling day at last! The must is probably still a little cloudy, but that is perfectly acceptable for real, unfiltered bubbly ciders. Remember to sterilize and rinse everything, including your hands. You'll need your primary fermenter, racking rig, brewer's spoon, bottling rig, and a small pot. Plus you'll have to sterilize your bottles and caps, and you should get your capper in place. Use beer bottles, recycled or new. Remember, ordinary bottles will burst under the pressure that bubbly cider creates as it primes, so you must use beer bottles.

Rack the must back into the primary fermenter, which will remove it from any remaining dregs, then place the fermenter on the table at about waist high and cover for the moment.

Sterilize all your beer bottles and caps and put the rinsed caps in a bowl. You'll need sixty-six of each, and I find it is helpful to prepare a couple extra in case you encounter a flawed bottle or cap. Also—AND YOU ONLY DO THIS STEP FOR BUBBLY CIDERS—heat one cup of water in the pot and when it's hot but before it boils add twelve ounces of white sugar, stirring gently, to make a sugar syrup. Then pour the syrup into the must and stir gently for two minutes to thoroughly dissolve it.

You'll need two people for the next step. Using your bottling rig, start a siphon going. One person will have to hold the rigid rod in the primary fermenter; the other will work the bottle filler. The bottle filler is a rod that has a small pressure-activated stop, and it only allows the must to flow when it is pressed down into a bottle. Start filling your bottles. Fill them all to about a finger's breadth from the top, then promptly cap them.

When finished, set the bottles aside someplace where they can be stored at room temperature. The remaining yeast will feed on the sugar syrup, creating gas that will prime (pressurize) the cider right in the bottle. After six weeks, open one and sample. If it's not adequately primed, you can drink it as wine but leave the rest to prime another six weeks. Bubbly cider needs no further aging. A note of caution, though. Do not confuse this stuff with store-bought bubbly hard cider. This is the real thing, made the Old Way, and it is as strong as wine. Take it slow. A single small bottle is an adequate portion for two.

Step Five for Cider Wine: You have been very patient and waited ten whole weeks. Your must should have clarified and is now a beautiful amber, a little darker or lighter depending on the character of the apple juice you started with. It is now ready to be bottled and become cider wine!

Remember to sterilize and rinse everything, including your hands. You'll need your racking rig and bottling rig. Plus you'll have to sterilize your bottles and the primary fermenter, and you should get your corker in place. DO NOT attempt to sterilize the corks.

Rack the must back into the primary fermenter, then place the fermenter on the table at about waist high and cover for the moment. Sterilize all your wine bottles and put the corks in a bowl. You'll need thirty of each, and I find it is helpful to prepare a couple extra in case you encounter a flawed bottle or cork.

You'll need two people for the next step. Using your bottling rig, start a siphon going. One person will have to hold the rigid rod in place in the primary fermenter; the other will work the bottle filler. The bottle filler has a small pressure activated stop, and it only allows the must to flow when it is pressed down into a bottle. Start filling your bottles, then promptly cork them. There is something so satisfying about this last step: the corking. Not only is it fun, but it feels right. Perhaps because you are participating in a timeless ritual involving the preparation of the sacred apple fruit. I imagine brewers of old felt this whether they were corking bottles in later centuries or stoppering ancient barrels and clay pots in prehistory.

When finished, sample a bottle. There is a lot of variety among apples and sometimes you will find the cider wine quite pleasant as is. If the wine seems a bit sharp or tannic, set the bottles aside someplace mildly cool and dark to age. During this time it will smoothen and develop complexity. Try it again three months later. If it has not yet aged to taste, let sit another six months. Rarely does apple wine need more than a year to peak, though I made a batch a few years ago that did not reach its best flavor for three years, and though it was a very long wait indeed, it was worth every moment when we finally broke into it. Brewing, especially in regard to wines, rewards patience above all.

The traditional skills you acquire brewing hard cider can be applied to creating a range of rare and much sought after beverages. Shown above are several borrowed from our wine cellar. Beginning from the upper left they are in clockwise order: cider wine, strawberry wine, peach mead (also called melomel), bubbly cider, and black ale.

You have just learned how to make two varieties of hard cider, but should you take an interest in brewing, you now know the fundamentals behind making meads, wines, and ales of every kind. If you want to pursue this interest further, I highly recommend *Making Wild Wines and Meads* by Pattie Vargas and Rich Gullins (© 2000). Also, chances are your local brewing shop offers courses in the brewer's arts.

So now, you've worked long and meticulously to create your vintage. In the doing, you've shared profoundly in the whole process of brewing the sacred fruit of the Britons and druids: the apple. You've participated in a cycle as old as time and perhaps gained a window into the love, attention, and cares of people long past, the very founders of our paths. And when the High Days come along, you'll have something very special to celebrate them with—a blending of the fullness of earth and the craft of your own heart and hands. So raise your goblet and toast the gods you follow with a beverage older than history. You've earned it. And don't forget to spill a drop for the Good Folk.

Conclusion:
Into the Green

Once upon a time the world was a wilderness with small settled enclaves scattered about: a village here and there, each surrounded by its pastures and meadows while vast untamed lands lay beyond. But whether in the village or on the last farm before the wood, the green permeated every-thing: the lives of farmers raising their crops, the activities of wives at the hearth, the work of local artisans. Balance with the green brought prosperity and happiness to everyone.

But the green also held mystery and sometimes frightening power. It was said that in the hedges faeries danced in dazzling circles, and in far moonlit places maidens walked with horned men. In the wilds were gob-lins and old gods of every sort, and children who wandered too far from home might find themselves lost in fairy tales. Some feared these natural mysteries, but certain cunning folk became more attuned than most to the ways of the green and learned to commune with the spirits of plants and understand the language of animals. They learned to see spirits and hear the old gods. They immersed themselves in the natural mysteries and found in the doing that they might touch the numinous. Those that sought the natural mysteries acquired titles like shamans, witches, and druids. They used their special knowledge to assist with child birth, raising crops, and safeguarding livestock, and they taught folk to honor the little spirits and remember the old gods.

But over the ages, masses of people spread everywhere and the green shrank in size and importance to the point one might say Nature itself is now the hedgerow. In the eighteenth century the Industrial Revolution came and a ravenous hunger for natural resources consumed humankind, which was disastrous for the natural world as species were wiped out and pollution spread. The rural ways gave way to factories, machines, and markets and the people who had lived so long close to Nature were forced to relocate to urban centers in order to find work. Their wisdom traditions had been vital, living things, but divorced from their ties to the land, they degenerated into empty rituals. Over a few generations, folk forgot the real reasons they once danced around the May Pole or harvested corn by the full August moon. The *raison d'etre* of their beliefs was usurped and their paths went the way of dying religions, devolving into esoteric pursuits for enlightenment through lore that had become half lost and occult.

Throughout the nineteenth and early twentieth centuries, there was an almost fanatical certitude that the way of industry and technology were inevitable and for the best. Science fiction writers speculated that man would soon create domed cities with fully regulated environments where everyone would live blissfully separate from the vicissitudes of summer heat and the inconvenient advent of thunderstorms. Captains of industry foresaw an era of plenty developing as technology increased their ability to produce heaps of goods for the mass market. The famed British leader Winston Churchill even dreamt of a time when farming as we know it would become obsolete and beef would instead be cultivated from massive slabs of naked flesh grown in giant cloning tanks.

Enamored by promises of universal wealth, abundant food, and endless trinkets to amuse, people failed to consider the long-term consequences of the new industrial way of life. They did not foresee a future where the planet would become so polluted that almost one in every two persons could expect to get cancer (Canadian Cancer Society, 2007). They could not imagine the day when it would be impossible to find someplace truly away from the ceaseless rumble of machines of industry and transportation. They could not have envisioned a time when their children would grow up so hyperstimulated by video games and a constant barrage of electronic media that their minds would be unable to stand still and hold focus. But in time some persons did begin to stop and take stock, and when they did they had to admit that for all the gains of the modern world, something invaluable had been lost. It was becoming apparent that human beings had a profound need for the green world. But it had been injured by avarice, and with the diminishment of the wild places its enchantment was perhaps only a shadow of what it had once been. Yet it remained out there, timeless, paced...waiting.

Finding the way back would not be easy, though. Centuries of living apart from the green had caused people not only to forget how to live with Nature, but most did not even understand what they had lost. The problem was confounding and might be likened to trying to teach a person who had never heard music how to play an instrument. To get back what had been lost, people had to first relearn how to experience Nature as an essential, integrated part of life. Only in this way could they reach the profound soul-deep *knowing* that the Native American medicine chief (cited at the beginning of this book), Eli Gatoga, spoke of.

When I first began to ponder this dilemma some twenty-five years ago, I began to ask myself how does one go about restoring that *knowing*. Having grown up on that little Cajun farm deep in the bayous where magic was as much a part of daily life as lost pecan groves and fried catfish, I knew that drawing close to the green was something best accomplished in the doing—by living close to the land, as the elders had, and practicing the traditions and skills they possessed. Thus, one might come to see through their eyes and weave oneself into the wild magic that began at the hedgerow. So without quite understanding what I was then undertaking, I began practicing what is now called primitive technology—learning through experimentation how to apply the life skills of the ancients.

Two interesting things often happen to persons who practice primitive technology. One: they discover many of the Old Ways are not only very doable, but they are also green, clean, and very satisfying. Old skills which have persisted across the millennia are by nature sustainable and low impact, and nothing says satisfaction like job done yourself. And since the old skills are very physical, they get you active and so are healthier. Two: for many practitioners primitive technology turns into a passion—a passion fueled by a sense of continuity with the ancestors. For example, it was only when Daphne mastered the challenge of baking bread in a cast iron Dutch oven on a wood stove that she came to perceive herself as more than just a female of the current generation. The simple act of baking bread traditionally revealed to her that she was part of a continuum of ancestors that ranged from the women of her family's distant past to the women of the unknowable future.

The practice of primitive technology reveals the inner minds of elder peoples who lived, perforce, much closer to the land than we do now. Daily life required they possess a deep understanding of the mystic and physical workings of the green world, so it stands to reason that emulating their lifeways will reintegrate us with Nature. The most striking personal experience with this happened for us when we moved into the Alaskan wilderness and began living much like the aboriginals had long before us. One simply cannot truly appreciate their perspective unless one has been there. There is an unbridled sense of victory in reaching spring that can only be known if you have worked hard to bring in firewood and food through five months of fierce subzero weather. You cannot imagine the joy of the gory work of gutting caribou unless you face a reality of going hungry without the meat. And when the land is the absolute source of sustenance as well as the ultimate challenge to daily survival, only then can you develop the keen love and solemn respect of it that is part of the aboriginal mind.

Drawing close to the land like this changes entirely how we perceive. Every experience becomes richer, deeper—pregnant with meaning. The subtle arts of gardening and animal husbandry do a lot to teach us to relate to the other life forms that share the world with us. Making cheese and brewing wines teach us both patience and flowing with Nature's timing. The act of hunting with a bow sharpens every sense and teaches a keen focus, and I don't know of anything to compare. Adapting to the challenges presented when Earth and Sky go against our plans teaches us to be sensitive to the moods and needs of the green world. Happiness becomes oriented toward contentment in the present as opposed to the post-Industrial era focus on evermore acquisition and accomplishment. It was David Louv who wrote, in his bestselling book *Last Child In the Woods* (©2008), that Nature amplifies time. It does so by expanding every part of daily experience.

And it is only when our awareness is so expanded that we can really progress spiritually. Whether we call the path we follow shamanism, witchcraft, druidry, Asatru, or any other label, it is only when our hearts and minds are aware of the instant and its true virtue that we can become immersed in the subtleties of the green enough to engage with it on a powerfully spiritual level. This, I believe, is at the heart of magic and communing with the numinous. Indeed, it is well documented that immersion in Nature is one of the essential elements of the peak experience (moments of timeless, perfect communion with the divine).

Ultimately, restoring the human relation with the green will even be essential to the survival of everything that shares this world. Our species is at a crossroad in history. It has the technology now to grant itself all sorts of material goods and marvels, but that technology comes at a staggering price—the consumption of vastly unsustainable amounts of natural resources and lifestyles that are exceedingly toxic to the environment. Or our species can choose to walk Nature's Way—a balanced, gentler path that is good for people and the sacred Earth. Humanity has historically been most motivated by its spiritual paths. Whole civilizations have risen, warred and fallen over spiritual paths. If it is to go a better way, redeem itself and save this one and only Earth, humankind must change at the level of spirit into something kinder and greener.

And so, we are just one little family on a small homestead deep in a wild place. What we can do is small, but we can test the Old Ways, and from the knowledge we garner we can share. We can teach. And perhaps through this book we can impart an essential bit of wisdom. It is just this: Spirit and enchantment and reality are bound together in a green world full of wonders. If you are intrepid enough to peer into it, it will heal you even as you will heal the Earth.

So the sacred year will spiral on. Nature will follow its timeless rituals and perhaps you will find your own means to walk its Way, just as we do. And as you go your Way, we Hollow folk bid you blessed be.

GET MORE AT **LLEWELLYN.COM**

Visit us online to browse hundreds of our books and decks, plus sign up to receive our e-newsletters and exclusive online offers.

- Free tarot readings • Spell-a-Day • Moon phases

- Recipes, spells, and tips • Blogs • Encyclopedia

- Author interviews, articles, and upcoming events

GET SOCIAL WITH **LLEWELLYN**

Find us on  @LlewellynBooks

www.Facebook.com/LlewellynBooks

GET BOOKS AT **LLEWELLYN**

LLEWELLYN ORDERING INFORMATION

 Order online: Visit our website at www.llewellyn.com to select your books and place an order on our secure server.

 Order by phone:
- Call toll free within the US at 1-877-NEW-WRLD (1-877-639-9753)
- We accept VISA, MasterCard, American Express, and Discover.

 Order by mail:
Send the full price of your order (MN residents add 6.875% sales tax) in US funds plus postage and handling to: Llewellyn Worldwide, 2143 Wooddale Drive, Woodbury, MN 55125-2989

POSTAGE AND HANDLING

STANDARD (US):(Please allow 12 business days)
$30.00 and under, add $6.00.
$30.01 and over, FREE SHIPPING.

CANADA:
We cannot ship to Canada. Please shop your local bookstore or Amazon Canada.

INTERNATIONAL:
Customers pay the actual shipping cost to the final destination, which includes tracking information.

Visit us online for more shipping options. Prices subject to change.

FREE CATALOG!

To order, call
1-877-
NEW-WRLD
ext. 8236
or visit our
website